Media for All

Edinburgh University Library

Books may be recalled for return earlier than due date;
if so you will be contacted by e-mail or letter.

University of Edinburgh

30150 024993674

APPROACHES TO TRANSLATION STUDIES
Founded by James S. Holmes

Edited by   Henri Bloemen
                 Dirk Delabastita
                 Ton Naaijkens

Volume 30

Media for All

Subtitling for the Deaf, Audio Description, and Sign Language

Edited by
Jorge Díaz Cintas
Pilar Orero
Aline Remael

Rodopi

Amsterdam - New York, NY 2007

EDINBURGH UNIVERSITY LIBRARY
WITHDRAWN
EDINBURGH UNIV. EDINBURGH

The copyrights of work by visual artists affiliated with a CISAC-organisation, have been arranged with Beeldrecht, Amsterdam.

Cover design: Studio Pollmann

The paper on which this book is printed meets the requirements of "ISO 9706:1994, Information and documentation - Paper for documents - Requirements for permanence".

ISBN: 978-90-420-2304-8
©Editions Rodopi B.V., Amsterdam – New York, NY 2007
Printed in The Netherlands

To Ian, Marcel and Evy

To Angelita, Tere and Eugénie

Table of contents

Acknowledgements   *9*

Media for all: a global challenge
Jorge Díaz Cintas, Pilar Orero, Aline Remael   *11*

Section 1: Subtitling for the deaf and hard-of-hearing (SDH)   *21*

Sampling subtitling for the deaf and the hard-of-hearing in Europe
Aline Remael   *23*

Access symbols for use with video content and information and
communications technology devices
Clive Miller   *53*

Deaf access for Deaf people: the translation of the television news from
English into British Sign Language
Christopher Stone   *71*

A world of change in a changing world
Josélia Neves   *89*

Subtitling for the deaf and hard-of-hearing in Brazil
Vera Lúcia Santiago Araújo   *99*

Section 2: Audio description (AD)   *109*

Sampling audio description in Europe
Pilar Orero   *111*

Accessibility: raising awareness of audio description in the UK
Joan Greening, Deborah Rolph   *127*

Towards a European guideline for audio description
Gert Vercauteren   *139*

A corpus-based analysis of audio description
Andrew Salway   *151*

From the visual to the verbal in two languages: a contrastive analysis of
the audio description of *The Hours* in English and Spanish
Julian Bourne, Catalina Jiménez Hurtado   175

Intersensorial translation: visual art made up by words
Karin De Coster, Volkmar Mühleis   189

Accessible opera in Catalan: opera for all
Anna Matamala, Pilar Orero   201

Verdi made visible: audio introduction for opera and ballet
Greg York   215

Audio description in the Chinese world
Jessica Yeung   231

Notes on contributors   245

Index   249

Acknowledgements

A collection of articles is as good as the contributions it contains. We would therefore like to start by thanking all our contributors for sharing their work with us. Furthermore, we owe thanks to our TransMedia colleagues: Mary Carroll, Anna Matamala, Jordi Mas, Josélia Neves and Diana Sánchez for all the energy that they put into the organization and running of the first *Media for All* conference in 2005, the catalyst for this publication.

We are also grateful to those who took time to reply to our questionnaires on subtitling for the deaf and audio description: Bernd Benecke, Bernard Dewulf, Chas Donaldson, Carlo Eugeni, Harry Geyskens, Veronika Hyks, Corinne Imhauser, Jurgen Lentz, Celia Quico, Joris Redig, Isabelle Couté Rodriguez and Susanne Verberk.

Jimmy Ureel has been the person in charge of revising and formatting the text and his work should be not only acknowledged but publicly recognized. Special thanks should go to our editor Marieke Schilling for her diligence, advice and encouragement, and to the series editors of Approaches to Translation Studies Henri Bloemen, Dirk Delabastita and Ton Naaijkens for their support.

We also owe thanks to the *Koninklijke Musea voor Schone Kunsten Brussel* for providing us with the reproductions of 4 paintings and sculptures, and to Beeldrecht in the Netherlands, for taking care of copyright procedures.

Those who live at home with the editors of the present volume deserve a few words to recognize their support, their generosity and understanding.

And we would also like to dedicate this book to all people with sensory difficulties, for whom we are working with the belief that the future will be better, wholly accessible and will hopefully arrive sooner than expected.

Media for all: a global challenge

Jorge Díaz Cintas

Roehampton University, UK

Pilar Orero

Universitat Autònoma de Barcelona, Spain

Aline Remael

University College Antwerp, Belgium

Technology is often considered to be both a blessing and a curse, and many people's everyday encounters with technology obviously corroborate this idea. However, the so-called curses of technology are not all inherent in its technical, non-human features. They are often related to how people or institutions make use of technology and to what end such forms of technology are used. That our world has become an information society is one of the results of technological advances worldwide and an idea we have become accustomed to, one that we now actually take for granted. The impact of quickly evolving new media and the way in which they determine information exchange, including who gets information and who does not, is central to the way society functions and will remain so throughout the twenty-first century. The degree of objectivity and the extent to which the information we receive is manipulated, both visually and verbally, are issues at the core of the freedom of speech in our free society.

In this book, we focus on how the combination of new information and communication technologies (ICT) with new professional translation practices can improve access for certain social groups to information and to entertainment widely disseminated via the Internet, on television, on computers and cinema screens, as well as in theatres, museums and other public spaces. Audiovisual media and improved high-speed travelling facilities allow us, as world citizens, to be connected to the rest of humankind at all times, through various technical platforms such as television and video conferences, but also through the increased mobility of international theatre and opera companies and fine arts exhibitions.

The majority of such events still address only physically able people. Another downside of recent developments is that the dissemination of cultural programmes and products, on the basis of ICT, happens at such a pace and makes use of so many hi-tech features that many users can no longer keep up. Again and again, they find themselves in the paradoxical situation of having to adapt to the rhythm of change imposed by a technological consumer society that does not always take into account its citizens, let alone those citizens with social or physical handicaps.

Indeed, we have not only become accustomed to the idea of living in a fast-consuming information society, but we are also well aware of the way in which this society determines wealth and, in Bourdieu's words (1986), cultural and social capital distribution in different ways. Access to information is crucial for participation in the benefits derived from globalization and economic as well as cultural growth. While some sections of our communities are developing at an extremely fast pace — both financially and socially — others are falling behind at the same rate. Exclusion from the information society may be the result of age (cf. the fast growing elderly population in Europe), physical problems, (remote) geographic location, and/or lack of funds and financial means. Such exclusion leads to social marginalization, which is why access to information was rightly identified in 2003 by the European Union as a human right.

The world's history of human rights abuses has taught us that such rights must be defended and protected, and 'abuse' in the present technical and media contexts usually takes the much less conspicuous shape of 'unfulfilled needs'. There is the need to have an Internet connection, the need to have the minimum hardware and software, but also the need to be able to use systems designed for users that are not physically or cognitively challenged. Not only age or social disadvantage, but also any physical or sensorial disability, which can affect human beings at any age, can instantly shift a person into a form of information limbo. Most institutional plans for the development of digital television and the Internet involve the provision of entertainment and education. It must ensured that they also make the most of these developments to provide information channels for sundry government communications as well as access to government services, projects and funding schemes. If digital television and the Internet are gradually becoming the only possible ways to access relevant information, and if applying for government services must be done via e-mail, this discriminates all population groups who are unable to read for whatever reason, for example the blind. One technically unproblematic solution might be making the Internet, and digital television, fully accessible aurally. In short, since the media have become central to the quality of our lives and, indeed, to surviving in today's world, it is only fair that these media, including more traditional ones, be made fully available and accessible to all citizens. The technology required to accomplish this aim already exists. The gradual transition from analogue to digital platforms, for instance, entails yet another increase in the quantity of information that can be made available, but also in the quality of reception, communication and access possibilities.

Europe seems to be well aware of this. The European Standardization bodies CEN and CENELEC recently (ISO/IEC Guide 71:2001) published Guide 6 entitled *Guidelines for Standard Developers to Address the Need of Older Persons and Persons with Disabilities*,[1] in which the use of the whole range of assistive technology that is already available today, whether it be in the form of equipment, software or services, is recommended. This obviously means a big boost to accessibility, a concept which is acquiring new meanings and has become a buzzword.

Until very recently, accessibility was a term mostly used in the context of providing assistance to people who are physically challenged, a very partial approach which ignores other needs and has had limited remedial impact. This has meant that new tools and emerging communication channels and platforms are first developed and only at a later stage are they adapted to 'different' users. With reference to websites, accessibility indicates the degree to which a particular existing portal can be accessed by people with disabilities. As far as museums and other buildings are concerned, it again designates the degree to which those buildings or spaces allow access to physically challenged people (e.g. the provision of wheelchair ramps). In the age of information and communication technology accessibility tends to refer more generally to the possibility for everyone to access and use technology and information products, regardless of physical or technological readiness, but always taking into account potential consumers with disabilities.

Although the use of accessibility in this sense sets specific population groups apart, it can be compared, to some extent, to translation and interpreting, still necessary evils for some, but at least evils that have become more generally accepted in our society. From immemorial times, translation has allowed population groups with different native languages to communicate and to access each other's publications and written heritage. Now, in the field of audiovisual translation (AVT), the professional practice of translating films, documentaries, cartoons, websites, video games and television productions has been added to the more traditional work done on paper or on a computer. Interpreting has granted conference goers access to other people's speeches since the 1940s, and today's community interpreting helps refugees gain access to medical care, whereas live interpreting for television provides viewers with interlingual translation of news and debates as the information is broadcast. More recently, the practice and study of AVT has been expanded even further. In addition to traditional forms of teletext subtitling for the deaf and the hard-of-hearing (SDH), the live subtitling of television news programmes produced with speech technology software is allowing the deaf and the hard-of-hearing to keep up with what is happening around the globe. Audio description (AD), on the other hand, offers blind people a verbal screen onto the world. Accessibility is a form of translation and translation is a form of accessibility, uniting all population groups and ensuring that cultural events, in the broadest sense of the word, can be enjoyed by all.

Accepting that accessibility is a human right means that policy-makers must watch over its implementation, as they (usually) do in the case of translation. It also means that industrial designers must incorporate the requirements of accessibility in the inception stage of new product design. This is the only way to ensure that products are accessible to all people who are disadvantaged, be it because of physical challenges, sensorial impairments, age, social issues, linguistic barriers or any other features that may set one population group apart from another. In this sense, accessibility concerns all of us and not merely a few so-called minorities.

Until very recently, lobbying for accessibility for all was mostly the concern of associations and individuals defending it on the basis of socio-cultural and medical human rights, and this is still the state of affairs in many countries. On the other hand, the European institutions are playing an increasingly important role, stimulating policy-makers at state levels to take action. Then again, when barriers are not tangible but rather technologically complex as well as changeable because of the pace of technological developments, overcoming them is a taxing exercise. Ensuring that existing products, structures and spaces become fully accessible and that new ones are made accessible from the start can be a financial nightmare in a capitalist system. This is especially true in developing countries, where social and political priorities may be different. Yet, it must be reiterated: if accessibility is not part of the original design or the inception of new technologies, its implementation becomes harder and costlier at a later stage. Legal provision involving sanctions for those who do not comply is therefore essential.

The different contributions in this volume highlight the concerns above from different angles, offering new directions for accessibility and translation practice and research. The varied and changeable approaches and situations in the field also confirm the need for unified criteria and standardization in areas such as technical format and linguistic contents. Both the industry and the users would benefit from increased standardization, be it curbed by national traditions, and advances in the West may well set the example for developments elsewhere in the world.

Media for All is the result of a long-standing friendship and collaboration between scholars and professionals working in different European university institutions and companies, committed to promoting and implementing Europe-wide, or even worldwide, accessibility. More concretely, this book is the offspring of an international conference organized at the *Universitat Autònoma de Barcelona* by the TransMedia international research group in 2005, gathering together some of the papers presented at the event and subsequent research. TransMedia has scholar members from the *Instituto Politécnico de Leiria* in Portugal, Roehampton University in the UK, the *Univer-*

sitat Autònoma de Barcelona in Spain, and University College Antwerp in Belgium, and also from professional AVT companies such as *Imaginables* in Barcelona and *Titelbild* in Berlin. Their research and collaboration focus on different aspects of media accessibility, and they are committed to ensuring that the needs of those presently excluded from the new information and communication technologies are included in the university curricula and made more visible in our society. The approach taken by TransMedia is interdisciplinary, since information content is always intertwined with various semiotic channels and with the different communication and dissemination platforms. Indeed, experts from different fields need to cooperate in order to address the current issues of accessibility, and this must be done, ideally, in consultation with members from the different target groups as well as with representatives of professional organizations and government bodies.[2]

Comparable concerns underlie the contributions collected in this book, some of which are authored by active professionals in the field. They help to mirror the state-of-the-art in media accessibility in Europe, offering a glimpse of what is already happening on other continents as well. As such, it is the first in its kind, but it has its limitations: the book is also a snapshot of a changing situation at a particular moment in time. Moreover, the growing interest in the possibilities that AD opens for both researchers and professionals explains the dominance of this fairly recent type of AVT in the present collection.

The volume is clearly divided into two main, distinctive sections: the first section focuses on the needs of the deaf and hard-of-hearing viewers whereas the second section takes the blind and visually impaired audiences into account. Both sections follow a similar structure and open with a survey or dossier devoted to the two most rapidly expanding forms of AVT and accessibility: SDH on the one hand and AD on the other. In *Sampling subtitling for the deaf and the hard-of-hearing in Europe* and *Sampling audio description in Europe*, written by Aline Remael and Pilar Orero respectively, the authors make use of the replies, provided by scholars, practitioners and members of relevant associations, to identical questionnaires sent by e-mail.[3] The questions were designed to provide answers shedding light on the following topics: the countries' sociohistorical backgrounds in SDH and AD; legislation and availability of the services; production and distribution processes; linguistic norms and conventions; the skills required; teaching, training and learning; the desirability of standardization; the impact of new developments (e.g. digital television); and the influence of practices in different media upon each other (e.g. television versus DVD or cinema). The two surveys tackle both questions and replies in their own ways while preserving a broadly parallel structure. The different (or sometimes limited) responses and different focuses of the respondents inevitably inform the structure and focus of the two dossiers. The choice of countries selected for discussion was made on the basis of a number of more or less pragmatic criteria: the information received was substantial and representative; the countries have different AVT traditions; and they are in different stages of development with regard to SDH and AD. Originally, the authors had hoped to be able to include contributions from outside Europe but, unfortunately, this information was not ultimately forthcoming. The dossiers do not have the ambition to offer a complete factual picture of the state of affairs in the countries under discussion, since this would inevitably lead to a mathematical list of dates, figures and percentages that could be obtained elsewhere. Instead, they discuss and analyse trends as well as compare developments and experiences and in so doing they sketch a general picture of what specific countries have achieved and how they have achieved this, what still needs to be done, what the expectations for the future are, and how different (research) communities can learn from each other. Both dossiers offer suggestions for further research and for improvements in the field of accessibility.

After the preliminary dossier on SDH by Aline Remael, the collection starts off with an article that falls outside today's most prominent forms of AVT within the domain of accessibility, but that is quite indispensable. Indeed, a first step to providing accessible media is to ensure that its target users are aware of the availability of accessible websites, television programmes, etc. In *Access symbols for use with video content and information and communications technology devices*, Clive Miller discusses the results of a research project whose chief aims are the development and testing of five international symbols denoting the availability of access ser-vices in the audiovisual media as well as the dissemination of these symbols to all relevant parties. The main access services covered by the project are: subtitling, audio description, sign language, speech output and spoken command, although tactile and auditory symbols are also investigated.

As it happens in other fields, the potential target audience of accessible translations is very diverse and not all deaf or hard-of-hearing individuals can or like to make use of subtitles (see Remael in this volume). In *Deaf access for Deaf people: the translation of the television news from English into British Sign Language*, Christopher Stone brings together the experiences of providers and users of sign language interpreting and explores the notion of a Deaf translation norm and its use in the rendering of English mainstream television broadcast news into British Sign Language (BSL). He claims that in order to ensure that the Deaf audience has an optimally relevant BSL text to watch and understand, the proposed Deaf translation norm incorporates enrichments and impoverishments into the BSL text, based on the bilingual interpreters' understanding and judgement of the English text as well as the video footage that is shown simultaneously on-screen. The result is a BSL text that utilizes and maximizes the multimedia environment to reduce the cognitive effort of the Deaf audience.

Turning to the generally best-known type of accessibility services, the article by Josélia Neves entitled *A world of change in a changing world* looks at the requirements for successful SDH in different media, as well as recent technical developments and needs. Neves discusses the impact that the digital age is having in the industry, primarily in the blurring of boundaries between originally distinct traditions. She claims that the potential offered by new technologies can open up avenues for more custom-made solutions, which are essential if one wants to reach the extremely diverse target group of viewers that normally consumes programmes with SDH. Her upbeat optimism about the future is based on the potential for further development offered by today's know-how. In *Subtitling for the deaf and the hard-of-hearing in Brazil*, Vera Lúcia Santiago Araújo expands the geographical scope of this collection of papers beyond the European continent, presenting an overview of the current situation with respect to SDH in Brazil, more specifically on television. She tracks its history, describes the specific characteristics of Brazilian SDH, and presents us with the most commonly used techniques and production methods, ending with an evaluation of the current situation.

The book then turns to the needs of the blind and partially sighted audience. After the general dossier on AD by Pilar Orero, the collection offers a total of eight articles that detail the use of AD in different media, discuss the politics of AD, sketch new research trends, and clarify some definitions and concepts.

First, Joan Greening and Deborah Rolph's article *Accessibility: raising awareness of audio description in the UK* paints a picture of what has been achieved by one of the forerunners in the field. Their article acknowledges that making sure that the receivers are aware of the existence of a particular service is an essential step in the development and effectiveness of that service. It then sets out to offer a detailed overview of the introduction of audio description in the UK, outlining the major developments that have taken place in television broadcasting as well as in the cinema, video, and DVD industries. The authors demonstrate that consumer feedback to the Royal National Institute for the Blind (RNIB) suggests that where audio description is accessed by blind and visually impaired people, it is appreciated as it enhances their global experience. The authors, however, point out that there is still much work to be done in order to raise awareness, even among the target audience.

Writing from an outsider's position, that is from a country where AD is still in its infancy, Gert Vercauteren examines what would be required to move *Towards a European guideline for audio description*. His paper compares some of the existing European guidelines with a view to providing a first outline of an international one, considering only guidelines for recorded audiovisual material. Given the diversity of even this one type of working material, the article suggests a subdivision into one general section containing standards that would be valid for all types of films and television programmes, and various subsections dealing with genre-specific issues.

Starting from existing English audio descriptions, Andrew Salway presents a corpus-based investigation into the language used for audio description in *A corpus-based analysis of audio description*. Salway outlines some avenues for future research that are in line with recent developments in translation studies generally, suggesting into the bargain that the use of language technologies may be an option for the future of AD production. In his opinion, this is due to the linguistic specificity of AD, explained in part by the fact that AD is produced by trained professionals following established guidelines, and in part by idiosyncrasies that are linked to the specific communicative function of AD. The production of computer-assisted AD could be an important cost-cutting factor, which is essential in a production environment determined by market competition.

Another cost-cutting exercise might be the translation of existing AD, as Julian Bourne and Catalina Jiménez Hurtado suggest in their paper *From the visual to the verbal in two languages: a contrastive analysis of the audio description of The Hours in English and Spanish.* On the basis of a case study, the authors analyse the different AD traditions in two countries where the practice is relatively well established. Their analysis covers word level, sentence level and larger units of discourse, unveiling some of the problems that might be encountered by attempts to translate existing AD scripts. Some of these problems are related to receiver expectations that are now in place in Spain and the UK respectively. However, the authors also point out that such difficulties are the staple diet of translators working in any other genre, concluding that the market possibilities offered by translating AD scripts certainly warrant more investigation.

Turning from television and pre-recorded audiovisual material to AD for museums and opera, the contribution by Karin De Coster and Volkmar Mühleis, *Intersensorial translation: visual art made up by words*, offers some reflection on the verbal description of works of art, more specifically its production and study. The authors introduce two key concepts that help provide a descriptive framework: 'visual intensity' and the 'narrative' of the work of art. They also distinguish between what they call 'clear signs' and 'ambivalent signs', as possible features of any work of art possibly influencing the work of the describer. Their contribution is illustrated by the analysis of two ADs of two very different paintings, one by René Magritte and another by Rik Wouters, as well as two examples of ADs of sculptures, one by Auguste Rodin and one by Eugène Dodeigne. All these descriptions were part of a pilot study carried out by the *Ligue Braille*, a Belgian non-profit organization for the benefit of blind and partially sighted people, aiming to throw more light on the accessibility to visual culture for people who are blind or visually impaired.

Two further contributions deal with AD for the opera. Anna Matamala and Pilar Orero investigate the beginnings of AD for the opera in Catalonia in *Accessible opera in Catalan: opera for all*. They discuss the different AD stages and tests which have taken place at the Catalan Opera House, the *Gran Teatre del Liceu*, to this date, in a bid to make opera accessible to all. Greg York, for his part, speaking as a practitioner with years of experience in AD for opera and ballet, introduces the concept of 'Talking Notes', which is also the name of the British company providing this service. In his paper entitled *Verdi made visible: audio introduction for opera and ballet*, he details the function and design of audio introductions, whose main objective is to provide a coherent account of the plot, and to illustrate it with vivid descriptions of sets, costumes, characterization and stage business. The production technique includes research, essential elements of scripting, the use of appropriate presenters, the relevance of musical examples, and methods of reproduction. In his opinion, a comprehensive AD must give enough colourful detail for the visually impaired patrons, helping them visualize the production before curtain up and allowing for uninterrupted enjoyment of the performance. Talking Notes provides audio introductions for the English National Opera and the Royal Opera House in London, where they are available during all performances.

The volume ends with an article written by Jessica Yeung, who expands the scope of the contributions on AD beyond European borders in *Audio description in the Chinese world*. Her article gives an overall picture of the state of affairs in mainland China, Hong Kong and Taiwan, foregrounding that the differences with regard to the way in which AD is carried out in these three territories are related not only to differences in economic capacity, but also to differences in attitude. In mainland China AD is non-existent, whereas in Hong Kong there is some fledgling research and the author herself has begun introducing the study of AD at university level. Remarkably, both research and training are carried out within the context of interpreting rather than translation studies. Still, research in Taiwan appears to be most advanced, at the cutting edge of AD, and the author describes this state of affairs with reference to what is being done in Europe. Taiwan is also ahead of its Chinese counterparts with regard to the provision of AD.

The present collection of essays reflects our shared interest in the field of accessibility in the audiovisual media. They all point to new avenues for interdisciplinary investigations into how communities care for their minorities, into which efforts are made by social and political agents to promote and guarantee free access to information for all and into which could be the best way(s) forward in the near future. The task of mapping accessibility and reinforcing its visibility in our society is large and challenging. We are fully aware of the need to combine resources, to broaden research, and to promote intercultural and accessibility training. We hope that this volume is a stepping-stone in the right direction.

---

[1] The whole text is available online at www.tiresias.org/guidelines/guide6
[2] More information about this group can be found online at www.transmediaresearchgroup.com/home.html
[3] The names and functions of all the respondents are listed in the acknowledgements at the end of each dossier.

References

Bourdieu, Pierre. 1985. "The forms of capital", in John G. Richardson (ed.) *Handbook for Theory and Research for the Sociology of Education*. New York: Greenwood Press, 241-258. Also available online at www.viet-studies.org/Bourdieu_capital.htm

The publication of this volume has received the financial aid of the Spanish R & D Project HUM2006-03653FILO.

Section 1

Subtitling for the deaf and
hard-of-hearing
(SDH)

Sampling subtitling for the deaf and the hard-of-hearing in Europe[1]

Aline Remael

University College Antwerp, Belgium

Abstract

Subtitling for the deaf and hard-of-hearing (SDH) has been around for quite some time and the practice is relatively widespread worldwide. In Europe, the first experiments with SDH on television largely coincided with the introduction of teletext. As new media gain popularity, new technologies are introduced and awareness of the need to provide information and entertainment that is accessible to all grows, the amount of subtitling also increases. Still, different countries go through different evolutions. They have different histories, traditions and priorities, and this has an impact on how much SDH these countries produce and broadcast and how they do this. Some of the major factors that have an impact on the development of SDH are: the political clout of groups representing people with hearing disabilities, the willingness of broadcasting companies to provide SDH even when there is no binding legislation, the swiftness with which such legislation is introduced, the availability of subtitling training, etc. This article, based on the results of an extensive questionnaire sent to professionals in a selection of western European counties, aims to provide a snapshot of an area in audiovisual translation (AVT) that is in a constant state of flux.

1. Introduction

Subtitling for the deaf and the hard-of-hearing (SDH) has been around for a number of decades virtually worldwide. This does not mean, however, that all is well with this particular type of audiovisual translation (AVT). The practice still needs to be expanded and improved, as well as adapted to new media and to the increasingly specialist and well-informed demands of its diverse audience (see Neves in this volume). In this dossier, we will consider the current state of affairs and, especially, the new developments that have taken place in a number of Western European nations. In these countries, as elsewhere in the world, the progress that has been made is the result of the concerted efforts of groups representing people with hearing disabilities, the work of volunteers, and the goodwill of some professionals, especially at the level of national television channels. Since the development of SDH is an ongoing process, this survey can be no more than a temporary snapshot.

The countries on which we shall be concentrating have been chosen for reasons similar to those underlying the selection made in the dossier on audio description (AD). Even though the countries represent the same geographical area, i.e. Western Europe, they have different AVT traditions – in terms of dubbing and subtitling – and are at different developmental stages with regard to SDH. Initially, we wondered whether a different AVT tradition might have an influence on the development of SDH in some media. However, the situation turns out to be anything but clear-cut. In what follows, the main focus will be on Flemish-speaking Belgium, Portugal (both subtitling countries/regions), Germany, Italy, Spain and Catalonia (all dubbing countries/regions), and the UK, a country that could be termed a 'grudging' user of subtitling for those rather few foreign-language productions that make it onto its small and large screens. Occasionally, we will also refer to data from France and French-speaking Belgium, both with dubbing traditions.[2] As we look into matters that our contributors consider to be new and promising or challenging trends in the field, we hope that our dossier will contribute to opening avenues for new and stimulating research.[3]

2. From the first initiatives to the present

In Europe, the BBC has always led the way in SDH, especially on television, which appears to be the medium that has traditionally heralded this type of AVT. As early as 1972, the BBC announced its Ceefax Teletext service, which would lead to the introduction of SDH seven years later (Robson 2004: 10) but by then the corporation had already been providing a weekly news programme with open subtitles (Donaldson). Flemish-speaking Belgium,[4] Germany, Italy and the Netherlands all started providing their first forms of SDH in the 1980s, while both Portugal and Spain joined the group in the early 1990s. In fact, many European broadcasters started developing teletext in the 1980s, and the introduction of SDH was directly linked to this development. On 1 June 1980, for instance, "videotext appeared in Germany in a national pilot project launched by the two public broadcasters ARD and ZDF.[5] From the outset, a part of this service was a limited amount of subtitling for the deaf and hearing-impaired" (Carroll).

Initially, the number of programmes to be provided with subtitles was very limited everywhere. Most channels started with the odd programme that was somehow thought to be of interest to a deaf audience and/or available for pre-recorded subtitling, and then expanded the service to news programmes. Dewulf states, for instance, that after some isolated experiments, SDH started with makeshift subtitling equipment in 1983 on the Flemish public channel VRT.[6] Initially, VRT focused on sports programmes and a selection of pre-recorded productions, and it was not until 1992 that SDH became truly important with the daily subtitling of the second news broadcast, at around 10 p.m., a repeat of the then main 7.30 p.m. news programme. In Italy, the first broadcaster to provide SDH was RAI,[7] in 1986, with the Italian-dubbed version of Hitchcock's *Rear Window*. Says Eugeni

The subtitles were previously recorded and projected simultaneously with the film on page 777 of the RAI teletext (called *Televideo*). After this first success, the state-owned company decided to continue exploiting the possibilities offered by *Televideo* and to expand the service to other kinds of programmes such as the TV news, TV series, some general interest programmes, and children's programmes.

Early developments in Spain are detailed by Orero, Pereira and Utray (forthcoming), who claim that

> the first specific subtitles for the deaf and hard of hearing were broadcast in 1990 by the national Catalan TV corporation CCRTV[8] and a few months later by the state Spanish TV TVE.[9] Once the SDH service was available the rest of the Spanish channels gradually started to offer it too.[10]

In Portugal, says Neves

> SDH was first introduced [...] on television on 15 April 1999, by RTP (*Radio Televisão Portuguesa* now *Radio e Televisão de Portugal*) thanks to an agreement, signed between the Portuguese government, RTP and the national association for the Deaf, the *Associação Portuguesa de Surdos*. At the time, the national public broadcaster, which ran two channels, RTP1 and RTP2, committed itself to offering 15 hours per week of intralingual subtitling on Portuguese-spoken programmes.

Meanwhile, the situation has evolved, albeit not as thoroughly and quickly as the deaf and the hard-of-hearing communities of Western Europe might wish. In almost all the countries under consideration, public television is far ahead of commercial channels, with the exception of the UK, where public and commercial channels alike provide SDH.[11] An increase in subtitling percentages has generally gone hand in hand with more extensive consultation of the target audience and with the development of new forms of subtitling like 'live subtitling', sometimes also called 'real-time subtitling' with or without recourse to speech recognition, to be more specific. The speed with which these developments took place (or not) has usually tied in with new legislation or other forms of agreement brokered between governments and, for instance, public broadcasting channels, following constant pressure from the deaf and the hard-of-hearing organizations. European guidelines, and in particular the Television without Frontiers directive from 1989 (updated in 1997), have no doubt been important, but such directives are not sufficient. As Carroll rightly points out, referring to Germany

> Public broadcasters are aware of the needs of the deaf and hearing-impaired, [but] limited funding is the main obstacle to their providing comprehensive SDH, a problem which they are not permitted to alleviate through income generated by advertising.

Legislation is obviously an important requirement, but it is not enough. All the same, and in spite of financial limitations, most public channels, and some commercial channels, are of course trying, though (rumour has it) the

German commercial channels are partly concerned about the negative consequences of any sanctionary laws.

Indeed, following the 1990 Broadcasting Act,[12] subsequent Acts of Parliament have gradually increased the requirement for subtitling on television in the UK, and have extended the scope of the initial act to non-terrestrial broadcasters. However, as Donaldson points out, "in spite of these positive developments [...] there is concern that the current legislation contains too many 'opt-out' loopholes and that Ofcom, the body responsible for monitoring the legislation, has not been strict enough in insisting on proper provision of access services". In other words, quality is suffering from the implementation of laws that aim at quantity only. *Television for All*, a BBC Research & Development publication (2003), indeed states that the BBC subtitled 80% of its programmes at the time of writing and that it intends to provide subtitles for all its programmes by 2008, thereby setting its own standards.

In Flanders, SDH is regulated by a 'management contract' between the public channel VRT and the Flemish government. The previous contract, which expired in 2006, stated no more than that VRT "should pay attention to minority groups" (Dewulf), but the new 2006 contract has become much more concrete, mentioning both SDH and AD explicitly. VRT has had to pledge to gradually increase SDH to 95% by 2010. In fact, all European countries offering digital television are aiming for 100% subtitling by that time. At present, the Flemish public channel is set to achieve 50% by the end of 2006. The state of affairs in the Netherlands is very similar. Here, a general management directive [*algemene maatregel van bestuur*] was also announced for 2006, stipulating that, by 2010, 100% of all Dutch language programmes must be subtitled on public television. It is expected that the commercial channels will also be compelled to start subtitling soon (Lentz), a situation that, once again, is echoed in Flanders. Some subtitling companies working for the commercial sector are certainly offering the service, as was confirmed by Verberk from The Subtitling Company, Brussels, but there is no legislation on the matter. In contrast, new legislation (20 September 2006) stipulates that all news broadcasts on the ten local Flemish channels must henceforth have teletext (page 888) subtitling for their news broadcasts.[13] This new subtitling service is expected to reach about one million Flemish citizens with hearing problems (Dewulf). The Flemish government has given each of the channels a lump sum of €50,000 for investment in subtitling equipment and is allocating €50,000 annually for employing specialized employees. This sum, however, is being used for training young journalists working for the local channels, not for training new translators in the field of accessibility.

In Italy, the Television without Frontiers directive of the European Commission has been regularly ignored by both the public and the private broadcasters (according to Eugeni), even though it was originally hoped that the so-called *Stanca* law (9 January 2004, with implementation guidelines as of 2005), would change this. Its objective is certainly comprehensive social inclusion. However, it aims, first and foremost, at literacy through the use of computers, and therefore IT accessibility rather than television. What is more, it entails obligations for the public administration, but RAI (the Italian public broadcaster) is not considered to be part of that administration. All the same, the law does ask all national television networks to increase their volumes of subtitled programmes and to try to make most of their services accessible.[14] At present, RAI is subtitling more than 70 hours a week (approximately fourteen per cent) of the programmes in winter time and up to 20% in summer time, when fewer real-time programmes and more old television series are broadcast. According to Eugeni, public awareness is increasing quickly.

In Germany, where legal matters relating to television are regulated on a state basis, the situation is different still, but again, the European directive is believed to be having an effect. Although German broadcasters are not yet required by law to subtitle any specific amount of programming for the deaf and hearing-impaired, an act entitled *Gesetz zur Gleichstellung behinderter Menschen und zur Änderung anderer Gesetze* [Act for the emancipation of physically challenged people and for the amendment of other acts] was passed in Germany on 1 May 2002

> giving associations representing the interests of the disabled the rights to negotiate with enterprises and other bodies to draw up 'target agreements' and to improve access. Several of the regional public broadcasters have self-imposed agreements to improve their accessibility and all are under some pressure from various lobby and interest groups to increase the amount of programming for the deaf and hearing-impaired.

The following, more detailed figures, also quoted from Carroll, describe recent developments in Germany from a quantitative point of view

> ARD [...] subtitles virtually all films and TV series during evening prime time viewing. Current affairs, documentaries, quiz shows and other entertainment programmes are normally still not subtitled [...] ARD subtitled 60,737 minutes in total (including the news and repeats) in 1998.
>
> Figures provided by Joachim Kotelmann of ARD Text in February 2006 show that ARD subtitled a total of 58,400 minutes in 965 programmes in 1999. Calculations for the year 2006 indicate a marked increase: in the first quarter of 2006, ARD subtitled 209 programmes, totalling 8,950 minutes or 150 hours. Provided this level is maintained, the amount of subtitling for the deaf and hearing-impaired on Germany's First Programme in 2006 will be approx. 20%, i.e. some 110,000 minutes or 1,833 hours.
>
> In 1998, public broadcaster ZDF subtitled 36,865 minutes (12,975 minutes new programming, 23,890 minutes repeats). In 1999, this figure was raised minimally to approximately 37,000 minutes. A 100% increase came between 2000 and 2001 with the launch of live subtitling of ZDF news broadcasts in 2001, which met with a warm response from deaf and hearing-impaired audiences. Currently ZDF subtitles three news broadcasts a day live as well as significant sports and current affairs programmes such as pre-election debates, and the repeat of a popular entertainment show, *Wetten dass*, which is broadcast six to seven times a year. Figures cited by President of the European Hard of Hearing Associa-

tion, Marcel Bobeldijk, in 2006 indicate that ZDF subtitled 18% of its programmes in 2005. In 2005, in addition to feature films, series and the like, 28,749 minutes of programming were subtitled live. In the first quarter of 2006, 9,371 minutes were subtitled live, an increase of 6,433 minutes over the same period in 2005.

In Portugal, SDH was introduced on television before legislation made it compulsory. The law that was in force when RTP first introduced teletext subtitling, *Lei 31A/98 de 14 de Julho* [Law 31A/98 of 14 July 1998] made no mention at all of the needs of hearing impaired viewers. According to Neves, this situation changed in 2002, with the *Lei 8/2002 de 11 de Fevereiro* [Law 8/2002 of 11 February 2002], when a new line (Line f) was introduced to article 44 stipulating that

> when passing out new broadcasting licences, priority would be given to Portuguese television broadcasters who offered equal opportunities to all citizens in their access to information and programmes in general, and that provided subtitling or sign language interpreting for the benefit of Deaf and hard-of-hearing viewers.

The law was enforced within the context of the Portuguese government's project for public service television, *Novas Opções para o Audiovisual 2002* [New Options in Audiovisual 2002], and with the 2003 RTP/SIC/TVI agreement. However, the obligation to make programmes accessible was later toned down as another Television Law, *Lei nº 23/2003 de 22 de Agosto* [Law 23/2003 of 22 August], reduced its reference to the matter to one single line, (*Art.47, al.2.f*), stating merely that television broadcasters must "*promover a possibilidade de acompanhamento das emissões por pessoas surdas ou com deficiência auditiva*" [promote the possibility for deaf and hard-of-hearing people to follow broadcasting] (Neves).

With regard to Spain, Orero, Pereira and Utray (forthcoming) write that while in the past SDH was provided on a voluntary basis there is now increased social awareness, and in June 2001 the *Ley de Fomento y Promoción de la Cinematografía y el Sector Audiovisual* [Law for the Promotion of Cinema and the Audiovisual Sector] (*BOE*, July 10, 2001) was passed, which offers grants for films with SDH and AD. There is a new *Ley general audiovisual* [General Audiovisual Law], which is now at a white-paper stage, and the objectives of this law are to merge current standards and adapt them to the new technological and social contexts. Regarding accessibility, article 62 regulates access for disabled people and establishes that all TV channels should make their contents available for people with sensorial disabilities through SDH, AD, and sign language. The objectives are clearly defined and a transitory provision draws up a calendar for the implementation of the services with which state-owned channels, national commercial licensees and other television channels with national coverage whose audience exceeds ten percent must comply.

The authors also provide the following draft calendar for assistive services on Spanish television from the white paper:

	2006	2007	2008	2009	2010	2011	2012	2013	2014	2015
SDH	40%	45%	50%	55%	60%	65%	70%	80%	90%	100%
sign language	1%	2%	3%	4%	5%	6%	7%	8%	9%	10%
AD	1%	2%	3%	4%	5%	6%	7%	8%	9%	10%

National broadcast licensees

	2006	2007	2008	2009	2010	2011	2012	2013	2014	2015
SDH	35%	40%	45%	50%	55%	60%	65%	70%	75%	80%
sign language	1%	1.5%	2%	2.5%	3%	3.5%	4%	4.5%	4.5%	5%
AD	1%	1.5%	2%	2.5%	3%	3.5%	4%	4.5%	4.5%	5%

Other national TV channels with more than 10% audience share

	2006	2007	2008	2009	2010	2011	2012	2013	2014	2015
SDH	15%	20%	25%	30%	35%	40%	45%	50%	55%	60%
sign language	0.5%	0.5%	0.5%	1%	1%	1%	1.5%	1.5%	1.5%	2%
AD	0.5%	0.5%	0.5%	1%	1%	1%	1.5%	1.5%	1.5%	2%

Figure 1. Draft calendar for assistive services in Spanish television.

3. Evolution in the subtitling process

3.1 'Pop on' or 'block' subtitles versus 'scrolling' subtitles and reading speed

Even though, generally speaking, all countries started with SDH around the advent of teletext, they do not all use the same system, and the manner in which subtitles are produced also differs depending on the medium for which the subtitles are meant. Before venturing into the new developments in live subtitling, a brief survey of the most currently used pre-recorded methods for television subtitling is therefore in order.

The major divide, technically speaking, is between 'pop on' or 'block subtitles' and 'scrolling' subtitles, a distinction that appears to go hand in hand with 'edited' versus 'verbatim' subtitling.[15] Edited SDH subtitling most closely resembles open subtitling: it requires summary, paraphrase and omission to various degrees, as a subtitle remains on-screen for a set number of seconds only, before being replaced by the next one, hence the term 'pop on'. Such subtitling always requires a degree of summary or paraphrase, even if it is sometimes allowed to cover three lines rather than the two lines customary in open subtitling. Indeed, three lines will sometimes be used in order to render speech as literally as possible, thereby limiting editing, but obviously the reading speed of such long subtitles can be problematic. This is especially true for a target audience of which some members have more limited linguistic skills. According to some, this state of affairs may be improving with better and more adequate schooling in some countries. In Belgium and in the Netherlands, for instance, the reading speed of (edited) subtitles was gradually increased, following reception research carried out by the television channels in the late 1990s. The VRT style sheet (Saerens & Dewulf 2000) refers to this audience survey carried out by the channel to motivate going from seven seconds for a full two-line subtitle to six seconds instead. However, the target audience is a very diverse group and this evolution is undoubtedly negative for some of its members.[16] Moreover, the results for one country cannot be automatically extrapolated to other countries in different stages of development and with different educational systems.[17] Besides, all SDH differs from standard subtitling in the additional specialized information it provides – although this often leaves much to be desired on DVDs (cf. infra). In this respect too, the style sheets that various companies use are often quite different (cf. infra), even though all SDH usually contains information about meaningful sounds, music and paralinguistic information such as intonation,[18] in addition to either a summarized or an almost verbatim rendering of speech. In all countries, deciding what should be included and how this should be done has been an ongoing learning process for the channels involved as well as for the researchers or target groups following up their evolution.

For instance, when SDH was first introduced by RTP in Portugal in 1999, the same norms as the ones used in open subtitling were applied, with the difference that SDH aimed to provide a verbatim transcription of the spoken words. A better understanding of the makings of this particular type of subtitle came with actual practice, and Neves points out that the situation changed gradually as

> major steps were taken when SDH was introduced on commercial television. The first Portuguese commercial broadcaster to offer SDH was SIC, who did so on 6 October 2003. This new service had the unusual situation of being introduced within the context of a PhD research project, which meant that new subtitling solutions were to be tested and a new 'tradition', with new norms, was to be established. In fact, the experiment would come to change the way SDH was being done at RTP and determine the way the other commercial broadcaster, TVi, would come to present its subtitles, which would be introduced on 30 October 2003.

RTP still has in-house subtitlers today, while the commercial broadcasters have chosen to outsource their work to different subtitling companies. The conventions followed by each broadcaster are different, but the broadcasters have taken on some of the solutions that were introduced by SIC, more specifically, the displacement of subtitles to identify speakers and the introduction of colour for specific effects. All Portuguese broadcasters, as well as all the other countries discussed in this dossier, now introduce information about music, sound effects and off-screen sound, although not all of them have experimented with smileys to convey paralinguistic information, which Portugal does (Neves). Spain and Germany, like Portugal, Flanders and the Netherlands use pop on, edited subtitling and here too pre-recorded programmes with SDH are done either in-house or handed out, depending on the channel. The amount of information conveyed may vary but even if some edited (pop on) SDH subtitles provide more information than standard open subtitles, they still differ fundamentally from the (scrolling) verbatim subtitles used by the BBC, for instance.[19]

Scrolling subtitles have the advantage of allowing a verbatim rendering of speech since the flow of speech is never interrupted and the system can accommodate a much higher word-rate. Although many viewers appear to prefer this system (or, in fact, any system that 'censors' as little as possible),[20] verbatim scrolling requires reading speeds with which parts of the deaf and hard-of-hearing audience may not be able to cope. Some may not be willing to admit this but most are simply not aware of the problem. The jury is still out on which method is better, and on whether it is better to summarize or render speech as faithfully as possible and both systems are currently still in use.[21] However, it seems improbable that a deaf audience would be able to manage reading speeds that are faster than those of open subtitles for a hearing public.

Irrespective of the system used, pre-recorded subtitles are timed and written with the help of software programs that are usually those used for open subtitling or closed subtitling for DVD. We will therefore not go into software technicalities here.[22] The situation in the UK, however, provides a bridge to our next topic. In the British Isles, says Donaldson

> most pre-recorded programme subtitling [for television] follows the traditional route of having a trained subtitler working with a copy of the programme to prepare subtitles according to his/her company's specific guidelines. Developments in equipment (shot-change recognition, etc.) have considerably speeded up this process over the years, reflecting the continuing pressure to reduce costs and turnaround times.

What is more, he points out that the most recent major development has been the onset of "speech input" even for pre-recorded subtitles.

3.2 Pre-recorded versus live subtitling and quality issues

Considering that no more than 20 years ago there was virtually no subtitling for the deaf and the hard-of-hearing, it is hardly surprising that receiving more subtitling was the first priority for both deaf and hard-of-hearing associations and legislative bodies in the past, and indeed continues to be so. This is demonstrated, for instance, by the demands of the *Samenwerkingsverband Ondertitel Alle Programma's* (SOAP) in the Netherlands.[23] It is also logical that SDH started with pre-recorded subtitling. The technical possibilities offered by Telenet were limited initially, and pre-recorded SDH has much in common with open television subtitling, with which some of the countries under consideration already had much experience. As the demand for the subtitling of current affairs programmes grew, the need for faster subtitling methods arose. Indeed, live subtitling requires that the speech of the interviewees, for instance, appears on-screen as they speak. In order to achieve this, different methods were developed and used over time.

Germany started with live subtitling at an extremely early stage. As Carroll points out, ARD was the first German broadcaster to introduce real-time or live subtitling of the news, starting with the popular 8 p.m. *Tagesschau* as early as 1984, and currently "the 4 p.m., 5 p.m. and 8 p.m. news on ARD provide real-time intralingual subtitles for most bulletins in the form of closed captions on Videotext page 150". ZDF launched live subtitling of news broadcasts in 2001 and currently "the channel subtitles three news broadcasts a day live, as well as significant sports and current affairs programmes such as pre-election debates." Live subtitling is fast gaining in popularity: "in the first quarter of 2006, 9,371 minutes were subtitled live, an increase of 6,433 minutes over the same period in 2005". As far as methods are concerned, German channels opted for speech recognition virtually from the start.

In Flanders, VRT was subtitling 50 hours a week in 2006. Of this number approximately 30 hours were pre-recorded, 20 hours semi-live[24] and live news programmes. Live subtitling on VRT is limited to real-time sports programmes and news programmes at the time of writing (December 2006), and it is solely done by means of speech recognition. However, Flanders started with experiments in what was then the 'craft' of live subtitling as early as 1981, with one person dictating the text and another typing as fast as they could, later switching to *velotype* (cf. below) for a limited period of time. Today, VRT uses the Softel subtitling program SWIFT with Dragon Naturally Speaking. The working method in Flanders and in most other countries working with edited subtitling and speech recognition is exactly the same as that for the Netherlands, described below.[25]

In the Netherlands, pre-recorded SDH subtitling for one of the major public channels, *Nederlandse Openbare Omroep* [Dutch Public Broadcasting], is done on SysMedia WinCAPS software.[26] Lentz specifies that the subtitlers use a headset and work through some 30 to 45 minutes of programmes in one day. If no time codes have to be added to the subtitles, as many as 60 or more minutes can be done in eight hours.[27] However, for live programmes, and hence live subtitles, different systems are used. One such system is *velotype*, the other speech recognition. For *velotype* subtitling, the collaboration of two people is required. A *velotypist* types on a special keyboard, which produces syllables rather than letters, while an assistant listens to the programme, summarizes and dictates. The subtitles appear in real time, but with some delay, usually referred to as lag. In the Netherlands, live subtitling with speech recognition is in full development, but Lentz states that even for this method two people are usually required. The delay is shorter than when subtitles are produced by a *velotypist*, an important condition being that speech recognition is good. One subtitler speaks into the microphone of the headset he/she is wearing to listen to the programme, and the speech recognition software, which has been trained to recognize the voice and articulation of the subtitler, produces subtitles on the screen. Theoretically, the recognizer will hear only the voice for which it has been trained and the subtitler speaks in a quiet environment, so that accurate results can be obtained. In practice, this is not always the case. A second person is therefore brought in to correct speech recognition mistakes (e.g. in spelling, when a word has been misunderstood, or replaced by a homophone) before the subtitles go on air. Correcting mistakes can be done by the person dictating the titles, but this is extremely difficult and feasible only for some programmes, provided that the commentator does not speak too fast. Whereas the delay tends to be shorter if the subtitler works alone, the number of incorrect subtitles will be higher, Lentz says, especially if the programme contains fast speech. He has found that team work delivers the highest quality in live subtitling so far.[28]

In the UK too live subtitling is mainly used for news, discussion and sports programmes, and is done in a variety of ways. The BBC started with live subtitling using stenographers[29] (former court reporters) in 1990, transferring to re-speaking in 2001 (Marsh 2006). The BBC now has some 650 hours of live subtitling per month (more in summer, less in winter), on different channels.[30] They use Via-Voice speech recognition software in combination with K-live, designed by the former BBC Research and Development department for the production of subtitles (Marsh 2006). In fact, speech recognition technology is even used for pre-recorded programmes, as the BBC's Research and Development department reported a few years ago (2003):

> For pre-recorded programmes, speech recognition can also be used to good effect albeit in an unusual way. We have developed a technique called Assisted Subtitling in which a speech recogniser is used to track through the script of a programme matching the written dialogue to the programme soundtrack. Having the script available beforehand means that the speech recogniser no longer needs to work out what is spoken but instead automatically

assigns a timing marker to each word in the script. Once this timing stage has been completed, the script is, in effect, synchronised to the programme soundtrack and from this, fully synchronised subtitles can be produced automatically.

At the BBC,[31] speech recognition is combined with verbatim subtitling and the scrolling technique, which it uses across the board for SDH. This means that, in some respects, its live subtitling method is very similar to the one described above, but also that it is dissimilar in a number of ways. Scrolling in live subtitling appears to have its own advantages and disadvantages. Indeed, the continuous procession of the words on-screen, without delays between subtitles, may be more convenient for live SDH production. The technique allows the subtitler to re-speak more fluently – although he/she must still edit and insert punctuation – than for the production of distinctly segmented and edited pop on subtitles. Recent research seems to indicate that respeaking for scrolling subtitles is closer to the skills (conference) interpreters are taught at translation and interpreting departments today.[32] A novelty at the BBC (2003) Research and Development department was that the corporation experimented with live subtitlers working from home on a network:

At BBC R&D we have developed a live subtitling system that allows subtitles to be created either by using speech recognition or stenography. The design offers the particular benefit of allowing subtitlers to work on any broadcast service from anywhere in the BBC, or even from home.

Since any form of interpreting is very labour-intensive and interpreters have to be relieved regularly, this system is extremely practical: the subtitlers who are on duty can monitor each other's progress online, on an internal connection, and take over when they are given the signal to do so. The software system that they use also allows for the addition of colours, for instance, at the touch of one key, while they speak.[33] At the BBC, it is claimed that live subtitling with scrolling makes it easier for one subtitler to work alone, since fewer tasks have to be accomplished at once (no or little summarizing) and subtitlers therefore make fewer mistakes. Still, mistakes as a result of faulty speech recognition remain and there are few quantitative data publicly available as yet which prove that this system indeed produces better results qualitatively as well as quantitatively.[34]

In Italy, apart from RAI and RTV,[35] all companies provide only prerecorded SDH. Rete 4, one of the three channels of Mediaset (with Canale 5 and Italia 1), the major private national broadcaster in Italy, subtitles two editions of the news a day, but one with sign language interpreters and the other one with pre-recorded subtitles. Both RAI and RTV subtitle the national TV news, or intend to do so soon, as we write. While RAI uses stenotypists only for the breaking news, RTV is planning to make use of respeaking both for real-time and for semi-live news reports (Eugeni).

In Portugal, significant investment in new subtitling equipment is being carried out and the country is now technically equipped to start providing live subtitling, but the service is not yet available as we write. Still, news bulletins and some live shows have been made accessible to Deaf viewers through sign language interpreting, which, according to Neves, is "an 'easier' solution at a time when pre-recorded teletext subtitling is still in its infancy and undergoing change and improvement".

The danger in the developments in live subtitling, which are the result of legislation and/or other agreements demanding more subtitling, and which will no doubt be taken up by other countries, is that quality might be sacrificed for quantity. This is the fear expressed by Donaldson about the situation in the UK: according to him live subtitling makes far more demands on the viewer than normal pre-recorded subtitling. He confirms that the transmission rate of live subtitles is often extremely fast, and that they therefore contain considerably more errors than pre-recorded ones. Moreover, live subtitles "are also more likely to be placed on different parts of the screen and to share the screen with other on-screen text, further increasing the difficulty of following such subtitles". He goes on to say that

> it is not enough to have a high proportion of material subtitled – such subtitles must be of an acceptable quality [...] Hearing people would not accept a soundtrack with words mispronounced, put in the wrong order, omitted or an entirely wrong word used. Why should the deaf and hard-of-hearing tolerate the equivalent of such errors in subtitling? [...] Nevertheless, there is at the moment little choice in the matter given the demands of the viewers for subtitles on live broadcasts (news, current affairs and sport in particular). Such 'live' subtitles as are prepared using normal keyboards tend to lag so far behind the on-screen action as to be almost unwatchable.

4. The feasibility of national/international guidelines and harmonization

The introduction of European (or worldwide) guidelines, and thereby standards, might improve the current situation in which each country develops SDH more or less independently and to the best of its abilities. Actually, all our respondents believe that uniformity would be a good thing, but only up to a certain point. All the researchers and professional subtitlers who responded to our questionnaire point out a number of difficulties (cf. below); some of these may be insurmountable, whereas others can certainly be overcome.

Most current national guidelines have been drawn up on the basis of acquired experience, but some channels have done (limited) research and/or have consulted empirical experts. According to Lentz, the written norms that are used by the public channel in the Netherlands, for instance, were drawn up by a group of senior subtitlers in co-operation with a partially deaf editor at *Publieke Omroep* [Public Broadcasting]. However, some reception research appears to have been carried out as early as the 1970s. Examples are the 1977 NOS publication and the continued NOS monitoring of viewer satisfaction through monthly tests, mentioned by de Groot (2001), in addition to the survey of literature on the accessibility of television programmes, carried out by van Son *et al.* in 1998. What is more, the NOS style book has been adapted to reflect new insights on different occasions and de Groot (2001) mentions versions from 1997 and 2001.

In fact, most channels have their own style books, and some are quite detailed. The VRT's instructions for SDH (2000) in Flanders run to 24 pages, including a brief survey of the target audience and its needs. The style book makes a distinction between pre-recorded and live subtitling, as well as between subtitling for fiction and non-fiction programmes. The document deals with reading speed, provides detailed instructions for adding paralinguistic and other information, stating what must be added and how this must be done (i.e. with reference to layout, the number of lines to be used, colours, capital letters, punctuation, etc.). This style book too was adapted following some target audience research in the late 1990s (Doens 2000). Verberk of The Subtitling Company, one of the firms working for commercial television in Flanders as well as for DVD, says that they apply their standard subtitling style sheet (which is always adapted to the customer's requirements), but that, generally speaking, the reading speed for SDH is actually higher than that of their interlingual subtitling for the general public. They further make use of colours and the positioning of subtitles to identify speakers. To the question whether a European standard might be a good idea Verberk replied that it would be hard to implement, given the variety in subtitling styles even within Flanders alone. Still, it would seem that many of today's stylistic variants (e.g. in the use of italics or dashes) are based on companies' personal preferences. Uniformity based on research would therefore simplify both the tasks of producing and using subtitles (cf. Neves on Portugal below).

In Germany, the situation regarding guidelines appears to be no different. Carroll confirms that

> a conglomerate of guidelines exist for SDH [...] Some television stations and DVD distributors have their own differing guidelines, which have developed over the years, based on experience gained with videotext rather than research. Subtitling companies generally have to adhere to these client-specific guidelines. Some providers (i.e., subtitling companies) have drawn up their own in-house guidelines, and standards. Berlin subtitling company *Titelbild*, for example, has a comprehensive set of guidelines, based on its experience with interlingual and intralingual subtitling and exchange with hearing-impaired groups [...] Research is needed to test and optimize standards.

In Italy, guidelines that are the result of collaboration between different parties are in use, but apart from the dedicated offices of the TV broadcasters, there is probably just one subtitling company, named Colby, that is devoting some efforts to SDH (Eugeni). The guidelines they drafted are the result of collaboration between the company and the *Centro Communicare è Vivere*

(CECOEV), an Italian association defending the rights of people with hearing impairments. There are other forms of collaboration as well, notably between the University of Bologna at Forlì, RAI and *Ente Nacional de Sordomudos* (ENS), but "the guidelines are not yet ready and their respect is neither guaranteed nor promised", says Eugeni, adding that "other subtitling companies offering SDH [in Italy] base their work on common sense and on non-systemic, one-off collaborations with the Deaf community".

There is no national norm in Portugal either. Broadcasters have chosen different ways to go about their services. Neves did set forward a proposal for a set of guidelines in the context of her PhD research project (2005). These guidelines are being roughly followed by the subtitlers working for SIC, and Neves's guidelines "are to be published under the patronage of the ICS – *Instituto da Comunicação Social*. They are presently seen as an embryo for future (national) norms for SDH". Meanwhile, all broadcasters have already taken on some of the solutions that were introduced by SIC (e.g. the displacement of subtitles to identify speakers, the introduction of colours), but since there is still no consensus as to what may be considered 'best practice', they are still trying to find their personal subtitling 'style'. This is a pity, Neves rightly points out, since many deaf and hard-of-hearing viewers say that switching between conventions when changing channels makes following subtitles more difficult.

Even in the UK, national guidelines do not exist. Each company does have its own internal ones, but there are no nationally recognized 'protocols', which Donaldson regrets, echoing some of Neves's concerns. The result is, again and even more so if one considers SDH in different media, "a variety of often radically different subtitling styles, which can of course be confusing for the viewer. The ideal situation would be for a nationally accepted standard, perhaps administered – and monitored – by Ofcom".

Spain appears to be the only country in our survey with national guidelines, but these guidelines are far from perfect. Sánchez writes that

> there are Spanish national guidelines covering SDH for teletext: UNE 153010. These guidelines were drawn up by a working group consisting of broadcasters, service providers and service users. They are broadly based on the [UK's] Ofcom guidelines.[36] Unfortunately, the guidelines are not based on scientific research which there is a marked lack of in Spain.

In fact, the effectiveness of UNE 153010 has been scrutinized in greater detail by Pereira Rodríguez and Lorenzo García (2005) on the basis of the data "obtained from preliminary studies of reception and the investigation and experience of professionals and researchers within the scope of subtitling". Their study focuses on "the elements which are different from the subtitles addressed to hearing viewers (locating and identifying speakers, number of lines and position, timing, transfer of sound effects)" (Pereira

Rodríguez & Lorenzo García 2005:21). The authors come to the conclusion that the UNE 153010 is an excellent starting point for drawing up unified SDH guidelines in Spain, but point out that in order to reach the majority of the deaf community at least two types of SDH ought to be produced for the two fundamentally different groups of SDH users. Meanwhile they suggest that the applicability and usefulness of the existing norm ought to be constantly monitored, adjusted and – for some subtopics – expanded, adding that it would be quite useful if some argumentation were provided motivating the proposed guidelines in cases where different SDH approaches to specific problems exist.

Generally speaking, there appears to be agreement among our respondents in as far as the need for uniform national standards and guidelines is concerned, as long as this goes hand in hand with an increased awareness of the need for diversification in accordance with the subgroups that constitute the target audience (Pereira Rodríguez & Lorenzo García 2005). On an international level, the matter becomes more complex. Eugeni rightly points out that until there is greater awareness of the need for SDH and what it should provide across the board, it is almost useless to talk about harmonization. Echoing the concerns about quantity versus quality discussed above, he states that

> the Italian SDH market is not developed at all and the Deaf have no idea of what a good subtitle is. All they ask for is more subtitles, they are not used to reading subtitles, and most of them do not even understand the text. Once they will be satisfied by quantity and fully used to reading a subtitled programme, it will be possible to talk about quality.

Eugeni ascribes this lack of awareness and insight to the fact that Italy is a dubbing country, not used to any kind of subtitling. On the other hand, it does not seem such a good idea to wait for acceptance to happen. Ideally, quantity and quality should go hand in hand. According to Imhauser, from Francophone Belgium, European guidelines could make the subtitling of a certain number of programmes compulsory, and could also set minimum standards to allow viewers to understand the colour codes, etc. The concept of 'minimum standards' appears to be crucial. Indeed, Eugeni points out that

> a good set of guidelines will never be useful if it does not focus on the target audience, especially in Italy. The linguistic competence and the reading speed of [some of the] Italian Deaf are, indeed, particularly basic and their comprehension of a subtitled programme is limited to some words.

The heterogeneity of the SDH target public, even within one country, is certainly an issue, and this heterogeneity will no doubt be greater still if one considers target audiences across countries with different educational and cultural traditions. Still, this does not mean, in our view, that the baby should be thrown out with the bath water.

The opinion expressed by Neves regarding European harmonization appears to be generally shared. She writes that any form of harmonization

> will necessarily need to allow for a certain amount of flexibility for viewers are usually set in their habits and changing them might not be easily achieved. Certain standards which cover technical or functional aspects, such as the European Telecommunications Standards Institute (ETSI) Standard ES 202 432 on access symbols for use with video content and ICT devices, might be relatively easy to implement on a wide scale; however, it will be more difficult to harmonise actual subtitling norms because viewers are used to their local practices and it will take time for people to accept changes. Furthermore, audiences' needs will necessarily differ for they result from intangible factors such as national character, educational and social background, among others.

She also states that

> even though standardisation and harmonisation are on the agenda of the policy makers of the European Union, I tend to believe that in the case of audiovisual translation in general and of SDH in particular, we are to witness a fragmentation of subtitling solutions rather than a harmonisation, though a great deal of harmonisation will be in order, to allow for compatibility and, consequently, diversity.

In other words, there is a need for harmonized guidelines up to a point, but both national identities and divergent technical developments catering for individual needs, make complete harmonization near-impossible. Sánchez agrees, adding another interesting comment:

> I would be in favour of harmonisation with regard to legibility. I think that studies conducted at EU level would be valid for all countries. However, with regard to readability, I think that studies need be conducted at national level because reading speeds amongst end users will vary depending on the history of SDH subtitling and the type of educational system which exists in each country. It is of course true that reading speeds vary considerably within each national group of those considered 'deaf or hard-of-hearing' and that one can never opt for a reading speed which will suit all. However, I think further study is needed at national level in order to ascertain the similarities and differences in the experience of SDH users in Spain and say, in the United Kingdom where more research has been done.

To conclude, Donaldson, speaking from a UK perspective, believes that harmonization is a good idea in as far as it is 'practical', and therefore most certainly achievable nationwide, given that different countries have their own, at times, contradictory methodologies.[37] He also believes that

> a generally accepted standard would be of particular assistance to countries performing SDH for the first time, as they would benefit from the experience of those countries which have been providing SDH for many years. There would also be cost-saving and time-saving benefits as training to an agreed standard would be expedited and file sharing (especially from English into subsequent languages) facilitated – a particular benefit given the high percentage of English-language material broadcast throughout Europe.

He rightly adds that any harmonization should be overseen by a "regulatory body responsible for adherence to quality".

5. Training, skills and the evolution of both these aspects

At first, SDH was taught exclusively on the job and most, if not all, SDH providers still offer in-house training. However, SDH is now also part of BA and/or MA programmes in Translation or Audiovisual Translation in several European countries. That, however, is where uniformity ends. Overall, a lack of consistent teaching methods and measurable standards still plagues the profession and, as a result, the professional prestige and remuneration of subtitlers. This lack of uniformity in training is, of course, tied in with the differing national traditions and stages of development described above. In our view, it would seem desirable for European standardization and harmonization of directives or guidelines, to devote considerable attention to training or possibly even training for trainers with a view to quality control.

All translation departments in Flemish colleges now offer subtitling either at BA and/or MA level and all departments entertain good working relationships with one or several commercial subtitling companies as well as the public television channel VRT. SDH is usually a subtopic in current courses, but the amount of time and attention, and especially hands-on training offered varies immensely. At University College Antwerp, for instance, occasional workshops are organized at BA level with professional subtitlers from various private companies, and working visits are paid to the VRT teletext department.[38] At ISTI (*Institut Supérieur pour Traducteurs et Interprètes*), Brussels, such workshops are taught within an MA programme in AVT by a former subtitler and sign interpreter, who works for *Radio et Télévision Belgique Francophone* (RTBF). In Flanders and in the Netherlands, the demand for SDH subtitlers is increasing rapidly as VRT and NOS have pledged to reach new targets by 2010, Flemish local channels receive limited subsidies, and commercial channels are under increased pressure to follow suit. This will hopefully have a positive impact on the types of courses offered, a hope that is shared by Dewulf (VRT). Until now, however, the choice is limited at best. Live subtitling with speech recognition is not taught at any of the departments for translation and interpreting in Belgium as we write, although University College Antwerp has incorporated the skill into its new Master in Interpreting, which starts in October 2007 and Hogeschool Gent also appears to be looking into the possibility of offering such a course within its MA programme. In Antwerp, a trial run of the course with a small group of volunteers is planned for the academic year 2006-2007 and an evening course in SDH more generally is envisaged for 2007-2008. Right now, both the Flemish public channel and subtitling companies still offer in-house training, but to newly hired personnel only. Verberk (The Subtitling Company, Brussels), for one, is in favour of more collaboration between companies and colleges/universities. In the Netherlands, the situation appears to be worse, with SDH subtitling training provided on the job only. Hogeschool Utrecht has sign language interpreting and written interpreting but no training in SDH, and nor does the *Vertaalacademie* [Translation Academy] at Maastricht, which is part of Hogeschool Zuyd.

In France, most subtitlers are still self-taught, although some universities offer courses, and professional subtitlers also tend to teach themselves the additional skills required for SDH, says Couté Rodriguez. In Germany, on the other hand,

> SDH subtitler training courses are currently provided by selected subtitling companies rather than by broadcasters who tend to provide ad hoc learning-by-doing induction for new subtitlers if and as required. In 2006 Titelbild ran an SDH training course for public broadcaster subtitlers. Very few universities in Germany teach any subtitling whatsoever so it is not surprising that SDH courses have not been taught at universities as yet. Titelbild works closely with Saarbrücken University and the *Sprachen und Dolmetscher Institut* (SDI), Munich, training both trainers and students. It is feasible that an SDH module will be included in future programmes with these institutions. (Carroll)

One would think that this state of affairs would be tied in with Germany and France being dubbing countries, and that in so-called subtitling countries, existing subtitling courses at universities and colleges would be more readily adapted to include SDH. However, the link between developments in SDH training and AVT traditions appears to be tenuous. Even though some countries are slightly ahead of their European neighbours, the development of university courses in SDH is only just beginning everywhere.

In Italy, another dubbing country, most of the SDH training is also done within existing subtitling companies and just a few university departments offer any AVT at all, but here too change is afoot. According to Eugeni,

> the Subtitle Project, directed by Dr Christopher Rundle of the University of Bologna, at Forlì (research department of Interdisciplinary Studies on Translation, Languages, and Culture), is working on special needs AVT in general, and on both real time and pre-recorded SDH in particular. [...] During one of the roundtables at the International Conference on Updating Research on Audiovisual Translation, held in Forlì from the 27th to the 29th of October 2005, all the Italian professional subtitlers complained of a lack of research on special needs AVT in general and on SDH in particular.

The *Scuola Superiore di Lingue Moderne per Interpreti e Traduttori* (SSLMIT) [the Higher Institute for Interpreters and Translators] of the University of Bologna at Forlì has meanwhile scheduled non-curricular undergraduate courses for the academic year 2006-2007, with the aim of teaching students the basics of pre-recorded SDH and of re-speaking. The pre-recorded SDH course is taught within the curricular course on interlingual subtitling, whereas the re-speaking course is part of the curriculum in simultaneous interpreting, a development that is comparable to that in Flanders.

In Portugal, a subtitling country by tradition, the introduction of SDH at SIC went hand-in-hand with research and with subtitler training (Neves 2005):

> SDH was first introduced at *Escola Superior de Tecnologia e Gestão de Leiria* in the academic year of 2002/2003. As far as it is known, this continues to be the only place in the country where translators are given initial training in SDH as a regular component of their undergraduate education. However, various workshops on SDH have been held at a number of universities, private schools and at subtitling companies.

In Spain, traditionally a dubbing country, there now appear to be subtitling courses "springing up all over the place" (Sánchez), but few of these deal with SDH. At the *Universitat Autònoma de Barcelona* (UAB), intralingual subtitling, which includes some notions of SDH, started in 2004-2005 within both the online and the face-to-face MA in Audiovisual Translation.[39] This is no doubt due to the fact that these MA programmes are fairly recent, set up at a time of increased awareness about the need for media accessibility. Indeed, from 2005-2006 the *Universitat Autònoma de Barcelona* has also been offering optional credits in media accessibility more generally, covering SDH, audio description (AD) and web accessibility. For its part, the *Centro de Formación Continua* of the *Universidad de Granada* launched an *Experto universitario en subtitulación para sordos y audiodescripción para ciegos,*[40] within the faculty and department of translation and interpreting in November 2005. The course addresses *diplomados* and *licenciados,*[41] as well as professional subtitlers who wish to expand their horizons or acquire more (theoretical) insight into the practice. At the University of Seville the *Master universitario en traducción audiovisual aplicada a la subtitulación y al doblaje* offers SDH as well as AD, and the University of Las Palmas de Gran Canaria started its *Master en subtitulado y audiodescripción* in October 2005.

To conclude with the UK, "most UK subtitling companies offer their own internal training schemes, usually taught by experienced subtitlers. The length of these courses can vary but – once again due to financial considerations – are rarely as long as they should be" (Donaldson). Besides, various universities have started offering SDH at undergraduate and/or postgraduate levels, within the context of broader curricula in AVT. Undergraduate courses, which basically offer an introduction to the subject, are available at Roehampton University and the University of Wales, Lampeter. SDH is included in postgraduate AVT programmes at Roehampton, Leeds, and Surrey.

It would seem that, irrespective of the country, the level and focus of university courses is rather unpredictable at present and varies even from institution to institution. This has prompted criticism on the part of some professionals. Among our respondents, both Sánchez and Donaldson, for instance, state that the courses taught at universities do not always meet professional requirements, and similar comments regularly surface in other countries as well. In Flanders, University College Antwerp has set up an evening course in collaboration with professionals from the AVT sector in order to train translators who did not have the opportunity to take AVT courses when they were students. According to Donaldson such courses should address both theory and practice in detail, but he feels that

> the widely-held perception of private subtitling providers is that academic courses focus on the former too much and need to take more account of the latter [...] any such course must include hands-on experience of subtitling under actual time constraints and should include experienced subtitlers amongst its tutors.

Likewise, according to Sánchez,

> any training in SDH should be in some way regulated in order for there to be a qualification which will ensure employers of a minimum standard of competency. Collaboration between industry and academia is basic. Employers need to be assured that a potential employee has completed a course and therefore reaches a certain level of competency.

On the other hand, the remuneration paid by some employers is not exactly a stimulus for good (future) translators to enter the AVT profession. It is an open secret that different companies involved in AVT across Europe (and probably beyond) sometimes prefer unqualified students over competent professionals in order to cut corners. The degree to which the work of translators in general and audiovisual translators in particular is appreciated, and protected, for example by copyright laws, is an issue that warrants more research in itself. A survey of standards and legislation regarding the professional status of translators working in AVT at this time would no doubt also yield variable results. In short, the issues of uniformity, standards and quality must be linked to 'good practice' in different senses and in different quarters, both in teaching and in the highly competitive profession.

And yet, 'good practice' in terms of employment and/or production quality aside, it is obvious that new developments in SDH will create more and different types of employment, which training courses will eventually have to incorporate. The steady increase in SDH production will require more training facilities, whereas the emergence of new forms of SDH will continue to modify the requirements such training must meet. As the need for media accessibility begins to dawn on an increasing number of people active in the field of translation, and as different types of (audiovisual) translation and (audiovisual) interpreting proliferate, merge and/or diverge, so must the courses that teach these new forms of oral, written and/or electronic text production.

It seems inevitable that, in time, different specialties will emerge within SDH, more concretely that of translators working in pre-recorded SDH and those working in live subtitling. Recent trends in curriculum development taking live subtitling with speech recognition on board, already appear to point in that direction, even though in practice, most broadcasters who use re-speaking are in a transitional phase. At present, Red Bee Media is not yet purposefully hiring interpreters, and its SDH subtitlers are expected to be flexible, working for pre-recorded as well as live subtitling (Marsh 2006). At VRT, three out of five recently (2006) hired subtitlers were interpreters (Dewulf), but 16 out of the 18 teletext subtitlers working for the channel also do live subtitling, at least occasionally.

Ideally, the development of new training programmes should be based on research or, at least, proceed in interaction with research. More insight into the needs of the target audience is essential, keeping the issue of quality versus quantity in mind, but also into the advantages of different production processes, the technology currently available and the best way of optimizing both software and hardware. Research should also yield better insight into the skills that are required (for re-speaking and SDH generally) and have an impact on how and within which institutional context or department, future subtitlers (in different specialties) should be trained.

In reply to the question about the skills a good subtitler in SDH should have today, most of our respondents reacted along the following lines, with minor variations. Since the traditional borders between AVT forms are fading, Neves (Portugal) states, for instance, that

> many of the techniques and characteristics of [...] different sorts of subtitling may now be found in the other. For instance, SDH is no longer necessarily intralingual, nor is the use of colour to identify speakers exclusive to SDH. The DVD market has contributed greatly to such changes. This means that, in principle, all subtitlers will be using similar skills when subtitling.

She adds, however, that is it fundamental for subtitlers to have "a deep understanding of the needs of the intended addressee". In the case of SDH, this means "an informed insight into the physical, psychological, educational and sociological implications of deafness", plus a highly developed "sound awareness" and the ability to determine when sound plays a narrative role or when it contributes, in an active way, towards character identification or composition, or towards the establishment of mood. On the production side, subtitlers have to be able to make the text 'readable' for people who cannot complement their reading with hearing, balancing quantity against acceptable reading speeds. The following view, offered by Donaldson (UK), summarizes most other concerns:

> The primary skills needed by any good (as opposed to merely competent!) subtitler are superb native language skills, including a detailed understanding of punctuation and grammar (skills which are increasingly difficult to find), a wide-ranging general knowledge and ideally good typing ability. Any well-planned training course should then be able to teach the

necessary editing and computer skills, etc., in addition to an understanding of the particular needs of the Deaf and hard-of-hearing audience (which would ideally include an understanding of lip-reading but very rarely does).

Eugeni (Italy), Lentz (Netherlands) and Dewulf (Flanders) add to that: interpreting skills for live subtitling, 100% concentration, the ability to do several things at the same time and to work under stress in difficult circumstances. The newer skills also include insight into how speech recognition works, its strengths and weaknesses, and the need to prepare the software program for specific broadcasts, notably by continuously expanding its lexicon. Finally, interlingual SDH is still in its infancy, appearing on some DVDs (mostly in English, German and Italian), but when it catches on all the above qualities will have to be combined with good translating skills in the more traditional sense.

6. Different media and the impact of digital television and DVD

That flexibility and adaptability are staple skills for anyone working in SDH will only be confirmed as SDH exploitation in the theatre, in the cinema, on DVD and on digital television expands. Not only does each medium offer its own possibilities for greater accessibility, it also poses its own challenges; and although television still appears to be in the vanguard for SDH across the board, there are some signs of change on other fronts.

In Germany, for instance, a minimum of 30 cinemas will have regular monthly and later weekly screenings with subtitles for the deaf and hearing-impaired by the end of 2006. According to Carroll,

> a number of major distributors have pledged their support for the project and reference cinemas are being equipped with the requisite facilities. If the project is as successful as anticipated, it is expected that additional cinemas and distributors will follow suit.[42]

By contrast, Neves writes that

> cinemas in Portugal mainly offer foreign spoken films that come with Portuguese subtitling for viewers in general. Deaf patrons are expected to follow films as they are given to hearers. They seem to be happy with the subtitles that are provided for hearers both because they have become used to following films with such subtitles and because going to the cinema is not one of the most popular forms of entertainment among the deaf. As far as it is known, there are no cinemas or theatres in Portugal with special facilities for Deaf and hard-of-hearing patrons.

The picture in Flanders and in the Netherlands, traditionally subtitling countries like Portugal, is very similar to the Portuguese one, but on the other hand, at this point not much appears to be happening in Italy, France or Spain. In fact, in both France and Spain standard open subtitling for the general public is only just beginning to gain some popularity. As for the UK, its SDH tradition is apparently spilling over into other venues, although, as always, the impetus for this service came from deaf people themselves. There are now some 160 cinemas in the UK which provide regular showings of mainstream movies with (open) SDH subtitles.[43] These subtitles are generally of good quality, albeit rather fast (Donaldson).

In the theatre, SDH, usually in the form of surtitling, is only just beginning too. In Belgium, there is SDH at the *Opéra de la Monnaie* in Brussels and in some French theatre festivals (Imhauser) but nothing appears to be happening in Flanders, apart from occasional interlingual surtitling of foreign language productions for the general public.[44] In the Netherlands and in Portugal, surtitles in the opera or the theatre are also done for the benefit of hearers rather than for that of hard-of-hearing audiences. In Italy and Spain, not very much is happening either, except for the odd event. In the UK, some theatres offer SDH but this is certainly not a widespread practice and the subtitles are often verbatim, ill-timed and therefore very difficult to follow. Sometimes, theatres are equipped with individual, small screens, on the back of the seats in the preceding row. In some venues, however, the screens are positioned on the ceiling under the balcony, i.e. halfway the theatre, forcing the target viewers to sit in the back, which reduces the chance of people with limited hearing impairments to make the best of the dialogue spoken on stage. To cut a long story short, research into what would be good practice for both cinema and theatre as well as a considerable amount of lobbying are still urgently needed in these areas. Accessibility obviously involves more than the provision of adequate subtitles or surtitles, and requires an interdisciplinary approach encompassing architecture and design that lies outside the scope of the present survey.

Moving on to the situation on the DVD market, one can observe the state of flux the market is in. DVD could have a beneficial influence on SDH in other media since DVDs are international, they reach many people, have almost unlimited quantitative capacities, and one language could be used as a template file. However, the DVD business is also a highly lucrative and competitive one, often subject to global cost-cutting exercises. Today some DVDs that are marketed in different regions, or 'territories' as the term goes, do have English and occasionally German and Italian SDH, but in the UK, Donaldson writes:

> Initially, DVD [...] demanded the highest possible subtitle quality (and an appreciation of this was reflected in very positive audience feedback). Unfortunately, this high quality did not influence television subtitling – and, indeed, some subtitling companies have split their subtitlers into two groups, DVD and television, with the former being their best (and better paid) subtitlers. Recently, however, the demand to cut costs has led in particular to an increased use of unsuitable (for the UK audience) 'reformatted' USA closed-caption files, with American spellings, reading speeds of 300+ words per minute and specific American 'protocols'.

Referring to the situation in Germany, Carroll does point out that

> it is still easier to find DVDs with English subtitles for the deaf and hearing- impaired than it is to access German SDH on DVDs. However, an increasing number of distributors such as Warner Bros. Entertainment are now including German SDH on virtually all DVDs released in Germany.

Carroll also hopes that the trend will continue and that the promotion of cinema SDH in Germany will boost public awareness.

Finally, the respondents who replied to our question about the influence digital television might have on the future of SDH, had high hopes for this new medium. Digital television, says Imhauser, will obviously offer many technical advantages, including advantages related to the 'physical' accessibility of the subtitles, briefly referred to above with respect to theatre and cinema. Besides, digital television will facilitate the production of different colours and fonts, and the positioning of subtitles in different places on the screen. Sánchez confirms that

> digital television allows for text-based or bitmap based subtitling, thus permitting a range of fonts and images. There will also be the possibility of more than one subtitle stream and this means that at least theoretically, more than one type of SDH could be broadcast, for example one stream could contain verbatim subtitles and the other subtitles which are adapted to fit a certain reading speed. I hope that this will open up the debate on readability / legibility and lead to research on reading speeds, etc.

Neves too stresses that the greatest asset of digital television will be the combination of increased flexibility with increased image quality and therefore legibility, but points out that it will no doubt call for an adjustment of technology and procedures from production, to file exchange, to broadcasting and all the way through to reception. She goes beyond the possibilities pointed out by Sánchez, claiming that

> digital television will allow for multi-layered, mix and match subtitles, allowing viewers to compose their personal subtitling solutions as if they were do-it-yourself kits. This may mean that subtitles will need to be conceived as separate modules that may be matched and mixed to suit the likes and needs of distinct users. Subtitling may soon find itself moving towards software localisation when all these new formats come to demand stricter technical parameters to allow for 'tailor made' combinations. Digital television will spur ahead wide scale normalisation, a fact which will inevitably dictate changes at a national level.

The prospects offered by digital television therefore appear to be a positive note on which to end this survey, especially since developments in one medium usually lead to developments in another. What is more, digital television, like DVD, is a global phenomenon and might therefore move us closer to harmonization, within the limits stipulated above. Finally, the possibility of digital television offering a way out of the verbatim versus edited subtitles-debate is certainly attractive, as long as the usual watchdogs make sure that standardization is not dictated on the basis of quantitative, financial and/or technological requirements alone.

---

[1] Unless indicated otherwise, all quotations have been taken from respondents' replies to the questionnaires sent to them by e-mail. All the researchers and professionals who have kindly agreed to provide us with information about SDH in the countries discussed in this survey are listed in the acknowledgements at the end of the article.

[2] The article by Araújo in this volume expands the scope of the survey to Brazil. Unfortunately, we did not receive any response from the colleagues and practitioners who we contacted in Australia, Canada and the USA.

[3] For up-to-date information about legal and other developments in SDH we would also like to refer to the Newsletter of the European Federation of Hard-of-hearing People (EFHOH). The September 2005 issue contains a table with SDH percentages and targets in Europe.

[4] For the sake of simplicity this part of Belgium will henceforth be referred to as Flanders.

[5] ARD is the abbreviation for *Arbeitsgemeinschaft der öffentlich-rechtlichen Rundfunkanstalten der Bundesrepublik Deutschland*, which today consists of nine independent broadcasters. ZDF is the abbreviation for *Zweites Deutsches Fernsehen*.

[6] The Flemish national broadcaster has two channels: VRT (*Vlaamse Radio en Televisie*) and *Canvas*. The youth channel *Ketnet* and the sports channel *Sporza* are subsumed under the latter.

[7] *Radiotelevisione Italiana*, the public national broadcaster, offering a 24-hour service by means of three channels (RAI 1, RAI 2 and RAI 3).

[8] *Corporació Catalana de Radio i Televisió* (CCRT).

[9] *Televisión Española* (TVE).

[10] The authors give full details in their article and also refer to Pardina i Mundó (1998, 2000), and to Méndez Braga (2002) for an overview of the Spanish panorama up to 2000. Pereira Rodríguez (2005) adds some new data for the following two years, of which Orero, Pereira and Utray (forthcoming) offer an update.

[11] Cf. the 1990 Broadcasting Act below.

[12] For details check online at: www.opsi.gov.uk/acts/acts1990/Ukpga_19900042_en_1.htm .The 1990 Act stated that all major television companies in the UK had to increase their subtitle output to 90% by 2010.

[13] ATM, *Antwerpse Televisiemaatschappij*, is one such example of local television, catering only for the city of Antwerp and its immediate surroundings.

[14] Information in English can be found online at:
www.innovazione.gov.it/eng/intervento/accessibilita_eng.shtml

[15] 'Pop on', 'block' and 'scrolling' or 'snake' subtitles (and other terms) refer to the technical features of subtitling production, whereas 'edited' and 'verbatim' refer to the linguistic contents of the subtitles. A survey of current terminology and the contexts in which it is used is actually in order, but beyond the scope of this survey. Terminological issues are further compounded in discussions of the similarities and differences between re-speaking, revoicing, rewording and interpreting.

[16] We wish to point out that the target group is, of course, very diverse, and that any discussion of it as a 'whole' risks being a gross generalization. As De Linde and Kay (1999: 11) point out: "The deaf community is made up of two distinct groups; those who are born deaf, and those who acquire a hearing loss later in life. Both groups differ in outlook and needs. The first group's main method of communication is sign language and their ability to use subtitles may be hampered by relatively low reading levels. The second group, people with acquired hearing loss, is more likely to have had an education within the hearing community and will consequently have average reading speeds".

[17] Cf. Eugeni's analysis of the situation in Italy in the subsection on standards.

[18] For a more comprehensive discussion see De Linde & Kay (1999), Robson (2004) and Neves (2005, forthcoming).

[19] See also Araújo on the situation in Brazil in this volume.

[20] A related development is that of the target audience demanding that SDH subtitles render even colloquial phrases or dialect, since the subtitles are their only contact with the spoken language (Santamaria & Rico 2004; Van Herreweghe & Slembrouck 2004). Eugeni also mentions that Italian deaf and hard-of-hearing viewers sometimes find the attitudes of subtitlers who stress the need for simplification, rather patronizing. According to him, many SDH users regard the subtitles as a didactic tool and use the subtitles to help them improve their linguistic skills. Oversimplified vocabulary is therefore not appreciated.

[21] Different views were aired by Neves (see article in this volume) and van Son ("Linguistic research and *status questionis* in the Netherlands") at the Barcelona *Media for All* conference in 2005, with van Son being in favour of complying with the wishes of the viewers who want more information.

[22] For an up-to-date survey of the different types of subtitling in use today, and of current subtitling software, see Díaz Cintas and Remael (2007).

[23] SOAP is the Dutch abbreviation for the Association for the Subtitling of All Programmes, a Dutch umbrella organization that joins all national groups representing people with hearing disabilities and that defends the rights of deaf and hard-of-hearing people (www.nvvs.nl/soap/oversoap/index.html).

[24] In the profession semi-live is sometimes used to refer to subtitling for which there is virtually no preparation time, i.e. the subtitler has a head start of minutes or seconds. On other occasions, it refers to pre-recorded subtitling that is broadcast live.

[25] In Spain, live subtitles are done for TVE with voice recognition, but the Catalan TVC has its very own system, the semaphore system. The system works by multiplexing five operators with QWERTY keyboards. Screens display a 'traffic light' green/red colour. When the screen displays a green line, the operator types what is heard through the headphones. When the red light appears, the operator stops writing. For more information see Orero (2006).

[26] Other software is probably also used. Working methods as well as software programs tend to develop very quickly, as channels experiment and try to improve their procedures.

[27] Apparently, the spotting is occasionally done by technicians in some countries. In France, Couté Rodriguez writes, discussing subtitling for DVD, the translator receives the dialogue after it has been spotted by the *laboratoire de sous-titrage*. The translator proceeds to translate much like he/she would do for open subtitles but adding the description of sounds, which have been spotted by a specialist. Once the translation has been finished, it returns to the lab, which puts the subtitles in the required font (e.g. in italics) in order to distinguish them from standard subtitles.

[28] In the Netherlands, NOB (part of NOB Cross Media Facilities), a company that is comparable to Red Bee Media in the UK, offers virtually all types of subtitling for television (intralingual, interlingual, open subtitling, teletext subtitling, etc.) at very short notice. It now works for public and private TV channels, private companies etc., but originally the service was part of the *Nederlandse Openbare Omroep*. The amount of SDH it offers is limited.

[29] See the article by Araújo about Brazil in this volume for more details about stenotype.

[30] BBC1, BBC2, including digital and satellite platforms, as well as various regional programmes (e.g. regional news five times a day).

[31] All subtitling for the BBC has been done by the private company Red Bee Media since 2006.

[32] Some pilot testing was carried out at VRT in preparation of a joint research project by VRT, University College Antwerp and the University of Antwerp, which started in January 2007. In fact, research into re-speaking and the technique itself seems to be an AVT buzzword with a discussion panel devoted to this topic at the *Languages & the Media* conference in Berlin (25-28 October 2006), and the symposium *New technologies in real time intralingual subtitling*, at the University of Bologna, Forlì (17 November 2006).

[33] BBC promotional DVD *Live subtitling with speech recognition*, viewed at VRT, June 2006. Working from home has been temporarily suspended by Red Bee Media.

[34] That is why the aforementioned research team at University College Antwerp and the University of Antwerp propose to investigate the advantages of 'rewording' (a term used by Eugeni) with verbatim scrolling and 're-speaking' with edited pop on subtitles, using the logging software *Inputlog* developed by Van Waes & Leijten (2006) at the University of Antwerp (www.inputlog.net). *Inputlog* keeps track of the delays incurred and the mistakes made by the speech recognition software.

[35] RTV is the television station of the Republic of San Marino, a local channel but RAI-owned and thus nationally owned.

[36] Some sections, including examples, are a translation, whereas other sections were modified (Sánchez).

[37] He too points out that "in the UK alone there are a number of different ways of indicating sound effects – e.g. (GUNSHOT), (gunshot), GUNSHOT, [gunshot], [GUNSHOT]. Such a confusion of methods is surely unnecessary.

[38] This is bound to expand with the start of the new MA in 2007, which has a strong AVT option.

[39] The face-to-face MA itself started in 1999, the online MA in 2003.

[40] An *experto* is the equivalent of a one-year MA.

[41] One is a *diplomado* after a three-year course of study and a *licenciado* after a four-year course. The latter degree is the Spanish equivalent of a BA.

[42] A pilot cinema projection with AD and SDH took place in Berlin on 20 October 2006.

[43] Further information about cinema subtitling in the UK can be found online at: www.yourlocalcinema.com.

[44] This type of surtitling for the theatre is actually becoming increasingly popular as more and more international theatre companies travel with foreign language productions.

References

BBC. 2003. *Television for all*. London: BBC Research & Development Department. www.rd.bbc.co.uk

de Groot, Vanja. 2001. *Zo gezegd, zo ondertiteld? Een verkennend onderzoek naar de taalkundige verschillen tussen spraak en ondertiteling voor doven en slechthorenden en de manier waarop deze bestudeerd kunnen worden*. Tilburg: Katholieke Universiteit Brabant. MA Dissertation.

de Linde, Zoé and Neil Kay. 1999. *The Semiotics of Subtitling*. Manchester: St Jerome.

Díaz Cintas, Jorge and Aline Remael. 2007. *Audiovisual Translation: Subtitling* Manchester: St Jerome.

Doens, Erwin. 2000. "Kwalitatief onderzoek van ondertiteling voor doven en slechthorenden". *VRT studiedienst*.

Marsh, Alison. 2006. "Re-speaking for the BBC". Paper given at the *First International Seminar on New Technologies in Real Time Subtitling*. 17 November. Forlì: University of Bologna. Manuscript.

Méndez Braga, Belén. 2002. *El subtitulado para sordos*. Vigo: Universidade de Vigo. BA Dissertation.

Neves, Josélia. 2005. *Audiovisual Translation: Subtitling for the Deaf and Hard-of-Hearing*. London: Roehampton University. PhD Thesis.

—. Forthcoming. *Audiovisual Translation. Subtitling for the Deaf and Hard-of-Hearing*. Manchester: St Jerome.

Orero, Pilar. 2006. "Real time subtitling: a Spanish overview", in Carlo Eugeni and Gabriele Mack (eds) *Intralinea* – Special Issue on Respeaking.
www.intralinea.it/specials/eng_more.php?id=450_0_32_0_M52%

Orero, Pilar, Ana María Pereira and Francisco Utray Delgado. Forthcoming. "The present and future of audio description and subtitling for the deaf and hard of hearing in Spain". *Meta*.

Pardina i Mundó, Joaquim. 1998. "El futuro de la subtitulación para personas sordas o con pérdidas auditivas".
www.terra.es/personal6/932108627/Articulos/arti3-C.htm

—. 2000. "Estudio sobre el Servicio Audiovisual de Subtitulación para personas sordas o con pérdidas auditivas en el mercado televisivo español", Dirección Audiovisual de la CMT.
www.cmt.es/cmt/centro_info/publicaciones/pdf/subtitula.pdf

Pereira Rodríguez, Ana María. 2005. "El subtitulado para sordos: estado de la cuestión en España". *Quaderns. Revista de traducción* 12: 161-172.

Pereira Rodríguez, Ana María and Lourdes Lorenzo García. 2005. "Evaluamos la norma UNE 153010: Subtitulado para personas sordas y personas con discapacidad auditiva. Subtitulado a través del teletexto". *Puentes* 6: 21-26.

Robson, Gary D. 2004. *The Closed Captioning Handbook*. Amsterdam: Focal Press.

Saerens, Gunter and Bernard Dewulf. 2000. *Stijlboek VRT Teletekstondertiteling*. Unpublished style sheet.

Santamaria, Laura and Albert Rico. 2004. "New guidelines for new readers". Paper presented at the *International Conferences Languages and The Media*, Berlin. Manuscript.

Van Herreweghe, Mieke and Stef Slembrouck. 2004. "Teletekstondertiteling en tussentaal: de pragmatiek van het alledaagse", in Johan De Caluwe *et al.* (eds) *Taeldeman, man van de taal, schatbewaarder van de taal*. Gent: Academia Press, 853-876.

van Son, Nic, Maarten Verboom and Hans van Balkom. 1998. *Toegankelijkheid van TV-programma's. Eindrapport van een bronnenonderzoek*. St. Michielgestel/Grave: IvD/CGL.

Van Waes, Luuk and Marielle Leijten. 2006. "Logging Writing Processes with Inputlog", in Luuk Van Waes, Marielle Leijten and Christine Neuwirth (eds) *Studies in Writing 17. Writing and Digital Media*. Oxford: Elsevier, 158-166.

Acknowledgements

EDINBURGH UNIVERSITY LIBRARY
WITHDRAWN

This survey mapping the status of subtitling for the deaf and hard-of-hearing in the audiovisual media in a selection of Western European countries has been written on the basis of information obtained by way of a questionnaire distributed by e-mail in the year 2006. I would like therefore to express my gratitude to the following respondents listed below. This article is theirs as much as mine: Mary Carroll (Managing Director, Titelbild Subtitling and Translation GmbH, Berlin, Germany; member of TransMedia); Bernard Dewulf (Editor in Chief, teletext subtitling for Flemish public broadcasting, Belgium); Chas Donaldson (freelance SDH lecturer and consultant, UK); Carlo Eugeni (PhD student researching RTS with speech recognition technology, University of Naples Federico II, Italy); Corinne Imhauser (professional interpreter and subtitler, coordinator of the Master in Multimedia Translation at ISTI – *Institut Supérieur de Traducteurs et Interprètes* – until 2006, now Head of the Interpretation department at ISTI Brussels, Belgium); Jurgen Lentz (Editor-in-Chief, teletext subtitling for Dutch Public Broadcasting, Netherlands); Josélia Neves (Assistant Professor, *Escola Superior de Educação, Instituto Politécnico de Leiria*; Portugal; Member of TransMedia); Isabelle Couté Rodriguez (freelance translator, France); Diana Sánchez (Head of Access Services of Imaginables inc. S.L, Barcelona, Spain; member of TransMedia); Susanne Verberk (Head of Translation Services, The Subtitling Company, Brussels, Belgium).

Access symbols for use with video content and information and communications technology devices

Clive Miller

European Telecommunication Standards Institute (ETSI), Sophia Antipolis, France

Abstract

Symbols can play an important role in assisting people to use products and services more effectively. Their application is optimized when the same symbol is always used to represent the same message, and standardization can provide a means for achieving this. In this project, five symbols have been tested and shown more effective than competing candidates. The testing methodology, carried out on the Internet, was mostly based on two standards defined for the testing of graphical symbols. These were: ETR070 June 1993: Human Factors (HF); The Multiple Index Approach (MIA) for the evaluation of pictograms and ISO9186 Second Edition April 2001: Graphical symbols – Test methods for judged comprehensibility and for comprehension. The symbols defined represent a set of access services, namely: subtitles, audio description, signing, speech output and spoken command.

1. Project summary

This project has been conducted under the auspices of the European Telecommunications Standards Institute (ETSI): ETSI STF286.

The aim of the project was to develop and test five international symbols denoting the availability of certain access services, then to disseminate these symbols to relevant parties. The access services covered were: subtitling, audio description, sign language, speech output and spoken command. In addition, tactile and auditory symbols were also investigated.

2. Definitions

Each of the access services involved in the project can be defined as follows:

- *subtitling*: a transcript of the spoken dialogue of audiovisual media, superimposed as text onto the visual element.
- *audio description (AD)*: an additional audible narrative interwoven with the dialogue which describes the significant aspects of the visual content of audiovisual media.
- *signing*: the use of sign language to convey the significant aspects of the audible content of audiovisual media.

- *speech output*: the ability of a device to communicate to its user using spoken language.
- *spoken command*: the ability of a device to accept and respond to spoken instructions from a user.

In addition, the following definitions should be noted:

- *sign language*: a language that uses a system of manual, facial, and other body movements as the means of communication. It has to be noted that there is no widely accepted international sign language. Many national versions exist together with local 'dialects'.
- *symbol*: a graphic device used to convey information. Symbols, pictograms and icons are all graphic devices used to convey information, either as complements to or as replacements for text. The word 'symbol' is sometimes used specifically to refer to abstract representations, the word 'pictogram' to refer specifically to pictorial representations, and the word 'icon' to screen-based graphical devices. In practice, these distinctions are often unclear and so the term symbol is used here generically. The symbols apply to all access services, ICT devices and associated media that provide the defined facilities.

3. Background

The Royal National Institute of the Blind (RNIB) in the UK was having difficulty promoting the AD service on digital television.[1] The AD service had been broadcasting for about three years but only a small handful of people involved in a trial were able to receive it, using special equipment. The difficulty seemed to be due to a circular problem: few people knew of the service so few people were using it; since so few people were using it, no manufacturers wanted to develop products for it; since no products were available for it, very few people knew about it. In fact, the only way the service had begun at all was because of a condition introduced to the broadcasters' licence in the 1996 Broadcasting Act, after much lobbying by the RNIB. However, nothing could be done to entice manufacturers to develop products until a large enough market could be established and this would never happen until more people became aware of the service. Although two products did become available (the Netgem i-Player set-top receiver and the Nebula DigiTV receiver for PCs), they presented considerable difficulties to the blind people intended to use them and consequently uptake was slow. The set-top box needed to be connected to a telephone line in order to install it correctly, which is not always possible. It features some 'voice tags', which announce channel names and give some guidance during the installation process. However, none of the menus or messages have voices, so any installation or usage problems that might occur leave a blind user stuck. The technical support was inefficient and its staff frequently did not understand how to deal with blind or elderly users. The PC TV receiver card software had not been written with accessibility in mind and did not always work well with users' screen readers.

Meanwhile, the Royal National Institute for Deaf People (RNID) in the UK was reporting similar difficulties with subtitles, even though they had been available for 30 years. Similarly, the difficulty was that people were failing to recognize where such services were available and know how to access them.

A proposed solution was to develop and establish symbols that people would recognize and associate with the respective access services. This in itself is a circular problem: a symbol is only meaningful once people become used to seeing it; but it only becomes widespread once it is well recognized. A number of different organizations had begun to use a variety of symbols, both for subtitles and AD, and there was a danger of more diverse symbols appearing in the future.

In order to combat this situation, a proposal was made to the Human Factors (HF) Technical Board of the European Telecommunications Standards Institute to develop a set of symbols. Not only should these symbols be used for access services such as AD and subtitles, they should also include other access services such as signing, speech output capability and spoken command input capability. The HF board carried the proposal through to the EC Design for All and Assistive Technologies Standardization Co-ordination Group (DATSCG). It was accepted and part funding granted, the remaining part to be met by contributions in kind, the RNIB being the main contributor.

4. Details of the proposal

The proposal was to develop and test five symbols, one each for subtitles, audio description, signing, speech output and spoken command. This would result in a European standard being established, with the intention of having it adopted by ISO to become an international standard. In order to do so, the testing had to comply with ISO standards, namely ISO9186. To satisfy the European Standards requirements, the testing had to be carried out subject to ETSI procedure as defined in ETR70. The EC required the testing to be carried out across a broad range of cultures within Europe.

Since some of the access services were specifically intended for visually impaired people, it was necessary to investigate the possibility of tactile symbols and auditory symbols, though not necessarily for all five symbols. It was reasonable to assume that if someone was using subtitles or signing services, their vision would be adequate not to need tactile assistance.

The symbols would be used to promote the services they relate to in every suitable context. These might include: DVD packaging, equipment, promotion of services, trailers for television programmes and films, television listings, websites, theatre guides and future media yet to be invented. This implied that the symbols had to work over a wide range of sizes from remote control buttons to huge billboards.

5. First selection

The first objective was to gather all the symbols that anyone had ever used for the five services. In addition, the project team developed some symbols of their own as well as contracting a professional artist to develop some more. The result was a total of 162 symbols: 42 for audio description; 37 for subtitles; 27 for signing; 30 for speech output and 26 for spoken command. Since it was impractical to carry out large-scale testing with so many symbols, the Human Factors Technical Committee was asked to assess the suitability of each of the candidates and to score the candidates accordingly. From the highest scoring candidates, the team selected six candidates for each of the services to go for full public testing. In the case of very similar symbols, only the highest ranking one went forward. The complete set of candidates can be seen in Annex A.

6. Testing according to ETR70

The ETSI method of testing graphical symbols defines seven parameters:

6.1 Hit rate
This index is the main parameter of performance and it is equivalent to the score of correct associations between the intended meaning and the symbol.

6.2 False alarm rate
The false alarm rate indicates in how many cases a symbol has been given an incorrect meaning.

6.3 Missing values
The percentage of missing values tells us in how many instances respondents did not answer a question presumably because they did not know the answer. Missing values represent usage situations in which users do not know which control to use to bring about a certain effect.

6.4 Subjective certainty

The subjective certainty index indicates how certain the respondents feel about their associations between pictograms and referents. If the users of a device are extremely uncertain about the effects of the controls of a device, they may decide not to use it at all, which in turn may seriously hamper the uptake of the device.

6.5 Subjective suitability

In addition to making associations between symbols and meanings and to indicating how certain they are about these associations, the respondents can tell us their subjective impressions as to how well symbols represent their intended meanings.

6.6 Symbol preference

The respondents indicate which of the candidate symbols represents best their intended meanings In this, we do not know which criteria (aesthetic or functional) the respondents apply.

6.7 Symbol set preference

This index is an indicator for which symbol set is preferred overall, mainly on aesthetic grounds. This test is ideally suited for a set of symbols that will always be used together as a complete family, for example on a piece of equipment. However, the symbols in question might be used independently or in small numbers, but almost never would all five appear together.

The way the test is conducted is for each meaning to be shown to respondents, together with all the candidate symbols of the set. The respondents would then be asked to pick which symbol best represents the intended meaning.

7. Testing according to ISO 9186

In order to maximize the likelihood of being adopted as an ISO standard, the ISO test strategy was also engaged. The standard used is ISO9186: Graphical symbols — Test methods for judged comprehensibility and for comprehension, second edition (1 April 2001).

The standard defines two tests: a comprehension test and a comprehensibility test. The comprehensibility test involves showing each respondent all the candidate symbols for each meaning in turn, along with an explanation of the meaning, and asking the respondents to decide how many people out of 100 would understand the intended meaning of each symbol presented. Any symbol which scores a mean that exceeds the acceptance level can be considered for standardization. Any symbol which scores less than the immediate acceptance level but qualifies for further testing should be subjected to a comprehension test. Any symbol which scores less than the qualifying level should not be tested further.

8. The online survey

In order to reach a wide range of respondents across a large geographical area, without incurring prohibitively high costs, the entire testing process was performed through a specially designed website on the Internet. This did introduce some difficulties in complying precisely with the requirements of either ETR70 or ISO9186, especially regarding the fact that none of the participants would be supervised during the test. In addition, there was no way to control the exact presentation of the test pages, as this varies with the user's browser, screen resolution and window size settings. Given these constraints, the test was designed to comply as closely as possible to satisfy both testing methodologies.

9. Opening questions

To assess that a wide range of respondents had participated, every respondent was asked the following questions:

- What is your full name?
- What is your e-mail address?
- What country do you normally live in? (Select from list)
- Are you male or female? (Male/Female)
- How old are you? (Under 16, 16 – 30, 31 – 50 or over 50).
- At what age did you finish full-time education? (Under 17, 18 – 20, over 20). [This was considered to give a simple measure of educational attainment that was unaffected by national differences.]
- What is your occupation?

- Do you have difficulties with any of the following?
  - Seeing
  - Hearing
  - Speaking
  - Walking
  - Using your hands
  - Understanding

An originally intended question asking "How would you describe your cultural background?" had to be dropped when it was found that nobody really knew how to answer the question, and it could not be readily translated into other European languages.

To encourage respondents, the front page of the website contained the following statement: "If you tell us your e-mail address, you could win a €50 voucher to spend on Amazon". The prize was awarded at the end of the testing by picking a respondent at random.

10. The test section

In the project, both the comprehensibility test and the comprehension test as defined by ISO9186 were run simultaneously, with all six variants being shown to each and every respondent of the comprehension test because it was unknown at the beginning what the results of the comprehensibility test were going to be. The standard itself does not define the two threshold levels of the qualifying score and acceptance score, but requires testers to obtain this information from the Secretary of ISO/TC145. The secretary reported that the acceptance level for non-warning symbols should be 60%.

The website address was www.accesssymbols.org and the website was available in seven languages. It was authored in English, then translated manually into Dutch, French, German, Greek, Italian and Spanish, and automatically translated into Russian. To judge the answers of the comprehension test, responses in a language other than English were translated into English automatically to allow the English judges to score them, though in some cases manual dictionaries and reference to native speakers did become necessary.

Respondents were sought by propagating the website address as widely as possible amongst consumer groups and related organizations.

Using an administration part of the website system, the three judges (in this case, the three experts in the team) completed the comprehension test by scoring each unique response as being one of:

- Correct understanding of the symbol is certain (over 80%)
- Correct understanding of the symbol is very probable (66% to 80%)
- Correct understanding of the symbol is probable (50% to 65%)
- The meaning which is understood is opposite to the meaning intended
- Any other response
- The response is 'Don't know'
- No response is given

11. Technical description of the website

The website was hosted by Compila.com in the UK, which offered a competitive service providing scripting and a database. PHP was the scripting language used with a MySQL database. The database was used for collecting information that the visitors entered, as well as some of the operational features of the website, such as providing the ability to manage and display the translations. No validation was enforced on the data that visitors entered, so if they wished to leave any questions unanswered, they were able to and still continue to progress through the survey.

The use of an online database provided an exceptionally powerful and flexible way to analyse the data collected, as scripts could quickly be written to perform a number of tasks such as calculating statistics and creating graphical representations of the statistics. A panel of judges provided the project team with the ability to allocate scores to all the answers given, whilst retaining the anonymity of the respondents and avoiding having to score the same answer more than once for each class of symbol.

12. Results

Since the team was able to monitor the statistics as surveys were being completed, it became apparent, partway through the testing, that ad01 (see Annex A), which was intended to mean 'audio description' was sometimes being confused with 'speech output'. Therefore, a modification was made to the symbol, taking it out of the television screen and changing the headphones into a speaker, to create a new symbol for 'speech output', so31. This replaced the worst performing symbol being tested, so27. In order to distinguish the symbol for audio description, this was modified by removing the 'document' element, creating a new symbol, ad43. For 'signing', the most popular symbol was sl27, but as this was not pictured in a television, it did not sit comfortably with the other symbols. It was therefore placed in a 'TV' element to create a new symbol, sl28, which replaced the worst scoring sl23.

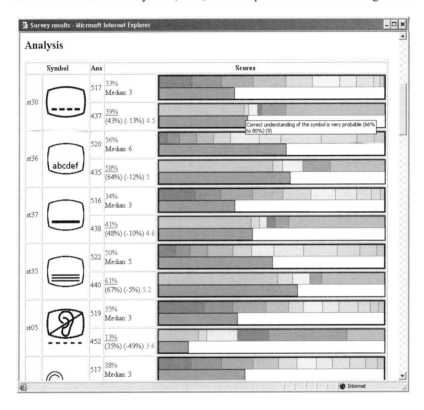

Figure 1. Example display of the analysis webpage

13. Discussion of the analysis webpage

The maximum scores for the comprehensibility test were 56%, 53%, 62%, 58% and 63%. These are quite low, considering the secretary's threshold requirement of 60%. Similarly for the comprehension test the maximum attained scores were 61%, 14%, 77%, 56% and 17% for subtitles, audio description, signing, speech output and spoken command respectively.

These results are not surprising. As stated earlier, the effectiveness of symbols is dependent on their users being familiar with them. Even road signs have to be learned, and their users are tested on them before being issued with a driving licence. Since none of the symbols tested are already in wide use, few people have had a chance to become familiar with them. The test itself is highly subjective: it is worded in such a way that not only asks what the respondents think, but what they think others will think. The exact words are "How many people out of 10 would you expect to understand this meaning?". So, even if the respondents felt confident about recognizing the symbol, they may have thought that others would not be able to. Without carrying out testing themselves, how could they possibly know?

The comprehension test is even more flawed, since many of the meanings of the symbols may not be familiar to the respondents. Recall that the primary objective of this project was to improve the awareness of the services.

14. Conclusions

The ISO9186 testing methodology is effective only if the respondents are already well acquainted with the subjects that the symbols are supposed to refer to. This is stated in the standard.

Other tests which have been done show that, for the comprehensibility test, not only scores should be collected, but also comments by respondents in order to apply some understanding to the scores. Additionally, when asked simply to score (for example, between 0 and 10), different people have different ideas of how much value those scores have. So, one person might feel that a 5 is quite a low score, but another might regard it as average. Fewer score options might give a clearer picture.

Perhaps a better approach would be to go through each intended meaning, explain it thoroughly, then offer all the candidates (maybe for other referents too, if sufficiently similar). Ask respondents to score 'very appropriate', 'acceptable' or 'not suitable', where the default option is 'not suitable'. Then, they pick out candidates they feel are suitable. In addition, a field should be provided to enter comments about any candidates they choose.

To test how memorable the symbols are, a recall test might be more effective. In this test, each respondent would be shown one of the candidate symbols, chosen at random, for each of the intended meanings, along with an explanation of the meaning. Then, the respondent would be asked a week later to identify the meaning of each of the candidate symbols that they had been shown.

Annex A: Complete set of candidate symbols

Subtitles

st01	st02	st03	st04	st05
st06	st07	st08	st09	st10
st11	st12	st13	st14	st15
st16	st17	st18	st19	st20
st21	st22	st23	st24	st25
			access	
st26	st27	st28	st29	st30
	ST			
st31	st32	st33	st34	st35
			Abcdef	
st36	st37			
abcdef				

Audio description

ad01	ad02	ad03	ad04	ad05
ad06	ad07	ad08	ad09	ad10
ad11	ad12	ad13	ad14	ad15
ad16	ad17	ad18	ad19	ad20
ad21	ad22	ad23	ad24	ad25
ad26	ad27	ad28	ad29	ad30
ad31	ad32	ad33	ad34	ad35
ad36	ad37	ad38	ad39	ad40
ad41	ad42	ad43*		

Signing

sl01	sl02	sl03	sl04	sl05
sl06	sl07	sl08	sl09	sl10
sl11	sl12	sl13	sl14	sl15
sl16	sl17	sl18	sl19	sl20
sl21	sl22	sl23	sl24	sl25
sl26	sl27	sl28*		

Speech output

so01	so02	so03	so04	so05
so06	so07	so08	so09	so10
so11	so12	so13	so14	so15
so16	so17	so18	so19	so20
so21	so22	so23	so24	so25
so26	so27	so28	so29	so30
so31*				

Speech command

sc01	sc02	sc03	sc04	sc05
sc06	sc07	sc08	sc09	sc10
sc11	sc12	sc13	sc14	sc15
sc16	sc17	sc18	sc19	sc20
sc21	sc22	sc23	sc24	sc25
sc26				

Annex B: Complete set of results

Results for subtitles

Symbol	Comprehensibility Test		Comprehensibility Test			
	Average	Median	ISO9186 score	ETR70 hit rate	ETR70 false alarm rate	ETR70 score
st30	33%	3	39%	43%	13%	4.5
st36	56%	6	58%	64%	12%	5
st37	34%	3	41%	48%	10%	4.6
st35	50%	5	61%	67%	5%	5.2
st05	35%	3	13%	35%	49%	3.6
st24	38%	3	23%	44%	34%	3.7

Results for audio description

Symbol	Comprehensibility Test		Comprehensibility Test			
	Average	Median	ISO9186 score	ETR70 hit rate	ETR70 false alarm rate	ETR70 score
ad25	31%	3	4%	6%	47%	3.1
ad27	35%	3	3%	4%	44%	3.1
ad42	27%	2	11%	14%	33%	3.5
ad01	53%	5	12%	15%	46%	3.3
ad41	29%	2	14%	17%	30%	3.6
ad32	26%	2	4%	5%	41%	3.2
ad43	44%	4	10%	15%	65%	3.1

Results for signing

Symbol	Comprehensibility Test		Comprehensibility Test			
	Average	Median	ISO9186 score	ETR70 hit rate	ETR70 false alarm rate	ETR70 score
sl26	62%	7	67%	71%	9%	5.3
sl05	57%	6	63%	66%	8%	5.2
sl23	27%	2	38%	40%	13%	4.5
sl16	52%	5	77%	80%	3%	5.7
sl24	58%	6	77%	79%	2%	5.7
sl08	47%	5	57%	60%	11%	5
sl28	44%	4	66%	68%	17%	5.2

Results for speech output

Symbol	Comprehensibility Test		Comprehensibility Test			
	Average	Median	ISO9186 score	ETR70 hit rate	ETR70 false alarm rate	ETR70 score
so30	37%	3	13%	19%	45%	3.4
so26	35%	3	13%	20%	33%	3.6
so19	41%	4	22%	27%	21%	3.9
so27	27%	2	2%	6%	31%	3.2
so24	42%	4	28%	36%	19%	4.1
so04	22%	2	6%	10%	34%	3.3
so31	58%	6	56%	68%	15%	4.9

Results for spoken command

Symbol	Comprehensibility Test		Comprehensibility Test			
	Average	Median	ISO9186 score	ETR70 hit rate	ETR70 false alarm rate	ETR70 score
sc26	63%	7	13%	26%	43%	3.5
sc25	59%	6	11%	23%	42%	3.4
sc22	43%	4	2%	6%	63%	2.9
sc21	33%	3	17%	22%	18%	3.8
sc04	19%	2	1%	6%	31%	3.2
sc24	27%	2	-1%	2%	65%	2.8

---

[1] See Greening and Rolph (in this volume) for details on the development of digital television in the UK.

Deaf access for Deaf people: the translation of the television news from English into British Sign Language

Christopher Stone

University College London, UK

Abstract

This paper explores the notion of a Deaf translation norm and its use in the rendering of English mainstream television broadcast news into British Sign Language (BSL). The Deaf translation norm incorporates the community identity and fluency of the translator/interpreter (T/I). Historically, this is a role that Deaf bilinguals have undertaken and, in part, involves the higher level of agency that the T/I exerts within the situation. In present day, this differs from a historic role now that the translation event happens in the public sphere rather than within the community. To ensure that the Deaf audience has an optimally relevant BSL text to watch and understand, the Deaf translation norm incorporates enrichments and impoverishments into the BSL text according to the audience's understanding of the English text and the video footage that is shown simultaneously on-screen. This creates a BSL text that utilizes the multimedia environment to reduce the cognitive effort of the Deaf audience.

1. The Deaf community

Convention has arisen that a person who has a Deaf cultural identity and is audiologically deaf is called 'Deaf' (Senghas & Monaghan 2002) and this distinction has been made within the community for several hundred years (Ladd 1998). Membership of the Deaf community in the past has predominantly been due to being born deaf or losing hearing at an early age so that no sense of loss is felt. Cultural identity was then forged by attending schools for the deaf in early life and Deaf clubs throughout the rest of one's life. As Ladd (2003: 44) says: "This traditional community therefore consists of Deaf people who attended Deaf schools and met either in Deaf clubs or at other Deaf social activities".

In more recent years membership of the Deaf community has been defined by Baker and Padden (1978: 4) as follows: "The most useful basic factor determining who is a member of the deaf community seems to be what is called 'attitudinal deafness'. This occurs when a person identifies him/herself as a member of the deaf community, and other members accept that person as part of the community".

The attitudinal deafness discussed by Padden clearly refers to the traditional community discussed by Ladd. As discussed by Ladd (2003: 42) the community is strengthened by 90% endogamous marriage. Five per cent of Deaf people born deaf have Deaf parents and a further five per cent have one parent who is Deaf (Kyle & Allsop 1982; Kyle & Woll 1985). The extent to which these families have many generations of Deaf is unknown, but there are known cases of one Deaf family having documented seven generations (with a grandchild resulting in eight generations) in Britain (Taylor 1998) although there are anecdotal stories from this family suggesting that there are ten generations (with a grandchild being the eleventh).

These multigenerational Deaf people are seen as the core members of the Deaf community. They are the ones who have experienced life, at least within the home, as a Deaf haven from a hearing world. As the guardians of sign languages, of Deaf history and culture there is an expectation that they will preserve and pass on Deaf ways of being in the world (Padden & Humphries 1988). Taking my Deaf T/Is from this group enables me to explore what a Deaf translation might be like if it were not for the 'hearing' institutional barriers that the T/Is face in the news studio.

The historical Deaf community is described as a collective community (Ladd 2003), and therefore allegiance is to the minority community rather than to the individualistic values of the (mainstream) 'hearing' community. Although this can be contested and, arguably, the present-day Deaf community is a heterogeneous community (Skelton & Valentine 2003a, 2003b), the Deaf T/Is in this study, from multigenerational Deaf families, adhere to traditional notions of collective identities (Smith 1996).

2. The research

The research draws on data from ethnographic interviews (Carmel & Monaghan 1991; Cook & Crang 1995; Spindler & Spindler 1992; Spradley 1979) of five Deaf T/Is (all of whom chose pseudonyms[1]) who regularly work in broadcast television news. All five have graduate level training in linguistics and experience both in working as and training interpreters. In an attempt to ensure that the research was Deaf-led or Deafhood (Ladd 2003) informed[2] (whilst Deafhood-informed ensures that research is undertaken in a Deaf culturally sensitive way it does not have to be carried out by Deaf people) semi-structured interviews of Deaf informants were used to generate grounded theories (Strauss & Corbin 1990). The research aimed to be Deaf-led and to explore what was deemed to be relevant to Deaf T/Is (the informants are quoted throughout this article) and as such no hearing interpreters were interviewed.

3. The British context for BSL on television

Under the 1996 Broadcasting Act[3] broadcasters are obliged to provide five per cent of programming by 2005,[4] either presented in or translated into sign language. This does not mean that the broadcasters feel any political affinity with the provision of BSL access but rather see it as a legal obligation which, like other equality laws, needs to be fulfilled (Squires 2004). There are institutional constraints on how T/Is work in broadcast media similar to the institutional constraints that interpreters face in other domains. Inghilleri (2003) considers interpreters within an asylum-seeking context. She discusses the need for the interpreters to ensure the believability of the interviewee by constructing their narratives as believable to the interviewer. This requires the interviewee to be perceived as a victim by the target audience within target cultural norms rather than constructing the story in a way that is believable and valid in the source language and culture.

This is mirrored by BSL T/Is working within a broadcasting context, although we see that the power dynamic flows in a different direction, from majority to minority audience. In the context of asylum seeker interviews, where the person's history must be seen as valid within a majority context from a minority context, there is no room for any of Venuti's (1998) suggestions for a translation preserving difference. Rather, there is the need for domestication and trying to ensure the naturalness of the TL.[5] This parallels the situation in the broadcasting context for BSL T/Is.

In this context, the audience comprises not only the Deaf target audience but also a mainstream audience that sees the in-vision T/Is. The T/Is must construct a product that is acceptable not only to the Deaf audience but also to the mainstream audience in terms of cultural expectation (Woll 2000) such as fewer grammatical facial movements and a speed perceived by the mainstream audience (themselves ignorant of the TL) to be appropriate in this medium.

Interpreted/translated television news in the UK is broadcast in two different formats, headline news summaries or weekly news reviews, with the T/Is finding themselves in two different situations. In the first situation, found in news week review broadcasts, the Deaf T/Is (as 'presenters') are acknowledged as being present and introduce themselves and the hearing anchor. They present some of the news stories and perhaps engage in some interaction with the hearing anchor in BSL. The Deaf T/Is in this role have had access to the script beforehand, have prepared how they will present this information, and are following the newsreader's autocue when presenting.

In the second situation, the Deaf T/Is are there to present the news stories of a reporter on location or with video footage and a voiceover. The Deaf T/Is have again seen the script beforehand and have prepared their presentation of the information. The Deaf T/Is will have been introduced by the anchor (hearing only, if during a news headlines format; hearing and Deaf during a news week review format) and will not be present other than to present the information in the news story.

In both situations the Deaf T/Is read an English script, prepare a BSL translation of that script and then read the English autocue whilst presenting their BSL version of the information. The situations differ, though, with regard to the status of the Deaf T/Is: in the first situation they co-present information with the newsreader (in the anchor position) and in the second situation they re-present pre-recorded news from a reporter.

When the Deaf T/Is are in the anchor position, the hearing anchors co-present information with their Deaf anchor colleagues from the same autocue and co-operate with each other so that the needs of the Deaf audience are taken into account, especially the speed at which information is presented in spoken English. The anchors work together creating greater space and time for the Deaf T/Is to make translation additions to the news stories so that the translation is relevant to the audience. As one of the informants says:

> I know that the news team they try to give me time, lengthen it per story, often, it depends on the producer, if they know when to slow down or give me longer, for some it's short and that's that, that can happen but it's rare. (Kim)

When the Deaf T/Is are translating reports, however, the English voice-over is prerecorded and this imposes a fixed time within which the translation must occur.

The space created whilst the Deaf T/Is are 'presenters' also allows for the Deaf T/I anchor to introduce things, for example, the names of protagonists and their ages. This can then make things easier for the Deaf T/Is translating the reports, since this information no longer needs to be included. The Deaf T/I anchors greet the audience but this is something that the Deaf T/Is as translators also try to do in any case, to build a good rapport with the audience. This act of being present in the second situation, however, is brief compared with the highly present nature of the anchor Deaf T/Is.

The Deaf T/Is do not see the task of 'anchor' and 'signer' differently in terms of an act of translation, but they are aware that they are labelled differently according to how they appear on-screen. Similarly, whilst the Deaf T/Is know that they are translating the English, they are doing this within a mainstream news programme and see themselves as newsreaders for the Deaf community. They are members of this community and one of the highest things valued by the Deaf T/Is is that they produce comprehensible TL for their target audience.

4. The historical roots

The Deaf T/Is understand the role that they undertake in television to be a role that bilingual Deaf people have undertaken for many years. Since the inception of Deaf clubs, the bilingual Deaf people have supported the community by translating letters, newspapers and information generally for se-milingual (Hinnenkamp 2005; Skutnabb-Kangas 1981) and monolingual Deaf people. This still happens today, is considered part of one's responsibil-ity to the community, and is an example of the reciprocal sharing of skills within the community's collectivist culture (Smith 1996). The rendering of broadcast news is the first time that this role has emerged in the public do-main.

It is worth bearing in mind that the Deaf community is not able to com-mission which news will be translated. Unlike when members of the commu-nity take their letters, or newspaper articles to be translated, the news being translated is that chosen by hearing, non-Deaf producers and journalists. The Deaf bilinguals exercised their judgements in informing the semilingual and monolingual Deaf people about events happening in mainstream society. So, to some extent the Deaf bilinguals acted as gatekeepers to the information being passed on to their community (Ladd 2003; Vuorinen 1995), in that if they did not think that the information was relevant then this information was not passed on to the community.

This is where the new role differs because neither the Deaf community nor the Deaf T/Is choose the news that is to be rendered for the Deaf commu-nity. And some of the news scripts that the Deaf T/Is are asked to work with are not judged, by the Deaf T/Is, to be of interest (or relevant) to Deaf audi-ences:

> Some of the reports are really coming from hearing culture, but we have to deliver the in-formation, we can't edit it or change it, but just deliver it. (Rebecca)

When using the script as a guide, the Deaf T/Is move towards considering themselves as bilingual newsreaders, both when they are anchors and when they are 'signers'. They do not consider themselves knowers of the informa-tion *per se*, but as deliverers of information approaching that information delivery from a translation perspective. One of the Deaf T/I informants states:

> If the text is clear then I can produce the information clearly, if the information is complex I don't repeat it complexly as the audience would not understand it, I need to make changes, what it means exactly, then I ignore the script, change the delivery so that I say exactly what the story means, then add the details and build it up so that it matches the meaning of the script. (Clark)

This action fulfils a role that, historically, proficient English readers would have had in the Deaf community:

> first interpreter been years ago … always have Deaf 'interpreter' always … I don't mean for example maybe hearing that then straight away sign it to Deaf, no I mean what's going on in society, tell Deaf that interesting, that, Deaf oh wow, interesting that, we've always had that, to me that's part of interpreting, like newspaper morning been read or TV been read then let people know, oh that was really bad, you know, and explain that Deaf really

> interested, that always have, or Deaf have letter, know someone excellent English, ask them to explain, always have but that has always been in the community rather than open and public. (Clark)

The historical role informs the translation style that the Deaf T/Is use; it is the precursor of the present-day Deaf translation norm. The translation act needs to be relevant to the constructed audience (Ruuskanen 1996):

> Maybe hearing in-vision I look between the subtitles and the in-vision interpreters and I think yes, but I would call it hearing structure, you don't want that, the audience it will fly over their heads, the subtitles are enough, what is the in-vision interpreter there for? It's a waste them being there, I always say that the subtitles and the in-vision interpreter should be really different, they should be different but the information that you understand for them should be the same, if they are similar then what is the in-vision interpreter there for? (Clark)

So that the viewer experiences a parallel understanding of the SL^6 information, the TL draws upon the visual information that is being seen on-screen:

> I have to create a clear mental picture for them, which means that I have to try to digest the information and then think how I can sign output which gives them a clear mental picture, by creating a clear picture for myself, then think that's it, I want the Deaf audience to have the same mental picture as me, not sign it so that the Deaf people have to build their own picture bit by bit. (Georgina)

By pointing towards relevant visual information and using this to inform some of the grammatical decisions, such as the visual shapes and sizes of objects (Supalla 1986), this ensures that the TL information is maximally relevant (Gutt 1998; Setton 1999; Sperber & Wilson 1986, 1995; Wilson & Sperber 2003) to the audience.

5. Relevance to the audience

The Deaf T/Is aim to use the English autocue interpretively (Gutt 1998), such that they are not creating a 'faithful' TL, but rather a TL that is optimally relevant to the Deaf audience. This involves including information that will have appeared either earlier during the week (for news week review programmes) or earlier in the broadcast (for news headlines). As information is the key to the news broadcast, that is given primacy over other parts of the message such as the metanotative qualities of the newsreader, i.e. the non-content characteristics that influence or determine a person's overall impressions of the speaker (Isham 1984:119).

Clark (one of the informants) questions some accepted notions of the skopos (Hatim 2001:73; Vermeer 2000) or goal of the translation and how the SL is to be used by the in-vision interpreter:

> I know that in training interpreters are told not to make additions to what someone says if they are monotonous or boring then you need to match their style to add things so that the audience think it's great ... that's a dilemma should you match the style of the person or just deliver the information not give their style over that's hard ... there is no easy answer if people specifically ask you to portray the character of the person then you are clear but I don't think that that is specifically needed in this situation what is important is information. (Clark)

In other words, the information in the script is understood and represented in a way that is pragmatically understood by the audience. The information that has been broadcast previously is used so that the TL can be re-edited to include both enrichments and impoverishments (Sequeiros 1998, 2002); whatever is required to minimize the effort on the part of the constructed audience (Ruuskanen 1996).

In some instances the implicatures that are constructed within the BSL text are different from the implicatures of the English text. This ought to be avoided: the in-vision T/I needs to ensure that the language is used in such a way that it points towards the same inferred meaning as the ST; the BSL needs to be presented as an ostensive utterance in an appropriate way. The TL interpretive utterance will then gain greater resemblance to the SL original (Gutt 1998).

The news headlines summary has the least amount of time available for a relevant BSL text. In order to create the most relevant BSL text, the Deaf T/Is therefore like to use the information already available to the Deaf audience via the subtitles and the visual footage in the more comprehensive news previously broadcast to create the most relevant BSL text. If they are to use the additional information previously broadcast to judge how the BSL can be made maximally relevant to the constructed audience, the Deaf T/Is need more information than is contained in the English news summary. One of the informants describes this below:

> There is background information on the news, the news from 6 to 25 past has lots of information and I read that to find out what they are talking about, then look at my script, much reduced information, if I feel it can be delivered as is I do it, if there is one word that is difficult I can take information from the larger script add it so that it has the same meaning with that background information, I only started doing this recently and Clark is the same, it's good restructuring and adding background information so that it is clear ... really for a Deaf audience it's only 30 seconds, what I feel is appropriate information from the larger script, I can't tell the script writers that their summary is poor so I add information, just one or two pieces so it's clear. (Rebecca)

So the Deaf T/Is not only enrich the SL, but also act as a journalist to the extent that they appropriately edit the larger story for the headlines summary. This happens within the constraints of the time and visual information that is being shown on the screen. It also fulfils the agency that they believe they should use to fulfil the Deaf translation norm.

6. Deaf translator role to interpreter role

One of the news review programmes changed its format slightly throughout the course of the research. Rather than just being a review of the week's news, the programme also included a preview of television programmes that were to be broadcast in the coming week. The floor manager also changed with the new format. The previous floor manager had worked well with the Deaf T/Is, so that they felt accepted as part of the team. The new floor manager saw the Deaf T/Is as outside of the team so that the Deaf T/Is felt that there was little acceptance of them as part of the newsreading team.

The Deaf T/Is felt that after filming a section in the new format, their agency was limited and changes could not be made. In the previous style programme, if the Deaf T/Is were not satisfied with their work, there was an opportunity for the section to be re-filmed. In the eyes of the Deaf T/Is this lack of agency was compounded by the format of the new style programme. It comprised many clips and short pieces of information, combined with video footage. This style of programming gave the Deaf T/Is little chance to re-structure or re-order the news and programme information. One of the Deaf T/Is, Kat, reported to me that they felt like a HEARING INTER-PRETER.[7] I raised this issue with the other informants and they agreed with this sentiment.

This seems to indicate that for the Deaf T/Is this confined role is more indicative of the 'hearing' (or non-Deaf) interpreter. The Deaf T/Is want more agency (Inghilleri 2003; Rudvin 2002, 2004) within the broadcast news. The hearing interpreters, from the Deaf T/Is' perspective, collude with the institution by not demanding greater time and space to include cultural and linguistic adjustments and enrichments in the TL.

The preliminary norm (Toury 2000) is one where Deaf T/Is are not able to choose the news items that are translated. In spite of this, the Deaf T/Is feel that in some contexts they are given enough agency to create some idea of ownership of the process and the information:

> On Newsweek or the headlines we are always talking about changing to match the audience ... we have to find out what the background information is, the script may not be clear, and so we need the background information so that we can put those in and sign it so that it is understood by the audience, we need to put in cultural information. (Clark)

When this agency is denied them, they feel used by the institution in perpetuating mainstream values:

> Some of the reports are really coming from hearing culture but we have to deliver the information we can't edit it or change it but just deliver it, sometimes they are trying to be funny and I would question whether the Deaf audience gets it or not, because it is a hearing thing, but I can't do anything about that that's beyond my control. (Rebecca)

This conflicts with the Deaf T/Is' historic and cultural rationale for being employed. Accordingly, the Deaf T/Is are unable to fulfil the skopos of the translation as they see it. The Deaf T/Is are not able to adhere to their Deaf translation norm. This Deaf translation norm is, however, a value that is shared by the Deaf T/Is and not necessarily identified by nor accommodated by the news broadcast institutions.

7. Presence

The Deaf T/Is see themselves as being more 'present' (Stolze 2004) when delivering the news information in BSL when compared with the hearing interpreters. They believe that this greater presence is a core part of the Deaf translation norm. The Deaf T/Is are re-presenting the information:

> We look at the whole thing, take it on board, chew on it, conceptualise the whole thing, what it is, then take on board that conceptualisation and present that in BSL. (Georgina)

So the information is not 'just' translated or interpreted into BSL but presented to the audience. There is no notion of neutrality embodied in that presentation. This presence means that the Deaf T/Is see themselves more closely in the role of bilingual reporter/journalist than interpreter. There is some ownership of the information and the way that this is presented to the Deaf audience:

> Simultaneous interpreting just goes on and on and on, you focus on processing and editing and reformulating information, and as you said relay the information, so I feel that for it to become Deaf you have to be in it, for it to become a full translation it has to be consecutive ... it is more BSL when you sign ... you have the information in your head and sign it clearly to the Deaf person, that creates instant rapport, with simultaneous you are out of the information. (Kim)

> If you are reading written materials understanding them and then translating them for an audience that is still consecutive because you take it section by section. (Kim)

So by not undertaking an online process, the Deaf T/Is are able to have greater rapport with their constructed audience. And this is how the Deaf T/Is create presence in their renderings.

This presence occurs more readily when the news stories are deemed relevant by the Deaf T/Is. When the news stories are viewed as inappropriate for a Deaf audience, then the Deaf T/Is move into functioning in the way they perceive the hearing interpreters to work. The Deaf T/Is become more detached from the information and less present when delivering the news story.

8. Translation performance

One of the things raised about the translation of the English into BSL is that there is still a performance factor to this task. Unlike the translation of two written languages, with the translation of a written language into an unwritten language there is a limit to the extent to which the TL can be edited. The longer the news story, the less the Deaf T/Is are able to construct a fully edited TL. And even with short news stories, if it is a live broadcast, once the broadcast has started any performance errors need to be corrected 'online'. This is also true to a lesser extent with pre-recorded broadcasts, if the Deaf T/Is are seen as part of the team and allowed to re-record stories.

This seems to be related to the nature of the interaction between having a prepared translation that is memorised and a scrolling autocue that acts as a prompt but is not a separately prepared autocue containing a gloss. The SL is still written English, but a translation has been mentally prepared. As such there is a translation performance issue because BSL is an unwritten language:

> I feel the task is interpreting when, if I have been mentally processing then that is interpreting, me if I have been processing, like TV news you are right, I feel it is translation, but I am still processing, reading the autocue, processing and changing it into sign, that means processing, so I feel TV news is a mixture of interpreting and translating. (Kim)

The English on the autocue is the same as that used by the newsreader and any notes in English or glosses are not prepared on a separate autocue for the Deaf T/Is. In this way the interaction differs from consecutive interpreting, where notes of the SL can be written down prior to reformulation. The reformulation is undertaken by the Deaf T/Is beforehand, but if this cannot be remembered due to the live nature of the translation, then the English autocue will still interfere with the TL production when being broadcast:

> If you do not remember the translation, the autocue is fixed ... that's difficult, sometimes I remember I can sign sometimes and not follow the autocue, it interfere influence our [Deaf T/Is] structure. (Georgina)

This is compounded by the lack of control that the Deaf T/Is have in a live broadcast when compared with interpreting in a meeting. The meeting can be stopped and clarifications can be made, but this is not possible during a live television broadcast. In a pre-recorded programme this is also something that comes into play:

Lots feel play safe stick to English order because it's live if it were pre-recorded it's better you have more control. (Kat)

The idea of translation performance is useful when thinking about translating BSL:

> Sometimes you finish feeling great because you have remembered the story and been able to reorder the information. Other times you are wanting the autocue to speed up so that you can be reminded of the next part of the story because you have forgotten what comes next, or what more needs to be said. (Georgina)

This is analogous to language competence and performance (Akmajian 1995) where internal language competence cannot be judged by performance errors. A native language user can have intuitions about the grammaticality of a sentence whilst making mistakes in production because performance errors occur. This happens in the case of translating oral languages, although signed languages may be the only example of unwritten languages being translated, when due to the performance of the translation errors occur. So, whilst the translator can construct an internal 'mental' translation using their translation competence, and judge the grammaticality of another translation, errors can still occur in the translations they produce themselves:

> Clark is really skilled at presenting sometimes you can tell if the script was given to him last minute but most of the time it doesn't bother him and he signs naturally Clark is good and one of the few compared to others and we know he can read and understand and memorise the information and you know he is skilled at translating he doesn't allow the or-der to influence him at all and so he just delivers the information sometimes he is reading but that doesn't affect his output but sometimes you catch him hesitating and you know that it is last minute information that he hasn't had a chance to fully digest but when he does have time he is great. (Kim)

Interestingly, when a story is repeated and the Deaf T/Is become more famil-iar with the information they are more able to act as information deliverers:

> Sometimes me nothing mentally processing, nothing sometimes, I read the script, translate it but I already know the information, I don't need to think, like if it is a repeated news story, like Soham the small girls murdered, that was repeated so I did not need to process. (Kim)

The less familiar the information is to the Deaf T/Is, the more likely they are to perform in a way that is perceived to be like a hearing interpreter.

> I feel I behaviour more like an interpreter when doing simultaneous interpreting,[8] watching the SL and signing the output is not mine, if I wait until I understand it and then tell the Deaf person what I understand that's it consecutive, that's Deaf, simultaneous is just pass-ing on information. (Kim)

Here the information is unscripted and so less familiar to the Deaf T/I than a scripted piece. Even though an interpreter will rely on prediction skills and will prepare for a job, there is still a different level of known information in a fully scripted SL to be translated when compared with a live meeting.

When space is given for the translation to be made so that a real connection can be made with the audience that is when one acts according to the Deaf translation norm. This relates to the idea that there have always been information sharers and their responsibility within the community is to ensure that the Deaf community members understand the information. In fact the notion of simultaneous interpreting clearly is not conducive with a Deaf translation style, and does not form part of the Deaf translation norm:

> I feel that it is hearing their rules, following this that and the other theirs hearing, if Deaf it would not be like that, Deaf rules are different. (Kat)

Hearing interpreters are deemed to follow their professional rules, which are seen as mainstream led and not Deaf culturally sensitive, rather than being involved in the information and involved in ensuring that the message is understood.

> Theirs, I feel interpreting hearing theirs, I feel the rules, how to behave, stiff, how to sign, all these rules, they are trained, like that, I feel that is there. (Kat)

> The information is signed outside of the interpreter. (Georgina)

This last quotation regards the language style that the hearing interpreters are seen to adopt by the Deaf T/Is. Rather than being involved in a scene and using either constructed dialogue or constructed action[9] the hearing interpreters use other devices (Quinto-Pozos, in press). This lack of involvement, described as empathetic and participatory by Ong (1982), compounds the lack of language adjustment on the part of the hearing interpreters.

It is important to say at this juncture that this neither describes all hearing interpreters (or Deaf T/Is as contrasting with the hearing interpreters), nor describes the needs of all of the Deaf community:

> The point is interpreters can hear the information and relay it, Deaf can relay the information too, but in a Deaf way, the Deaf can follow, suits Deaf way but if they don't that becomes like interpreting. (Kat)

The comments of the Deaf T/Is are couched within the notion of the differences between Deaf T/Is and hearing interpreters where those differences could be seen as problematic. There are hearing interpreters who are able to take control of communicative situations (and, conversely, Deaf interpreters who are not). There are those in the community who are less empowered because of their language usage and need greater action on the part of the interpreter in terms of ensuring that the message is understood. In this situation, the Deaf T/Is describe the need for a Deaf T/I to be brought in to act as an intermediary. This greater action to ensure that the message is understood is something that the Deaf T/Is also take within the media. To that extent the Deaf translation norm is not just about doing a 'good' translation but creating a TL that is understood.

> Again lots of the time we all think that we are aiming for people like us and those that we mix with, often we forget grass roots Deaf people and it's worse for grass roots Deaf people because the newspaper isn't accessible because it's in English, the TV subtitles don't provide access, so really the programme is for them not to others who have access, they have it already. (Kat)

9. Identity

The Deaf T/Is are well aware of their core membership in the community. This comes from being born into and growing up in the Deaf community. The Deaf T/Is still socialise with the Deaf community, as that is their home community. This reinforces the Deaf T/Is identity and adeptness at modifying their language so as to be understood by other members of their community.

The Deaf interpreters make decisions in relation to their translations according to how they construct themselves as core community members who regularly interact with the Deaf community:

> Deaf people identify those [language] factors without thinking about it and adjust their language without training, they just adjust their language because this the community they mix in, so they just know how to adjust their language. (Clark)

When the Deaf T/Is categorise 'hearing' (non-Deaf) interpreters as non-members of the Deaf community, they then do not want to license these non-Deaf interpreters to make similar decisions with respect to the TL:

> [hearing] interpreters dip in and out of the [Deaf] community, if a hearing interpreter was deeply involved in the community all the time then maybe they could take on board all of these factors perhaps, but most interpreters now a days dip in and out, that's it, they work in the community and then leave, it's rare that interpreters now a days are like those in the past, that was different, they were part of the community and socialised within it, it's different now. (Clark)

> as I read down the text I pick out what my mental picture which is automatically the same as Deaf people but those interpreting read the information and try to change the order but the picture they have isn't right. (Kim)

The aim of the Deaf translation norm is to remove traces of the SL so that the TL audience members perceive the text as their own:

> No they are different I don't know how hearing interpreters create their mental pictures I can talk about Deaf interpreters as one of them or how I understand/receive information from hearing interpreters so what I normally do is read the piece of text and try to think of the Deaf audience I have to create a clear mental picture for them which means that I have to try to digest the information and then think how I can sign output which gives them a clear mental picture by creating a clear picture for myself then think that's it I want the Deaf audience to have the same mental picture as me not sign it so that the Deaf people have to build their own picture bit by bit. (Georgina)

In this way the Deaf T/Is use this space on televised news broadcasts to create a Deaf space:

> Maybe Deaf read the script, have understanding of it, they have their experience, their background, their own, this they relate to the script, and add cultural knowledge, maybe hearing read the English autocue or hear it, they think, oh yes, I know, before, have over there, relate to autocue, I feel hearing maybe have limit, through have to be Deaf to empathise, same Deaf have limit through English script. (Kat)

Similarly it is reported by the Deaf T/I informants that there are some Deaf T/Is using hearing interpreters as role models:

> Hearing interpreters should copy Deaf interpreters but it's happening the other way round Deaf interpreters are copying hearing interpreters why is that? (Kat)

This seems to imply that the Deaf interpreters are not following the Deaf translation norm, but rather using models that are used by hearing interpreters. It is a complex matter, because hearing interpreters are the norm in most situations other than television. The hearing interpreters can interact with the mainstream majority and theirs is clearly the dominant discourse within the sign language interpreting profession.

The Deaf translation norm is something that has evolved and developed within the Deaf community. It is this home grown quality that is important in creating a Deaf space on television. A translation that the Deaf constructed audience identify with:

> Although there are some Deaf in-vision here and elsewhere the rest are not suitable, they are not native users of BSL, sign with bad articulation, fingerspelling, not clear, shame that group not better, more groups then can compare, at the moment too many learn BSL late, become in-vision, it's a mess, some hearing interpreters better than them, yes. (Rebecca)

> Not criticism but hearing interpreters good but not have some specific skills, like really hearing will never have those skills, same Deaf with never have some skills that hearing have never, I think it's possible for us impossible for them, through influence from sound, impossible, way of thinking, impossible, do your best fine, but Deaf natural, grow up natural, comma full-stop from head, you tell me I've been I don't know why, not taught in school, how to move head nothing, just using language naturally have head movement there natural.. (Rebecca)

So notions of naturalness are an important part of the Deaf translation norm and that comes from growing up in the community and being natively fluent in the language. Similarly, it would appear that this is not something that hearing interpreters can achieve, although there are aspects of this translation norm that can be achieved. If an interpreter is Deaf (hearing), then they have grown up in the community and potentially have a high degree of fluency, but cannot reduce the influence that hearing sound has on their way of thinking.

10. Institutional limits

In striving to achieve a TL product that is understood with minimal additional processing effort on the part of the audience, when compared with BSL that is not a translation, the Deaf T/Is still have to work within the limits of the organization for which they are working:

> I'm in their hearing news, me in hearing, their news, I do not make big changes to Deaf-cultural their way, me no, at first when learning it was a struggle, now I do not always sign in a strong Deaf way, really should and can float between strong Deaf and less strong, me not so strong Deaf, I have thought why, of course it is because it is hearing news, their structure, that means how can I radically change it to Deaf's if it is based on English, based on hearing structure, it would have to be the other way round with me sitting at the desk and the hearing person standing at the side, that would be Deaf. (Kim)

The Deaf audience relies solely on the ability of the Deaf T/Is to provide access to the hearing news, without any support during the broadcast from the hearing institution. The autocue is the feed that the hearing newsreader has and an additional camera with autocue, with a different BSL structured script, could easily be set up for the Deaf T/Is. This is not necessarily the preferred way of working for the Deaf T/Is, but it is the minimum that the television studio could do to accommodate Deaf T/Is to perform a live translation of the news.

It would be interesting to interview the television newsreaders and others within the institution to have a greater understanding of their motivations for having Deaf T/Is on the news. Now that there is legislation that a specified percentage of broadcast television is mandated to have BSL interpretation or be a BSL based programme, as well as the official recognition of BSL in 2003, this may influence their behaviour in accommodating the Deaf T/Is. The question that this raises is whether there is a genuine commitment to access for the Deaf community with BSL as a first or preferred language, or if the prime motivation in having Deaf T/Is is to satisfy legislative obligations and that the Deaf T/Is must work within the limits set by the institution.

[1] These were Clark, Georgina, Kim, Kat and Rebecca.
[2] An idea mooted by G. Turner and recently explored at REMEDES 2004.
[3] www.hmso.gov.uk/acts/acts1996/96055--h.htm#20
[4] www.ofcom.org.uk/tv/ifi/codes/ctas/#content
[5] Target Language in this case BSL
[6] Source Language in this case English
[7] The BSL signs are glossed using upper-case lettering (e.g. HEARING).
[8] There are times when Deaf T/Is work between two sign languages such as BSL and ASL (American Sign Language – an unrelated sign language to BSL).
[9] This is the sign language equivalent of reported speech where the person signing either becomes the person and reports their speech or enacts their actions.

References

Akmajian, Adrian *et al*. 1995. *Linguistics: an Introduction to Language and Communication* (4th ed.). Cambridge, Mass. and London: MIT Press.

Baker, Charlotte and Carol Padden. 1978. *American Sign Language. A Look at its History, Structure, and Community*. Silver Spring: Linstok Press.

Carmel, Simon and Leila Monaghan. 1991. "An introduction to ethnographic work in deaf communities". *Sign Language Studies* 73: 411-420.

Cook, Ian and Mike Crang. 1995. *Doing Ethnographies* (Vol. No 58 Quantitative): Environmental publications. http://eprints.dur.ac.uk/archive/00000060/01/Crang_ethnographies.pdf

Gutt, Ernst-August. 1998. "Pragmatic aspects of translation: some relevance-theory observations", in Leo Hickey (ed.) *The Pragmatics of Translation*. Clevedon: Multilingual Matters Ltd, 41-53.

Hatim, Basil. 2001. *Teaching and Researching Translation*. Harlow: Longman.

Hinnenkamp, Volker. 2005. "Semilingualism, double monolingualism and blurred genres - on (not) speaking a legitimate language". *Journal of Social Science Education* 1. www.sowi-online.de/journal/2005-1/semilingualism_hinnenkamp.htm

Inghilleri, Moira. 2003. "Habitus, field and discourse: interpreting as socially situated activity". *Target 15*(2): 243-268.

Isham, William P. 1984. *The Role of Message Analysis in Interpretation*. Paper presented at the RID Conference Interpreting: The Art of Cross Cultural Mediation.

Kyle, Jim and Lorna Allsop. 1982. *Deaf People and the Community: Final Report to Nuffield Foundation*. Bristol: Bristol University, School of Education.

Kyle, Jim and Bencie Woll. 1985. *Sign Language: the Study of Deaf People and their Language*. Cambridge and New York: Cambridge University Press.

Ladd, Paddy. 1998. *In Search of Deafhood: towards an Understanding of British Deaf Culture*. Bristol: University of Bristol. Unpublished PhD.

—. 2003. *In Search of Deafhood*. Clevedon: Multilingual Matters.

Padden, Carol and Tom Humphries. 1988. *Deaf in America*. Cambridge, MA: Harvard University Press.

Ong, Walter J. 1982. *Orality and Literacy: the Technologizing of the World*. London: Methuan.

Quinto-Pozos, David. In press. "Can constructed action be considered obligatory?". *Lingua*.

Rudvin, Mette. 2002. "How neutral is 'neutral'? Issues in interaction and participation in community interpreting", in Maurizio Viezzi & Giuliana Garzone (eds) *Perspectives on Interpreting*. Bologna: CLUEB, 217-233.

—. 2004. "Cross-cultural dynamics in community interpreting. Troubleshooting", in Gyde Hansen, Kirsten Malmkjær and Daniel Gile (eds) *Claims, Changes and Challenges in Translation Studies*. Amsterdam and Philadelphia: John Benjamins, 271-283.

Ruuskanen, Deborah D. K. 1996. "The effect of pragmatic factors on the definition of equivalence in translation". *Language Sciences* 18(3-4): 883-895.

Senghas, Richard and Leila Monaghan. 2002. "Sign of their times: Deaf communities and the culture of language". *Annual Review of Anthropology* 31: 69-97.

Sequeiros, Xosé R. 1998. "Interlingual impoverishment in translation". *Bulletin of Hispanic Studies* 75: 145-157.

—. 2002. "Interlingual pragmatic enrichment in translation". *Journal of Pragmatics* 34: 1069-1089.

Setton, Robin. 1999. *Simultaneous Interpretation: A Cognitive-pragmatic Analysis*. Amsterdam and Philadelphia: John Benjamins.

Skelton, Tracey and Gill Valentine. 2003a. "'It feels like being Deaf is normal': an exploration into the complexities of defining D/deafness and young D/deaf people's identities". *The Canadian Geographer* 47(4): 451-466.

—. 2003b. "Political participation, political action and political identities: young D/deaf people's perspectives". *Space and Polity* 7(2): 117-134.

Skutnabb-Kangas, Tove. 1981. *Bilingualism or not: The Education of Minorities*. Clevedon: Multilingual Matters.

Smith, Theresa B. 1996. *Deaf People in Context*. Washington: University of Washington. Unpublished PhD.

Sperber, Daniel and Deirdre Wilson. 1986. *Relevance: Communication and Cognition*. Oxford: Blackwell.

—. 1995. *Relevance: Communication and Cognition* (2nd ed.). Oxford: Blackwell.

Spindler, George and Louise Spindler. 1992. "Cultural process and ethnography: an anthropological perspective", in Margaret D. LeCompte (ed.) *The Handbook of Qualitative Research in Education*. London: Academic Press.

Spradley, James P. 1979. *The Ethnographic Interview*. Fort Worth: Holt, Rinehart and Winston.

Squires, Judith. 2004. "Equality and New Labour". *Soundings: A Journal of Politics and Culture* 27: 74-85.

Stolze, Radegundis. 2004. "Creating 'presence' in translation", in Gyde Hansen, Kirsten Malmkjær and Daniel Gile (eds) *Claims, Changes and Challenges in Translation Studies*. Amsterdam and Philadelphia: John Benjamins, 39-50.

Strauss, Anselm and Juliet Corbin. 1990. *Basics of Qualitative Research: Grounded Theory and Procedures and Techniques*. London: SAGE Publications.

Supalla, Ted. 1986. "The classifier system in American Sign Language", in Colette Craig (ed.) *Noun Classes and Categorization*. Amsterdam: Benjamins, 181-214.

Taylor, Philip (writer) 1998. "Looking for Thomas... a search for my roots [Television]", in Terry Riley (producer) *SeeHear*. United Kingdom: BBC.

Toury, Gideon. 2000. "The nature and role of norms in translation", in Lawrence Venuti (ed.) *The Translation Studies Reader*. London: Routledge, 198-211.

Venuti, Lawrence. 1998. *The Scandals of Translation: Towards an Ethics of Difference*. London: Routledge.

Vermeer, Hans J. 2000. "Skopos and commission in tranlsational action", in Lawrence Venuti (ed.) *The Translation Studies Reader*. London: Routledge, 221-232.

Vuorinen, Erkka. 1995. "News translation as gatekeeping", in Mary Snell-Hornby, Zuzana Jettmarová and Klaus Kaindl (eds) *Translation as Intercultural Communication*. Amsterdam and Philadelphia: John Benjamins, 161-171.

Wilson, Deirdre and Daniel Sperber. 2002. *Relevance Theory*. Paper presented at the Working Papers in Linguistics 14, UCL.

Woll, Bencie. 2000. *Exploring language, culture and identity: insights from sign language and the Deaf community*. Paper presented at the Language Across Boundaries Conference, Anglia Polytechnic University, Cambridge.

A world of change in a changing world

Josélia Neves

Institutico Politécnico de Leiria, Portugal

Abstract
The introduction of digital technology is making many of the dreams of the past become realities of the present. This is certainly a fact when the issue under consideration is subtitling for the deaf and hard-of-hearing (SDH). At the beginning of the twenty-first century, SDH finds itself in a crucial stage of its development. The foundations have been solidly planted by strengthened television transmission services such as those provided by closed subtitling and teletext systems. Developments are equally visible in the growing offer of SDH at cinemas and on DVDs. Convergent technology is rapidly blurring frontiers, making it quite difficult to delimit the media where SDH may now be found. In response to such changes, subtitling methods have gradually adapted themselves to the special needs of an ever-growing number of specific contexts. The existence of different norms accounts for the wealth of experiences that have been taking place in many corners of the globe. In addition to providing an overview of the makings of SDH, this article hopes to set forth the discussion of how, in the present scenario, much may be done to make the most of the technical conditions currently available, and of the expertise that has been gained in the last decades, in the hope of coming closer to catering for the needs of all those who may use SDH as a tool to access audiovisual texts.

1. Introduction

A quick glance at the latest publications (Gambier 2004; Orero 2004) and at the programmes of recent conferences makes it clear that much has been changing in the field of audiovisual translation (AVT) in this last decade. It is also obvious that a new topic – accessibility to the media – has gained the interest of scholars and professionals, making itself visible in publications on audiovisual translation in general and in the growing number of specific works on subtitling for the deaf and hard-of-hearing (SDH) and audio description (AD) for the blind and partially sighted, in particular.

In this new context, the term accessibility is no longer viewed as referring to special services for people with disabilities but as referring to solutions that take into account the needs of all, including those who have special needs. Gambier (2003:179) also refers to this all-encompassing concept of AVT when he says that "the key word in screen translation is now accessibility". In so doing, he makes it clear that audiovisual translation's *raison d'être* is to take multimedial texts to receivers who would otherwise be deprived of the full message, either because they do not know the language of the original or because, for some particular reason, they cannot access some of language features, such as sound or image.

Still, even though this call for integration is no doubt sound special viewers with sensorial impairments need to be offered services that have been devised with their particular needs in mind if they are to be given equal opportunities when watching audiovisual texts. This is the case for both AD and SDH, which have gradually come to be known and used by ever-growing numbers of both impaired and non-impaired viewers.

In everyday life, this newly acquired interest on the part of academics and AVT professionals means a world of change to those for whom the access to information and culture has, for far too long, depended exclusively on the expertise and the goodwill of friends or family who (with greater or lesser competence) used to relay (and continue to relay) their versions of the original texts. And even though the changes are obvious now, this world of change has been slow in its making. It is the result of a gradual change in attitude and the strong determination to change practice, to improve technology and even to draw up and to impose legislation, especially on the part of those who are most concerned. In addition, change is frequently motivated by less than altruistic motives, particularly when benefits are foreseen to come in the form of increased audiences and/or greater income, as has happened in Portugal (Neves 2005).

And yet, the change has not been sudden. It has been taking place, here and there, for over twenty years, despite the fact that, until recently, the existence of solutions for impaired viewers was almost unknown to most. AD and SDH have been around for quite some time so why this great interest now? Is this yet another trend? There are reasons to believe that this newly found concern is the result of a growing awareness of the needs and the rights of all people regardless of their conditions.

2. A changing world in technology

The advent of SDH as we know it today dates back to the 1970s and 1980s when, in the USA, closed captioning, and in the UK, teletext subtitling, were simultaneously developed to allow for the presentation of closed subtitles on television. These systems were to determine most of the SDH solutions and strategies to be used throughout the world to the present day. However, the history of SDH did not begin with these two technologies nor is it to stay with them forever. According to the Captioning Media Program (CMP n.d.), the first subtitles for the hearing impaired actually appeared in the 1940s, when Emerson Romero, a deaf man and himself an actor in the times of silent films, tried to adapt old films for deaf viewers. He used the techniques available for silent films and spliced in text reproducing dialogue between frames. This meant that text and image would alternate rather than coexist as was the case later. In 1949, two years after Romero's first experiments, Arthur Rank provided a subtitled feature length film at a cinema room in London. Skilled hearing operators slid pieces of glass, with etched words, in and out of a projector. The captions were shown on a smaller screen to the bottom left of the screen of the movie, in synchrony with the dialogue. This technique was not very successful for it made viewers look away from the action to read the subtitles; however, the underlying idea would be taken up in Belgium where the first open subtitles were printed directly onto a master copy of the film. One decade later, in 1959, the US government passed the first law (Public Law 85-905) to promote the provision of subtitles for hearing impaired moviegoers. Another 10 years would pass before subtitles found their way into television. The first preview of a subtitled TV programme happened at the First National Conference on Television for the Hearing Impaired, held at the University of Tennessee in 1971. This conference is seen as an important date in the history of subtitling for it brought together representatives of all major TV networks in the United States (ABC, NBC, CBS and PBS), producers, federal agencies, Deaf/hearing-impaired people, professionals, parents and teachers to discuss important issues that ranged from technology to the needs of consumers with hearing impairments. The first TV programme to be aired with subtitling for the deaf was an episode of the *French Clef* to be followed by an episode of the *Mod Squad*, both broadcast in 1972. These first subtitles were open and hidden subtitles became common practice only in 1980.

In the 1970s, the British followed in the USA's footsteps and set out to provide subtitling for the deaf and hard-of-hearing on television using the teletext system, which – like the closed captioning system used in the USA – concealed the teletext signal in the VBI (vertical blanking interval). However, instead of resorting to line 21 alone, the teletext system allowed for the concealment of information at the end of each of lines 6 to 22 and 318 to 335. At the time the British system competed with the French system ANTIOPE – *Acquisition Numérique et Télévisualisation d'Image organisées en Pages d'Ecriture* – first used in 1977. It gave way later to the teletext system that would be adopted by various countries throughout Europe, Asia, Africa and the Pacific. The teletext system has since been in use in analogue television systems throughout Europe. Its technical potentialities and limitations have determined a great deal of the quality of SDH offered today.

With the emerging digital age, closed subtitling and teletext subtitling may soon become obsolete. As it is, SDH is no longer offered exclusively on television. It is one of the many features on audiovisual products of all types, besides television: VHS, DVD, the Internet and video games, among others.

It is clear that, as far as technology is concerned, we are now facing rapid and quite impressive changes. Great improvements are envisaged with the growing dissemination of digital media. The new technical conditions made available will allow for subtitling solutions that, in the era of analogue technology, could be regarded simply utopian. Interactive digital television and convergent media call for a review of the present notions of 'mass media' and 'audiences'. In the future, audiovisual programmes might not even be provided as finished products. People will be able to interact with the original text adjusting it to their particular needs and wishes. This means that accessibility services, such as subtitling or audio description, may come to be available on call, and be tailored to the individual needs of each viewer. More concretely, a development that could soon be in order may well be multi-level or multi-track subtitling, which would allow people to determine the characteristics of the subtitles they want to receive. This would mean the possibility to choose from a number of graded subtitle types, moving from verbatim subtitling, across edited to adapted subtitles, to suit the needs of different readers. Hard-of-hearing viewers and fast readers might then choose to have verbatim subtitles, whilst slow readers might opt for simplified versions. What is more, this might also entail the development of other varieties of subtitles, for example, subtitles containing supplementary information such as an explanation of concepts or detailed information on particular features to be activated by those who have an interest in accessing metatextual information. The possibility to activate extra information on sound effects and/or music would also make watching subtitled programmes a richer experience, particularly for those who need other ways of accessing sound.

In addition to the possibility of selecting specific contents, the possibility to 'pick and choose' would allow viewers to select the actual appearance of subtitles. One may be able to decide upon the use of colour or subtitle positioning on the screen. The decision to use colour or subtitle displacement to identify speakers will be used by those who find it an asset, whilst others who may find these solutions annoying or distracting may take to other subtitling styles to suit their preferences.

Subtitle size would also be changeable, catering for the special needs of those people who, in addition to suffering from a hearing impairment, may also have poor eyesight, a condition which is common in an ageing society. At this point we can only guess at what will be technically possible in the future but we can obviously start preparing for what is to come.

The fact that audiovisual translation is greatly determined by technological factors makes it clear that a world of change is needed if we are to keep up with a changing world.

3. A world of change in attitudes and practices

Even though technological changes are undoubtedly important, technology alone cannot account for what is of vital importance for the attainment of true accessibility: Real improvements will be made possible only if and when those involved in the provision of audiovisual materials in general become aware of the special needs of many of their receivers.

Subtitling for the hearing impaired has been around for more than half a century. As far as television is concerned, it has been technically viable for over 30 years; however, only recently has SDH gained widespread visibility. In an initial phase, SDH was only a fact in countries with strong lobbying Deaf communities. In countries where subtitling is normally used for hearers, it took longer for people to become aware that certain viewers were not getting their share. Subtitling for the hearing impaired has lived the story that characterizes most innovations. Initially, there was an urge to make it happen and subtitles were introduced. Then, there was a need to increase quantity, and countries such as Great Britain set forth impressive benchmarks of 100% by 2008. Now the time has come to address a new challenge, that of quality.

Even though very little attention is being dedicated to quality standards and different countries are working at different tempos and with distinct underlying objectives, that which best characterizes these recent years is an honest effort to introduce or to increase SDH output, particularly on television. This generalized drive has happened for a number of reasons.

General awareness of disability has been raised thanks to the promotion of events such as those organized in 2003, The European Year of People with Disabilities. In the course of the event, many European countries passed laws and regulations to ensure equal opportunities and equal rights; many countries introduced SDH as a regular television service; and others took action to increase the amount of SDH then being offered. Within this context, it was only natural that the introduction of digital television should include measures to ensure greater accessibility to impaired viewers. Transnational projects such as TV for All (Stallard 2003) and the urge to standardize digital media brought about greater visibility and conveyed a new importance to a matter that had, until then, been limited to those directly concerned.

Recent years have also witnessed a growing interest in SDH on behalf of scholars and researchers. This is particularly visible in the amount of research projects that have been or are being carried out in this field. Empirical research has led to a better understanding of the profile of hearing impaired viewers, providing important insights into their preferences and needs (Gregory & Sancho-Aldridge 1997; de Linde & Kay 1999; Franco & Araújo 2003; Neves 2005). The findings that derive from the study of quantitative and qualitative data can shed light on important issues that are often disregarded for being considered irrelevant or difficult to address. A better understanding of aspects such as language and reading skills or viewing habits has allowed for new approaches to the analysis of present SDH formats and for the proposal of solutions for improvement of present standards.

Such studies, when articulated and shared with all the agents involved – broadcasters, subtitlers and the viewers themselves – may result in significant improvement in quality standards and in valuable tools for professionals on the job. Furthermore, they may be used in the training of future professionals, who will no doubt benefit from teaching programmes that develop the skills considered to be required for the provision of high quality subtitles.

4. What it takes

A better understanding of the makings of SDH may allow us to arrive at a number of interesting conclusions. As is generally known, subtitling for the deaf and hard-of-hearing calls for much more than is required from subtitles for hearers. It is a fact that no AVT solution is adequate for all viewers. As happens with viewers in general, SDH receivers are an extremely heterogeneous group, covering people with different types and degrees of deafness, different cultural, educational and linguistic backgrounds and therefore, quite distinct needs. It is clear that the requirements of Deaf viewers are different from those of their hard-of-hearing counterparts, and it is common to hear both the first and the last complain about how different their 'ideal' subtitles should be. Still, the fact that these two audiences would benefit from substantially different subtitles does not mean that it is not worth pursuing the achievement of subtitles that might be reasonably adequate for the majority of receivers.

Regardless of the type of linguistic transfer that may be in order – intralingual or interlingual SDH – or the media or the genre in which the subtitles are to be shown, there are parameters that are equally valid to all. Briefly speaking, the overriding concern will always be to make subtitles readable and enjoyable, conveying all the important information normally made available through acoustic signs. This will obviously mean playing a balancing act between time and space, contents and form, text and receiver. Subtitles for the deaf and hard-of-hearing live as much from their contents as from their form. What you say and how you show it are equally important because the sounds must, of necessity, be rendered visually and all means available are therefore valuable if they result in greater economy and higher efficiency. A formula for adequate SDH may read as follows:

- Readable subtitles will be those that are clearly legible because of their font type, their colour, their positioning and their alignment.
- Readable subtitles will also be those where the form directs readers to its content, through adequate line breaks and subtitle divisions.
- Readable subtitles will be the ones where reading time is proportional to syntactic structure and semantic complexity.
- Readable subtitles will also be those that are in synchrony with the overall rhythm of the text, respecting cuts and visual cues.
- Readable subtitles will compensate for bumps, such as stylistic nuances, with extra reading time.
- Finally, readable subtitles may mean simplification and reduction, but may also mean explicitation and addition.

And here again, another important balancing act is in order, i.e. between what is to be omitted and what is to be added. Two words designate the criteria to be followed – redundancy and relevance – omit what is redundant and add what is relevant.

Redundancy is a natural component of all language, which means that special care is due if minimal redundancy is to be left for the benefit of greater linguistic efficiency. Furthermore, what may be redundant to hearers may not be so to those who cannot hear, which makes it important to establish whether redundancy is expressed through visual codes or not.

An apparently easier matter is that of addition. In fact, SDH is often defined as a type of subtitling that adds information about sound effects and speaker identification, and there are cases in which the SDH differs from subtitles for hearers only because they carry a few extra lines with such information. Indeed, there is a need to add information about sound and music and it is essential to identify speakers. On the other hand, this is not a straightforward matter and raises additional issues.

The identification of speakers has been dealt with in a number of different ways: the addition of identification labels, the use of colours and the displacement of subtitles to match speakers' positions on screen have been among the most common solutions. However, these may result in added problems, for they may overload perception and become cumbersome to deaf receivers.

Offering simple denotative information about sound effects, as in 'telephone rings', is also a simple and efficient way of going about conveying sound visually. All goes well when sound is denotative in nature. Problems occur when sound goes beyond its denotative value and carries hidden messages. Sound, in all its forms, has the power to suggest worlds of its own and to carry emotion, which may be conveyed with subtlety through rhythm, pitch or cadence. Words, sound effects and music are modulated and convey meanings that are sometimes difficult to interpret and even more difficult to convey through other signs, in this case usually words.

The emotion that is carried on the human voice can change meanings and suggest what goes unsaid. Finding a way to express the emotion of the human voice has been on the agenda of many people working on SDH, a fact that is particularly visible in in-house style guides and codes of good practice. Various solutions have been suggested: the use of expressive punctuation, the exploitation of font type and colour, the inclusion of explanatory labels, the resource to emoticons and smileys or emoticons both in their alpha-numeric format and in the more elaborate round faces. Just as happens with the human voice, other voices may also carry emotion. Animal sounds can convey urgency, danger or contentment, features that can be understood only when the manner in which they are produced is decoded. Sound effects too can speak of emotions. The way a doorbell rings, a door bangs or a car hoots may say a lot about that very moment. In addition, music too is more than a melody. It speaks for much that goes unsaid. According to Prendergast (1992:213-226), it establishes mood, underlines actions, punctuates the action and all, quite often, with no resource to words.

This question then remains to be answered: how can such subtleties be conveyed through visual signs? The way in which all these features can be conveyed through subtitles is perhaps one of the greatest challenges for many working in the field. Very few innovative solutions have actually been tested and many deaf viewers are highly critical of what is being offered to them for reasons that span from under-presentation to over-presentation. The use of smileys, for instance, has gradually gained the approval of many viewers in Portugal and Spain, but they have been considered most distracting, particularly by hard-of-hearing viewers and by people who have been using traditional subtitles for long. Here, as in many other cases in audiovisual translation, habit often dictates likes and dislikes and it can take time and persistence to get people to enjoy less conventional solutions.

5. A quick look into the future

The challenges are many and making subtitles that are simultaneously readable and comprehensive is perhaps the aim that will guide the present into the future. The challenges become greater still if we take into account the profound changes that technology is imposing on audiovisual translation in general and on subtitling practices in particular.

The fact that with Interactive Digital Television, subtitles may soon take the form of 'DIY kits', rather than text that are presented as 'finished wholes', may lead subtitling to share ground with software localization, in that subtitles will be broken down into apparently non-contextualized strings that will become meaningful only when integrated with each other. The boundaries that now exist between subtitling, dubbing and audio description as separate genres, for instance, may soon disappear and we may well be speaking of new audiovisual translation types that allow for the overlay or convergence of various solutions at any one time. Subtitles may also grow away from their verbal form and appear in iconic or multi-dimensional forms, conveying sound through visual or tactile solutions. Even if this may appear very close to science fiction today, the technical conditions are now realities begging for creative exploitation.

The challenges that come with such progress are diverse. In this context, issues such as standardization, research and development, and translator education and training, among others, may be questioned anew. If, at present, standardization may be seen by many as impossible or even undesirable, it may become an essential component when so much compositional choice is passed over to viewers. Interactivity is bound to demand greater standardization and homogeneity. The Television Without Frontiers Directive (European Union 1989) anticipates many of the problems that come with digital technology and calls our attention to the steps that need to be taken if we are to keep up with the times. Adjustments will also be in order in the development of software packages to assist professionals in the new tasks that they will need to carry out. Finally, in order to keep up with such developments and to make space for the new demands, translator education and training will be required to reassess curricula and teaching methods and to invest in new equipment and specialized teacher training.

If technical development is accompanied by thoughtful national and international policies and if technology is supported by conscientious professionals who understand their role as facilitators bridging gaps between different 'worlds', the future of SDH, and that of audiovisual translation in general, may be bright. Perhaps, then, true inclusion will be achieved because services will be supplied to all alike, allowing for subtle adjustments that will guarantee adequacy to viewers as individuals.

While the picture sketched above is still in the making, much can be done to improve present standards. All that is done within the present context – legislative measures, technological development, research and translator training, to name but a few – will result in a better future for the millions of people who need special solutions if they are to have equal opportunities when receiving audiovisual texts. In short, this means accepting the fact that people with impairments are entitled to enjoy watching television, go to the cinema, the theatre or the opera, play video games or surf on the Internet, and that all this can be made available through accessibility services.

References

CMP. n/d. *How Bird Hunting in North Carolina Saved Captioning.* Captioning Media Program.
www.cfv.org/caai/nadh36.pdf

de Linde, Zoé and Neil Kay. 1999. *The Semiotics of Subtitling.* Manchester: St. Jerome.

European Union. 1989. *Television Without Frontiers Directive* (89/552/ EEC), adopted on 3 October 1989 by the Council and amended on 30 June 1997 by the European Parliament and the Council Directive 97/36/EC.
http://europa.eu.int/comm/avpolicy/regul/regul_en.htm

Franco, Eliana and Vera Araújo. 2003. "Reading television". *The Translator* 9(2): 249-267.

Gambier, Yves. 2003. "Introduction. Screen transadaptation: Perception and reception." *The Translator* 9(2): 171-190.

— (ed.). 2004. *Traduction audiovisuelle.* Special Issue of *Meta* 49(1).

Gregory, Susan and Jane Sancho-Aldridge. 1997. *Dial 888: Subtitling for Deaf Children.* London: ITC.

Neves, Josélia. 2005. *Audiovisual Translation: Subtitling for the Deaf and Hard-of-Hearing.* London: University of Surrey Roehampton. Unpublished PhD thesis.

Orero, Pilar (ed.) 2004. *Topics in Audiovisual Translation.* Amsterdam and Philadelphia: John Benjamins.

Prendergast, Roy M. 1992. *Film Music: A Neglected Art.* New York and London: W.W. Norton.

Stallard, Gerry. 2003. *Final Report to Cenelec on TV for All. Standardization Requirements for Access to Digital TV and Interactive Services by Disabled People.*
www.cenelec.orgNR/rdonlyres/5C6E5124-6034-422A-1CC62B2229746C3/664/inalreportTVforall.pdf

Subtitling for the deaf and hard-of-hearing in Brazil

Vera Lúcia Santiago Araújo

State University of Ceará, Fortaleza, Brazil

Abstract
The aim of this paper is to present an overview of the current situation regarding closed subtitling in Brazil, more specifically on television. It touches on the history of closed subtitling and describes its main characteristics, its techniques and its production methods. The paper ends with an evaluation of the status questionis.

1. Introduction

Subtitling for the deaf and hard-of-hearing (SDH) began in Brazil in 1997 when *Rede Globo*, the most popular television channel in the country, decided to subtitle its most famous daily news programme *Jornal Nacional* [National News]. Two years later, a bill mandating SDH on open TV was sent to the Brazilian parliament to be voted on. According to this proposed piece of legislation, almost all open television programmes must be subtitled. The only exceptions are TV commercials and late night programmes.

Still, subtitling is not common on Brazilian TV and has not been used again on Brazilian open TV since 1997. As open channels rarely broadcast foreign productions, translated programmes are not seen very often on TV screens in Brazil. In addition, when translation is needed dubbing tends to be the main audiovisual translation (AVT) mode chosen. Cable TV channels, on the contrary, broadcast many foreign films and programmes and they usually have open subtitling as their preferred mode of translation.

While parliament is still discussing the above-mentioned regulation, *Globo* has continued to subtitle a variety of programmes, ranging from feature films to news programmes, talk shows, and television serials (*telenovelas*). Three years after *Globo*'s pioneering initiative, other Brazilian TV networks, like *SBT* – *Sistema Brasileiro de Televisão* [Brazilian Television System] and *Rede Record de Televisão* [Record Television Network], have started to use SDH to make their productions more accessible. *SBT* subtitles most of its programmes, while *Record* uses SDH to translate just one daily news programme called *Jornal da Record* [Record News].

2. The production of closed subtitling

Brazilian SDH follows the standards of the closed subtitling North American model (namely closed caption), which inserts the subtitle in line 21 of the vertical blanking interval – the black horizontal bar between individual television images – in the video signal. The subtitles are visible only by means of a decoder accessed by the remote control of the television set. The making of these subtitles is completely different from the open subtitles aimed at hearing viewers. The main distinction between these two forms of subtitles is the extent of condensation. In Brazil, SDH is almost a full transcription of the speech in its verbatim version, whereas subtitling for the hearing provides an edited version of the speech. People responsible for SDH in Brazil seem to believe that deaf people are better readers. In what follows, we will see that some research on the subject proves them wrong.

Closed subtitling is produced by a company called *Steno do Brasil* and transmitted by satellite to *Globo TV*. The professional in charge of the task is a stenocaptioner, who operates a stenograph, a machine equipped with a stenotype keyboard. As the company is not specialized in subtitling, the stenocaptioners are not translators. Their main task is to provide intralingual verbatim transcriptions of what is said in business meetings, courtroom and parliamentary sessions. In other words, they do exactly the opposite of what interlingual subtitlers do, i.e. they do not condense speech. Consequently, the subtitles simply scroll onto the screen and speech and image are hardly synchronized. Table 1 shows this lack of subtitle-image synchrony in a *Globo* talk show sequence from *Programa do Jô* [Jô's Show]. This show presents 30-minute long interviews with people from different professional occupations and walks of life. The interviews tend to be very dense, with reading speeds of about 184 words per minute. Following the North American model, 70% of the speech is translated. As a consequence, the subtitles remain visible almost five seconds after speech and image.

Table 1. Subtitles from *Programa do Jô*

Speech	Beginning (time)	End (time)	Caption
(JO) hei hei hei hei uou , uou !	0.12	0.18	*[Aplausos e assobios da* [Clapping and whistles from
gente destemida adora experimentar,	0.18	0.19	*platéia]* audience]
comer qualquer comida para sentir	0.20	0.24	*Sexteto* [Band plays]
o paladar, seja na terra no mar ou	0.25	0.27	*Gente destemida* [Bold people]

no ar, o homem consegue provar,	0.28	0.29	adora experimentar. [love to experiment.]
seja na terra no mar ou no ar, o	0.30	0.31	Comer qualquer comida pra [Eat every food to]
homem consegue provar !	0.32	0.33	sentir o paladar. [feel how it tastes.]
	0.34	0.35	Seja da terra, do mar ou do [Whether from the earth, the sea or the]
	0.36	0.37	ar. [air.]
	0.38	0.39	O homem consegue provar. [One can try.]
	0.40	0.42	Seja da terra do mar ou do [Whether from the earth the sea or the]
	0.43	0.44	ar, [air,]
	0.45	0.46	o homem consegue provar. [one can try.]
	0.47	0.48	>>Jô: Boa noite! [>>Jô: Good evening!]
	0.49	0.50	[aplausos e assobios] [clapping and whistles]

The stenograph is a computerized piece of equipment with 24 keys that can be pressed simultaneously. Robson (1997:73) claims that it "allows the stenocaptioner to write entire syllables or words with a single hand motion (known as a 'stroke') rather than having to type one letter at a time". This is one of the reasons why it is faster than a standard keyboard. Another reason is that words and syllables are not typed as they are spelled, but as they are heard according to sound, i.e. phonetically. This means that "the entire language of stenocaptioning is phonetic" (ibid.). The last reason that accounts for the speed of the equipment is that the stenocaptioner needs to type only a few sounds and the computer will start a search for the desired word in a built-in dictionary. It is rather surprising that, in spite of the system's complexity, the various television channels do not seem to have looked into other alternatives to provide real-time subtitling in Brazil.

The stenotype keyboard is similar to the keyboard used in court and its keys are not the same as the ones on a standard keyboard, which allows the fast typing required in real-time captioning. Robson (ibid.) explains how it works:

> The seven keys on the left (STKPWHR) are stroked by the fingers of the left hand to create initial consonants (sounds at the beginning of a syllable). The ten keys on the right

(FRPBLGTSDZ) are stroked by the fingers on the right hand to create final consonants. The thumbs write the vowels (AOEU).

As can be seen, not all sounds are represented in the stenotype and the stenocaptioner has to use a combination of the existing keys to produce the non-existing sounds. For instance, to produce the sound [I], one has to press [E] and [U] (ibid.:74). In the case of vowels, there is also a differentiation between short and long vowels, which can be distinguished by means of different combinations.

In order to write a number, the stenocaptioner has to press the number bar located at the top of the stenotype. Then the numbers show up with the following positions: 1234 on the left, 6789 on the right, and 05 at the bottom. From left to right, any combination can be created in one stroke; so, one can write 369 by pressing the keys simultaneously. This is not the case with numbers like 693 for which individual strokes are required.

3. Types of closed subtitling

Brazilian TV uses two types of subtitling: roll-up and pop-on. Roll-up subtitles scroll continuously from the bottom to the top part of the screen, reaching up to four lines at a time. Words come out from the left to the right side of the screen. It is the type of subtitling used in programmes requiring real time translation, such as talk shows and news programmes.

Picture 1. Roll-up closed subtitles[1]

Picture 1 shows a roll-up subtitle from a *Globo* news programme called *Jornal Hoje* [Today's News]. The open and closed subtitles are superimposed. The open subtitle, meant for hearing viewers, was also used because the woman's speech was not sufficiently audible as her voice was disguised so as she would not be identified. This kind of overlapping – open subtitles for the hearing and closed subtitles for SDH – is very common on Brazilian TV. As only the open subtitle is synchronized with speech and image, the two types of subtitling contain two different kinds of information. The open subtitle provides the woman's speech ('My only dream was buying a sewing machine') whilst the closed subtitle is still translating what the reporter was saying before introducing the woman's story ('It was a Cinderella dream, as in most of the cases'). As indicated above, SDH in Brazil produces subtitles which are displayed from two to five seconds after speech and image have moved on.

Another interesting aspect with regard to picture 1 is the occurrence of an error caused by the incorrect use of the stenotype. Due to its complexity, where the striking of a wrong key can produce a completely different word from the one intended, many errors are made. Robson (1997:76) is of the opinion that these mistakes do not cause many difficulties to the deaf viewer's reading experience as the wrong words do not make sense in the context provided. In my view, based on previous research (Franco & Araújo 2003), the resulting subtitle may indeed introduce an unnecessary additional difficulty to Brazilian deaf viewers, as it is hard for them to read and write in Portuguese. When dealing with deaf people in a specialized school in my hometown, I delivered some multiple-choice questionnaires to verify if they could understand the contents of a subtitled programme after they had been exposed to it. Contrary to my expectations, multiple-choice questions did not facilitate deaf viewers' participation. Rather, it took the sign language interpreter hired to mediate the session a great amount of time to translate and explain the questions. This fact demonstrated that our deaf participants were not proficient readers in Portuguese. It also anticipated the research results which suggested that more condensation is needed in SDH for deaf Brazilian viewers to enjoy television by means of subtitling.

Pop-on subtitles are similar to open subtitles. Unlike roll-up subtitles, they pop on and off the screen, in synchrony with speech and image. *Globo* television makes use of these subtitles especially in feature films and fictional series.

Picture 2. Pop-on closed subtitles

Picture 2 shows this type of subtitling from the TV series *Jesus* broadcast by *Globo*. Even though pop-on closed subtitles are similar to the open subtitles that Brazilians are familiar with, their rates differ considerably. There are two reasons for this. Firstly, closed subtitles have to include additional information, such as indications as to who is speaking, sound effects, soundtrack noises, paralinguistic information and other acoustic signs that are not visible but audible. Secondly, *Globo* closed subtitled films are less condensed than open subtitled ones, because the former tend to give a full transcription of the source speech. This transcription is, in turn, generally based on the Brazilian Portuguese dubbed version of the film. Editing is carried out only for the sake of image and subtitle synchrony. This means that other features involved in the reception of closed subtitles (text readability for the deaf audience, oral discourse markers, shot changes, etc.) are not taken into account.

4. Assessing the subtitles

In order to find out if closed subtitles meet the needs of Brazilian deaf and hard-of-hearing viewers, two experiments were carried out in 2002 (Franco & Araújo 2003; Araújo 2004) at the Ceará Institute of Education for the Deaf. The first experiment tested some subtitled sequences of *Globo* programming. The second one proposed more condensed subtitles for the same programmes. The pilot study assessed eight different sequences, five programmes with roll-up subtitles and three films with pop-on subtitles. The results suggested that most of the deaf were unable to follow the programmes because of the lack of synchrony and the high reading speed required to read the subtitles (an average of 168 words per minute).

The roll-up subtitle programmes were not synchronized with the image and this proved to be very hard for the deaf. The only broadcasts they were able to follow were a talk show and a report on football from a news programme. There were two reasons for these exceptions. In the first case, in spite of its lack of synchronization and high reading speed, the deaf viewers did not depend on the images in order to watch the talk show (*Jô's Show*) while using the subtitles. There were very few shot changes and the camera was either on the host and his guest or on the audience most of the time. As for the second item, as the deaf viewers already knew the subject of the report – a final match of the national football championships – it probably did not take much effort nor did it require many subtitles for them to understand what went on visually in terms of football. What is more, the championship score was probably known to most deaf viewers (Franco & Araújo 2003).

Globo pop-on closed subtitle films make use of fully synchronized subtitles and it was expected that whenever there was speech-subtitle-image synchrony, the reception of closed subtitles and the understanding of the contents would be facilitated. The results, however, refuted this assumption. The deaf viewers had huge difficulty in watching the films, whose subtitles were denser and less edited than the open synchronized subtitles which Brazilian audiences, including the deaf, are used to. The reason for these differences resided in the subtitles being a pivot translation, that is, they were a condensation of the film's dubbed version.

The results of this first experiment suggested that more editing was needed for the deaf viewers to enjoy subtitled programmes and a second study was then proposed in order to test this hypothesis. The same eight sequences were retranslated and new research was carried out. The procedure employed for the new translation was similar to the one used in video and television open subtitling in Brazil, that is, *Globo* subtitles were reduced to maintain synchrony with speech and image. They had to be converted to open subtitles, because the computerized stenograph was not available. The parameters used were the following:

1 second	–	half a line (16 characters)
2 seconds	–	1 line (32 characters)
3 seconds	–	1 line and a half (48 characters)
4 seconds	–	2 lines (64 characters).

The new subtitles translated around 50% of the speech. The reception was much better this time, but the deaf viewers still complained that the subtitles appeared too fast (Araújo 2004). As these results were not conclusive, many other reception studies with different groups of subjects from different locations inside and outside Brazil are needed in order to check, compare and validate the speculations offered here.

5. Concluding remarks

Although SDH in Brazil started about a decade ago, the situation has not changed much since then. It continues to be carried out by stenocaptioners, without the participation of professional subtitlers. As a consequence, the stenocaptioners still produce an almost verbatim version of what is spoken. Given that the correct use of the stenotype requires long training, it would seem to make sense that the task could be performed more efficiently with both stenocaptioners and professional subtitlers working together. The stenocaptioner could operate the equipment, while the subtitler could translate/edit the speech. Training courses continue to be offered by stenocaptioning companies only and Brazilian universities do not seem to be willing to enter this field. Unfortunately, research being carried out at college level does not have any impact on the making of closed subtitles. Although there are no concrete negotiations at present, we hope that collaboration between companies and universities will be possible and fruitful in the near future.

SDH in Brazilian Portuguese also continues to be available exclusively on TV. Unlike what happens in other countries (Díaz Cintas 2005), DVD, cinema and theatre offer only interlingual subtitling in Brazil. Even though the Brazilian deaf community can benefit from these other subtitles, it is widely known that these subtitles do not meet the community's needs. Moreover, the Brazilian deaf have access to the national film production only when it is released on DVD, since all foreign productions are dubbed. Perhaps the situation will improve when the bill mandating SDH is finally passed.

---

[1] All photos used in this paper are courtesy of Cid Barbosa.

References

Araújo, Vera L.S. 2004. "Closed subtitling in Brazil", in Pilar Orero (ed.) *Topics in Audiovisual Translation*. Amsterdam and Philadelphia: John Benjamins, 199-212.

Díaz Cintas, Jorge. 2005. "The ever-changing world of subtitling: some major developments", in John D. Sanderson (ed.) *Research on Translation for Subtitling in Spain and Italy*. Alicante: University of Alicante, 17-26.

Franco, Eliana P.C and Vera L.S. Araújo. 2003. "Reading television: checking deaf's reaction to closed subtitling in Brazil". *The Translator* 9(2): 249-267.

Robson, Gary. 1997. *Inside captioning*. Castro Valley, California: Cyber Dawg.

Section 2

Audio description (AD)

Sampling audio description in Europe

Pilar Orero

Universitat Autònoma de Barcelona, Spain

Abstract

Developments in audio description in Europe and worldwide have not taken place evenly and while some countries started describing TV programmes for their blind populations a long time ago, others have not even started yet. There do not seem to be any fixed, international guidelines to help in the preparation of an audio described script and much controversy still surrounds the question whether it is best for the writer to read the script or simply write it. In addition to these challenges, the technical reception of audio description is also a complex issue where technological requirements may sometimes clash with audience expectations. This dossier investigates all these issues from a historical perspective and attempts to map out the current situation. It also reflects on the different skills needed to become a professional describer and investigates some of the existing guidelines that propose ways of producing high quality audio description scripts.

1. Introduction

Audio description (AD) is far from being a standardized mode of media accessibility in its technical support, its logo (see Miller in this volume), its formal features, or its contents (see Vercauteren in this volume). To be able to understand AD and to put forward fundamental as well as comprehensive research it is crucial to look at some of the most representative traditions in Europe today. This was the idea behind the drafting of this dossier on AD and it was considered important to ask specialists in the field to offer an overview of their experience and the practices in their countries.

This dossier presents AD overviews for Belgium, Germany, Portugal, Spain and the United Kingdom. These five countries were chosen because of their different backgrounds in audiovisual translation (AVT) and their language situations. While Spain and Germany have a dubbing tradition, Belgium and Portugal have a subtitling tradition. In the UK, translation of audiovisual material is an altogether rare occurrence. These countries also represent different stages in the development of AD: from the UK, where AD is widely available in cinemas and on TV, to Spain with hardly any AD but with fully developed national standardization for the creation of ADs, and Belgium (Flanders) as the absolute beginner.

2. A short history of audio description in Europe

Let us start with the country for which we have the first dated AD: Spain. In the 1940s, AD was first offered on the radio. Gerardo Esteban, a journalist, began a weekly broadcast of a film with AD comments in *Radio Barcelona* just after the Spanish Civil War. Arandes, in his interview published in *JoSTrans* in January 2007, and in the radio programme *Un día cualquiera,* [1] explains all the details of this professional practice and how audio described films enjoyed an important space in prime-time radio programming in the 1940s and 1950s until the birth of television. This radio experience, along with the European project Audetel (cf. infra), which was set up by the EU in 1991, was the basis for the Spanish system Audesc. The Audesc system has been used by one of the Spanish blind associations, ONCE, for the production and distribution of audio described films among its members (Hernández-Bartolomé and Mendiluce-Cabrera 2004). As for television, Orero, Pereira and Utray Delgado (forthcoming) write that television broadcasting of closed commercial AD started on the Andalusian autonomous channel *Canal Sur* on 22 February 1995. Films were broadcast until the end of 1996, and 76 films were aired in total. Later on, in October 1997, a new programme *Cine para todos* [Cinema for all] offered both subtitling for the deaf and hard-of-hearing (SDH) and AD, and it was on air until December 2001, broadcasting 132 films. Two years later, in 1999, the Catalan television Channel TV3 – the CCRTV's main channel – [2] started to broadcast the sitcom *Plats bruts* with Catalan AD (Vila 2006:128). The work of AD was jointly done by TV3 and ONCE, and they have also worked together on the sitcoms *Majoria absoluta* (2002) and *L'un per l'altre* (2003-5). The Barcelona Opera House, Liceu, has been offering AD services in six operas per season since 2004 (see Matamala and Orero in this volume) and several theatres in Madrid and Barcelona offer closed AD, that is AD only to those patrons who chose to connect their headphones during some plays each season. AD on DVD first started in Catalan with the sitcom *Plats bruts* but the availability of AD on DVDs is still very scarce.

In the UK, Hyks points to the theatre as the pioneer initiative-taker of AD (see Greening and Rolph in this volume). A small family-run theatre in Nottinghamshire gave a described performance to an invited blind audience in the mid-1980s. The theatre manager, recognizing the potential of such a service, inspired the Theatre Royal Windsor to set up a regular service, which began on 6 February 1988. With regard to television, on the other hand, it was the Audetel Project, set up by the EU in 1991 to coincide with the year of the disabled, which set the ball rolling. The British television regulatory body, the Independent Television Commission ITC (now Ofcom) put together the EU-funded Audetel consortium to explore the issues associated with setting up a description service for television. The work of the consortium included the development of descriptive styles for all types of programming falling under its responsibility as well as of the digital technology required to convey the describer's voice across the television network. Extensive testing of the sound quality on the descriptions was also carried out with elderly people to ensure that it was intelligible to those with less than perfect hearing. The electronics firm Softel developed a software package and computer workstation for the preparation and recording of the AD.

In Germany it was in 1989 when, inspired by a presentation of AD at the Cannes film festival, the first film was described by a group of four people at the Bavarian Association for the Blind, which included both Bernd Benecke (now head of AD at *Bayerischer Rundfunk* BR) and Elmar Dosch (who is a blind person). The film, the US film *See no evil, hear no evil*, directed by Arthur Hiller, was presented in a cinema, and was followed by two similar projects in 1990 and 1992.

1993 saw the projection of Michael Verhoeven's *Eine unheilige Liebe* [*An Unholy Love*] with live AD at the Munich film festival. This film then became the first film with AD on German television, shown in November 1993 by broadcaster *Zweites Deutsches Fernsehen* (ZDF). The following years ZDF showed one or two films a year until 1996. At the time, the AD was paid for by the German Association for the Blind, but today it is the broadcasters who pay for the service.

In Portugal, television viewers had the opportunity to first experience AD in December 2003, when the public broadcaster *Rádio e Televisão de Portugal* (RTP) transmitted the Portuguese film *Menina da Rádio*. In order to access the AD narration it was necessary to have a radio device near the television set. In the course of that same year, RTP provided AD with at least two more films and one programme of the fiction series *A Ferreirinha*. Then, in December 2004, *TV Cabo* and *Lusomundo Gallery* (a premium cinema channel) were the first to broadcast AD using a digital television service, enabling the viewers to access the AD contents through a digital television set-top box. *Lusomundo Gallery* regularly broadcasts new Portuguese films with AD on a monthly basis, in addition to some repeats. The total number for 2006 was 106 films.[3]

In Belgium, it was in 1995 that AD began when a Flemish blind organization, *Blindenzorg Licht en Liefde*, had contacts with Markus Weiss from the British Royal National Institute of the Blind (RNIB) during the 1991 European project Audetel. That same year there were two experiments in Flanders with AD: an episode of the police series *Langs de kade* [Along the Quay] was adapted and presented to an audience of visually impaired people, and a second experiment involved the performance of a Shakespeare play *Driekoningenavond* [Twelfth Night]. This was provided with live AD at the then City Theatre in Antwerp on 9 April 1995. After a period of silence another experiment followed in January 2006: the description of a popular soap opera episode, *F.C. De Kampioenen*, broadcast by the public channel *Vlaamse Radio en Televisie* (VRT), was presented to an audience of about 120 visually impaired people.[4] The episode, which involves a blind character, was shown at the public broadcasting channel's theatre *Het Amerikaans Theater* in Brussels on 16 January 2006. As we write, no episode has been broadcast on television yet. Still, MA students at University College Antwerp provided the first Dutch-Flemish feature film with AD (*Karakter*, van Diem 1997) and their work was presented to the press on 2 October 2006, in a joint press conference organized by BCBS and UCA. Finally, on 17 October 2006 the Flemish film *De Zaak Alzheimer* (Van Looy 2003) was projected with AD at the Ghent International Film Festival. For this film the AD was the work of a local association that is a member of the umbrella organization BCBS. Meanwhile, negotiations are under way for the Brussels-based firm The Subtitling Company, to provide the first DVD with AD of the Flemish film *Windkracht 10*, based on the television series with the same title.

3. Technical reception of AD

How AD is broadcast versus how it is received are very interesting and distinct issues since it may be the case that AD legislation and AD services are actually being provided in some countries but with technical problems as far as its broadcasting is concerned.

The situation in the UK is most interesting. When the service was launched in 2000, it was received by only a sample of 45 households equipped with the prototype receiver. Three years later, by which time the minimum quota of AD broadcasts had risen to 6% of more than 20 television channels, only the same small number of people were able to benefit from it, because the hope for a commercially developed decoder still had not materialized. Manufacturers seemed unwilling to invest in a decoder with only a rather limited application as they saw it, and at that stage, they, unlike the broadcasters, were under no legal obligation to do so. After some upheavals (see Greening & Rolph in this volume) the reception of AD is still not universal, but it is available in most homes.

The same is the case in Portugal where *TV Cabo* and *Lusomundo Gallery* broadcast AD in a digital television service, enabling the viewers to access the AD contents through a digital television set-top box.

In Spain, television broadcasting of closed commercial AD has been developed and broadcast in two different ways. The Andalusian television channel *Canal Sur* used radio and television simultaneously. Those who wanted to listen to the AD version had to tune in to *Canal Sur Radio* as well as watch the television programme. Catalan television has opted for the NI-CAM DUAL stereo system, which means that AD cannot be heard by everyone, but only by those who want to listen to it. For live AD in the theatre patrons are provided with a headset, and the live AD is transmitted using an infrared system, similar to the system used for simultaneous interpreting in conferences. For the opera, headsets are plugged into the TFT screens,[5] which offer subtitling (see Matamala & Orero in this volume).

For the television broadcasting of AD in Germany a two-channel-sound system is also used, which – in analogue times – meant that the stereo signal was separated into the two mono channels. On the left you would find the normal soundtrack, and on the right a mix of the soundtrack with the AD (one-stream-model). The switch-over to digital television brought with it some serious problems for AD providers – since they now actually have to transmit both analogue and digital, and this via air, cable and satellite.

In German cinemas two techniques are in use. The first is similar to the Cinema Subtitling System (CSS) developed by Digital Theatre Systems (DTS) used in the UK, and was developed by the Dolby Company. The AD is on a CD connected to the time code of the film and is transmitted via infra-red signalling to headphones in the audience. It is not mixed, which sometimes gives problems in adjusting the right sound level when the film has a very dynamic soundtrack.

The other system consists of a premix presented through the normal sound system. The problem here is that everyone is forced to listen to the AD, so the method is useful for only special screenings. On the other hand, the premix can be used again later for DVD and television. In 2005, only three movies were made available with AD in German cinemas.

Likewise, there have been only a few described performances in German theatres until now. In 1999 a performance of Chekov's *Uncle Vanja* at the *Schaubühne* in Berlin had an AD presented live via infrared headphones. The same technique was used in October 2006 in Kiel, in northern Germany, for the classic *Das Kätchen von Heilbronn* by Heinrich von Kleist, and for *Miss Sara Sampson* by Gotthold Ephraim Lessing in Munich in February 2006. The problem, says Benecke, is always that of securing funding, because theatres, even if they are interested, are not willing to pay for the description.

Digital decoders are often not able to separate the two mono-parts of the one-stream, so people sometimes get a mix of both mono and complain. The solution is called two-stream, which means the listener receives the original soundtrack in stereo and an independent second stereo stream for the AD on top of that. Any decoder used for AD should be able to offer this. Some German broadcasters, like ZDF and Arte, already use it.

In Belgium, an infrared simultaneous interpreting system was used for the one theatrical performance with AD in 1995, whereas the film projection at the Ghent Film Festival in 2006 was shown with open AD. As for television, there has been no AD whatsoever up to now.

4. The process of AD

In the UK, the AD process itself remains the same irrespective of the material that is being described, although the approach to the text itself and the contents do vary, as does the delivery of the description. Feature films are delivered on reels which are put through the telecine machine to create a working copy at the video speed of 25 frames per second. Television programmes tend to arrive on digibeta and these already have the correct speed. The assets are cached onto a central server, which can then be accessed by the whole team involved in the AD process. Indeed, there are times when more than one person needs to work on the same project.

AD scripts are prepared using dedicated software. They are checked for accuracy and style before being recorded. In problematic cases, when it is not clear if the information provided is explicit enough, a visually impaired adviser is consulted. The head of the AD unit decides who will record the description unless the client has made a specific request.

Once the description has been recorded, it is checked for sound quality as well as fluency and delivery. Once approved, the sound files are laid back onto the digibeta or whatever technical format is being used. More and more sound files are being sent and stored electronically.

Live television AD is not yet being attempted because the programme selection process tends to be made months in advance. However, in the event of 'as live' programmes where there is some delay before transmission, it might be possible using a speech recognition system. Hyks, for instance, would like to see major national occasions such as state funerals or weddings being audio described because visually impaired audiences seem to be forgotten in those instances. She has described live events such as the Queen Mother's birthday and circuses, where with the right preparation and background information AD can be effective. It is a specialized skill resembling radio broadcasting of a live event.

In Germany, the descriptions of television programmes and films are written by a team of three, of which one person is blind. This follows the idea that two people, who watch the same scene, will not always see the same things, so in the team they can control and complement one another. The blind member of the group will tell where he/she needs the description and how much and what kind of information is necessary. This text is then revised at *Bayerischer Rundfunk* (BR) by Dosch and Benecke. Finally, it is recorded with the narrator and mixed into the film soundtrack.

Films shown on the German public television channels ZDF and *Südwestrundfunk* (SWR) are produced by the company *Deutsche Hörfilm GmbH* (founded in 2001), which also produces descriptive narration for video and DVD. *Deutsche Hörfilm GmbH* trains its own describers because the company has a different way of doing the AD compared with *Bayerischer Rund-funk*: it works with just one author and one blind 'tester'.

In Spain, as in Germany or any dubbing country with a language other than English, AD is epigonic to translation and dubbing. The Spanish process of creating the AD is similar to that described by both Hyks for the UK and Benecke for Germany, though there has been one case which may set the trend for future ADs where the AD script was originally written in a foreign language and then translated. The AD of Woody Allen's film *Match Point* (2006) was created in English and then translated into Spanish (Sanchez 2006). Though this practice may be an exception now, in future it may be one of the many possibilities of creating AD scripts, as proposed by Orero (forthcoming).

5. Training in AD

Generally speaking, training in AD is available at two levels and in two places: at universities and at companies that offer the service in the form of in-house training.

In the UK, as AD began to be recognized as a skill, the national training programme Audest was set up by the RNIB and the few practitioners active in the field. However, the course soon outlived its usefulness, having no academic accreditation attached to it and something else was clearly needed. At that stage, theatre managers still regarded AD as an unnecessary added burden or amateur pursuit and there was little enthusiasm to add it to their already overloaded work schedule and responsibilities. To help raise the status of AD, the Audio Description Association (ADA), a registered charity, was founded in 1999 and work began on devising an accredited training course for theatre describers which would be administered by a university or its equivalent. The level 3 course was submitted to the Open College, attached to Leeds Metropolitan University, and courses administered by the Open College but run by trained trainers (all experienced describers) began in 2001. The courses may be paid for by a theatre management that wants to set up its own in-house AD team and more recently individuals have also been able to apply and be assigned to an existing course if they pay their own way. It is important that each course comprises a group of learners with a minimum of two in order to understand the teamwork aspect of the work. In order to be accurate a describer needs a second pair of eyes to verify what he/she has described. It is also important to be able to take criticism from another person, because only then can the best quality of description be achieved. In 2005, the ADA started to develop add-on modules to the core course, namely AD for television, museums and galleries, as well as dance. This is to enable theatre describers to work in a broader environment.

Having the ADA accredited qualification does not automatically mean that a theatre will pay for the service, or that the trained describer, who is not attached to a particular theatre, will automatically walk into a job. However, with the latest ADA requirements, Hyks's comments are as follows: "I think that audio describers will soon be hired on a payment basis, as are signers, who were never part of the voluntary/charity sector and have always been paid a professional fee".

The ADA OCN course, run by two trainers, comprises five days of tuition spread over several weeks, in order to allow the learners time to prepare the required tasks. As part of a team, they learn how to prepare a set of introductory notes before the start of a show. The introduction will last approximately ten minutes, comprising an introduction to the play, any relevant information about the work and its author, and the cast of characters, their costumes, and the set(s). Learners must show that they understand how the sound system works in each venue and must produce a set of instructions for using the headsets. They must be acquainted with the kind of access features that public buildings need to provide. They must give a practical demonstration of how a blind or visually impaired person should be guided along a prescribed route, be familiar with personnel in the theatre and demonstrate that they know the background to the 2005 Disability Discrimination Bill. Finally, the summative task is to prepare and deliver a 20-minute continuous description of a performance selected by its level of difficulty.

Both the University of Surrey based in Guildford, and Roehampton University in London offer an AD module as part of their MA in Audiovisual Translation. Industry also offers AD training. Service providers like IMS, itfc and Red Bee Media (for the BBC) offer in-house training using their dedicated software. Whereas five years ago each company had a full-time team, the tendency is now to limit the number of permanent staff members and to employ freelancers on a daily basis or a per job basis.

In Belgium, the *Hoger Instituut voor Vertalers en Tolken*, at University College Antwerpen will offer training in AD as part of its MA in Translation with AVT specialization from October 2007. In the private sector Joris Redig, manager of The Subtitling Company in Brussels, has recently added the service to the company's AVT package, and it normally trains the staff it has hired in-house. They offer French and Dutch AD and sometimes, says Redig, "the same person does the creation of the AD script and voices it, but we prefer professional talents using a professional studio". Besides these two initiatives, nothing much is happening so far.

In Germany, BR runs training and continuing training seminars and workshops for AD authors – when there is a need for new ones – in order to guarantee high-quality standards. Normally, all candidates have some kind of experience in developing texts and in understanding film, and have had some contact with blind or visually impaired people. After the first training module there is a year of on-the-job training, which allows the describers to work on 'real films'. They are remunerated but still receive precise and extensive feedback after each film. Actually, twelve describers are doing all the work in Germany and only one or two of them are able to earn a living as describers, all the others do some other work too.

Basis for the training are the German Guidelines written down in the brochure *Wenn aus Bildern Worte werden* [When images are turned into words] by Dosch and Benecke (2004). BR has also provided help to other German broadcasters, such as ARTE, *Norddeutscher Rundfunk* (NDR), *Westdeutscher Rundfunk* (WDR) and *Mitteldeutscher Rundfunk* (MDR) in developing their own audio described programmes. These broadcasters all use the describers trained by BR. Other firms such as *Deutsche Hörfilm GmbH*, which also produces descriptive narration for video and DVD for ZDF and SWR, trains its own describers because of its different approach to the AD, as explained above.

In Spain, AD training is offered by both official training institutions such as universities and in-house service providers like *Mundovisión* or *Aristia*. At university level and for undergraduates, the *Universitat Autònoma de Barcelona* offers a course called Media Accessibility, which is open to any student on campus. The course provides the basic concepts and techniques on media accessibility: SDH, AD, web accessibility. Students gain an insight into the many problems which disabled people face and also how they may be avoided to some extent through media accessibility. At postgraduate level, universities such as Granada, Seville, Castelló and Las Palmas offer post-graduate degrees (i.e. an *Experto*) in subtitling for the deaf and audio description (Pereira & Lorenzo 2006). Within its MA in Audiovisual Translation – both face-to-face and online – the *Universitat Autònoma de Barcelona* started offering modules of SDH in 2004, and it expanded to AD in 2006/7.

While in Portugal there is no formal course at university level, two different training sessions have been organized. The *Escola Superior de Tecnologia e Gestão do Instituto Politécnico de Leiria* and the *Centro de Línguas & Culturas da Escola Superior de Educação, Instituto Politécnico de Castelo Branco* organized an AD workshop with Joel Snyder, describer for the US National Captioning Institute in 2004 and with Bernd Benecke, audio description editor at the German *Bayerischer Rundfunk* (BR) in 2006 respectively.

6. What is the profile of the professional audio describer?

According to Hyks

> a competent describer can summarise effectively, describe colourfully and accurately and convey the verbal pictures in a vivid yet objective manner. This applies to both the writing

and the delivery. An effective audio describer delivers the text in a tone that matches the programme material, at a measured pace, distinctly but never stealing the scene.

Orero (2005c) mentions that the skills needed to be an audio describer – as those stated (provided in their promotional leaflet) by the Audio Description Association in conjunction with the Open College Network West and North Yorkshire in the UK – are:

- the ability to summarize information accurately and objectively
- a good command of the working language
- a clear and pleasant speaking voice
- good sight and hearing (whether aided or unaided)
- the ability to work as part of a team
- the commitment to access for disabled people, and the provision of quality audio description to blind and partially sighted people.

But the aforementioned skills are drafted from the UK, a country with little import of media products in other languages other than English. In other countries where there is a large import of audiovisual programmes, such as Spain,[6] much of the accessible work may be done by the translators who can extend their professional profile from strict audiovisual translator to describer. Who does the recording of the AD is another issue. While in some countries both writing and recording are done by the same person, in Spain there is a dubbing union which protects the working rights and conditions of those who record voices for films, advertisements, documentaries, etc. It may be the case that only those with an equity card will be allowed to record ADs in future.

To end with Portugal, Quico lists: excellent writing skills, a good knowledge about the contents being described, attention to detail and, finally, a true passion for accessibility issues and users' needs.

7. Standard or guidelines for AD

Since one of the contributions in this book looks specifically at the issues of standards or guidelines for the creation of AD, we refer the reader to this article. Vercauteren analyses current guidelines in Flanders, Germany, Spain and the United Kingdom, proposing a classification which is a much needed starting point for a possible European collaboration towards drafting a harmonized European Standard for AD.

8. Legislation regarding media accessibility

In Germany, there are no national regulations, only some regional laws which advise television broadcasters to expand their AD (and SDH) services. For example, legislation concerning AD in Bavaria is quite weak.[7] It explicitly states in Article 14 that *Bayerischer Rundfunk* (the public television broadcaster) and the private channels should provide AD and SDH, but there are no figures as to how much should be provided or how the figures should be increased. Since there are no sanctions, only public broadcasters provide AD in German and the percentage of audio described programmes on public television is less than one per cent.

In Spain, there is a new audiovisual law entitled *Ley general audiovisual*, which is now at a white paper stage. Its objectives are to merge current standards and adapt them to the new technological and social contexts, and to regulate the laws on television and radio in a general sense. Regarding accessibility, Article 62 regulates access for disabled people and establishes that all television channels should make their contents available for people with sensorial disabilities through SDH, AD, and sign language. The objectives are accurately defined and a transitory provision draws up a calendar for the implementation of the services with which state-owned channels, national commercial licensees and other television channels with national coverage whose audiences exceed ten percent must comply. Figure 2 below, taken from Orero, Pereira and Utray Delgado (forthcoming), shows the draft calendar for the implementation of assistive services on Spanish television, drafted from the white paper *Ley general audiovisual*:

	2006	2007	2008	2009	2010	2011	2012	2013	2014	2015
SDH	40%	45%	50%	55%	60%	65%	70%	80%	90%	100%
sign language	1%	2%	3%	4%	5%	6%	7%	8%	9%	10%
AD	1%	2%	3%	4%	5%	6%	7%	8%	9%	10%

National broadcast licensees

	2006	2007	2008	2009	2010	2011	2012	2013	2014	2015
SDH	35%	40%	45%	50%	55%	60%	65%	70%	75%	80%
sign language	1%	1.5%	2%	2.5%	3%	3.5%	4%	4.5%	4.5%	5%
AD	1%	1.5%	2%	2.5%	3%	3.5%	4%	4.5%	4.5%	5%

Other national TV channels with more than 10% audience share

	2006	2007	2008	2009	2010	2011	2012	2013	2014	2015
SDH	15%	20%	25%	30%	35%	40%	45%	50%	55%	60%
sign language	0.5%	0.5%	0.5%	1%	1%	1%	1.5%	1.5%	1.5%	2%
AD	0.5%	0.5%	0.5%	1%	1%	1%	1.5%	1.5%	1.5%	2%

Figure 1. Draft calendar for assistive services in Spanish television.

The UK has the most veteran bill in Europe. The 2006 Broadcasting Act stipulates that ten years from service start-up, ten per cent of programmes must be audio described. If a 24-hour channel transmits 168 hours of programming a week, 16.8 hours should theoretically be being described by 2010. There are now over 40 channels on British television but some have only just come on stream. There will be a wide range of provision over the next ten years. Initially, many channels interpreted the percentage provision as air time including repeats and often chose to describe programmes that were transmitted at non-peak viewing times and repeated several times during the week, in an attempt to minimize costs. The RNIB is lobbying to change this practice (see Greening & Rolph in this volume).

In Flanders, the new management contract involving the public channel VRT and the Flemish government, states that part of the social surplus value of the public channel is its role in promoting social cohesion. This involves subtitling television programmes for the deaf and hard-of-hearing and making them accessible for the blind and visually impaired (VRT 2006). The channel now pledges that it will undertake concrete experiments aimed at improving accessibility for blind and visually impaired audiences. In a first stage the financial, technical and operational implications of setting up such a service will be investigated. If the exercise proves to be feasible some initial experiments with AD will be carried out for *Ketnet*, the youth channel.

Since this is a move from no mention of the needs of blind viewers at all, this is a first step in the right direction. However, the contract does not specify how programmes should be made accessible, or how many, nor does it impose deadlines. Being a subtitling country, some people in the blind community are saying that a first step might be the audio subtitling of foreign language interviews in news broadcasts, for instance. Since audio subtitling is a matter of applying technology, using existing subtitles, this solution is less costly and might therefore be given priority, at least on television. Nothing is certain at this point, even if those audiences who have witnessed AD performances are enthusiastic advocates of the system.

9. AD on national television

In Germany, only public broadcasters do AD and the percentage is less than one per cent. In Spain the percentage nowadays is even less than in Germany, since AD is only offered sporadically, and in Belgium the public channel has merely started talking about the possibility. In Portugal, the only channel which has been consistently broadcasting contents with AD is *Lusomundo Gallery*, between six and twelve films per month, which means that approximately two per cent of its contents has AD. Only the UK has a significant percentage provision, even if some programmes are repeats that were transmitted at non-peak viewing times and broadcast several times during the week. This means that there is a noticeable difference between public and private broadcasters as far as AD output is concerned, even though the percentages are very low.

This phenomenon has a direct impact on the number of professional audio describers needed and the number of firms offering their services. If there is no market, or a very small market, the situation is, of course, reflected in the needs for training, professionals, and firms offering the services. This may change in the near future with the shift from analogue to digital television and some EU regulations which may force in some way, perhaps not sanctioning but rewarding, the offer of media accessibility. All in all, it seems as if AD is growing, if not in volume, at least in interest and awareness – which may be a first step towards a generalization. There is no doubt that the EU directives on media accessibility will have to be implemented in each European country. When this will take place and who will be responsible for the cost is still to be seen.

---

[1] Broadcast on 7 May 2006 in RNE1. The interview in Spanish can be accessed online at: www.rtve.es/rne/audiocast/noes/files/neudc-060507-tertulia.mp3

[2] The CCRTV (*Corporació Catalana de Ràdio i Televisió*), the Catalan state-owned radio and television corporation has many other channels: TV3, Canal 33, 3/24, *TV3 Internacional* and *Catalunya Ràdio*.

[3] The breakdown is as follows: six films in January, eight in February, eleven in March, seven in April, seven in May, seven in June, twelve in July, twelve in August, nine in September, ten in October, six in November and eleven in December.

[4] This experiment was the result of collaboration between the director of the soap, Guido De Craene, the umbrella organization *Belgische Confederatie voor Blinden en Slechtzienden* (BCBS) [Belgian Association for the Blind and Visually Impaired] and University College Antwerp (UCA), with Aline Remael (UCA) and Harry Geyskens (BCBS) providing the AD.

[5] Short for *thin film transistor*, a type of LCB flat-panel display screen, on which each pixel is controlled by one to four transistors. TFT technology provides the best resolution of all the flat-panel techniques, but it is also the most expensive. TFT screens are sometimes called active-matrix *LCDs*.

[6] The linguistic reality in Spain also means much translation work between the four languages which coexist: Castilian, Catalan, Basque and Galician.

---

[7] The full text in German from the *Bayerisches Gleichstellungsgesetz* can be found online at: www.stmas.bayern.de/behinderte/politik/baybgg.htm

References

Arandes, Jorge. 2007. "Interview". *The Journal of Specialised Translation* 7. www.jostrans.org

Benecke, Bernd. 2006. Audio description workshop. Centro de Línguas & Culturas da Escola Superior de Educação, Instituto Politécnico de Castelo Branco.

Hernández-Bartolomé, Ana I. and Gustavo Mendiluce-Cabrera. 2004. "*Audesc*: translating images into words for Spanish visually impaired people". *Meta* 49 (2): 264-277.

Orero, Pilar. 2005a. "La inclusión de la accesibilidad en comunicación audiovisual dentro de los estudios de traducción audiovisual". *Quaderns de Traducció* 12: 173-185.

——. 2005b. "Teaching audiovisual accessibility". *Translating Today* 4: 12-15.

——. 2005c. "Audio description: professional recognition, practice and standards in Spain". *Translation Watch Quarterly* 1: 7-18.

——. Forthcoming. "¿Quién hará la audiodescripción comercial en España? El futuro perfil del descriptor", in Catalina Jiménez (ed.) *La subtitulación para sordos y la audiodescripción en España*. Berlin: Peter Lang.

Orero, Pilar, Ana María Pereira and Francisco Utray Delgado. Forthcoming. "The present and future of audio description and subtitling for the deaf and hard-of-hearing in Spain". *Meta*.

Pereira, Ana María and Lourdes Lorenzo .2006. "La investigación y formación en accesibilidad dentro del ámbito de la traducción audiovisual", in Consuelo Gonzalo and Pollux Hernúñez (eds) *Corcillum. Estudios de traducción, lingüística y filología dedicados a Valentín García Yebra*. Madrid: Arco/Libros, 649-658.

Sanchez, Diana. 2006. "Making and breaking the rules: media access guidelines in Spain". Paper given at the conference *Multidimensional Translation. Audiovisual Translation Scenarios*. 1-5 May. Copenhagen: University of Copenhagen. Manuscript.

Snyder, Joel. 2004. Audio description seminar: the visual made verbal. Escola Superior de Tecnologia e Gestão do Instituto Politécnico de Leiria.

Vila, Pere. 2006. "Accesibilidad en Televisión de Cataluña", in Álvaro Pérez-Ugena and Francisco Utray Delgado (eds) *TV digital e integración ¿TV para todos?* Madrid: Universidad Rey Juan Carlos & Dykinson, 127-130.

VRT. 2006. *Beheersovereenkomst 2007-2011 tussen de VRT en de Vlaamse Gemeenschap. De opdracht van de openbare omroep in het digitaal tijdperk.* 20 July.

Acknowledgements

This survey mapping the status of audio description in the audiovisual media in a selection of Western European countries has been written on the basis of information obtained by way of a questionnaire distributed by e-mail in the year 2006. I would like therefore to express my gratitude to the respondents listed below. This article is theirs as much as mine: Veronika Hyks (Independent Media Support, IMS, UK), Bernd Benecke (*Bayerischer Rundfunk*, Munich, Germany), Harry Geyskens (Belgian Confederation for the Blind and Partially Sighted, Belgium), Celia Quico (*PT Multimédia / TV Cabo*, Portugal), Joris Redig (The Subtitling Company, Brussels, Belgium).

Accessibility: raising awareness of audio description in the UK

Joan Greening

Royal National Institute of the Blind (RNIB), London, UK

Deborah Rolph

Universitat Autònoma de Barcelona, Spain

Abstract
This paper explores the provision and awareness of audio description (AD) across the visual media, from its availability since 2001 to viewers of digital television through to its inclusion in both cinema and DVD film releases. This paper sets out to describe the background to the introduction of AD in televisual broadcasting, cinema, video and DVD, and to outline the major developments that have taken place in the UK. Consumer feedback to the Royal National Institute of the Blind (RNIB)[1] suggests that where AD is accessed by blind and visually impaired people, it is appreciated as it enhances their total experience. However, there is still work to be done in order to raise the awareness of all blind and visually impaired people of the value of AD. The need to train retail staff and the availability of the appropriate technology is highlighted. As the leading organization representing the interests of the two million blind and visually impaired people in the UK the RNIB is seen as being in a unique position to bring together the key players in the media industry for the benefit of blind and visually impaired consumers.

1. Introduction

Audio description (AD) is the addition of a descriptive narrative to accompany the key visual elements of theatre, television, cinema and other visual media. In films or plays, the description is delivered in the natural pauses in the programme's dialogue with minimal interference to the original audio. It includes features such as the characters' facial expressions, background scenery and the action taking place on-stage or on-screen. The main purpose of AD is to describe those images important for conveying the storyline so that blind or visually impaired people can experience a more complete picture of what is being shown, enabling them to enjoy the presentation more fully.

2. Television

2.1 Background and some history

The Independent Television Commission's Audetel Project was undertaken between April 1992 and December 1995 with the aim of enhancing television viewing for blind and visually impaired people by providing spoken commentary in addition to the normal programme dialogue (Ofcom, n.d.). Audetel (Audio Described Television) was a European-wide consortium of regulators, consumer associations and broadcasters formed to research and develop audio description. Created in 1991, the project began by carrying out a survey of the practical requirements of blind and visually impaired people with regard to their television viewing. It conducted research on the best methods of manufacturing and supplying low-cost decoding equipment to transmit the signals required for the broadcast of AD for television. This technical research entailed the development and production of a prototype receiver. A field trial was conducted by the BBC in 1994 using the technology developed by Audetel in which 50 of these receivers were placed in the homes of blind and visually impaired television viewers selected at random from an RNIB database of 60,000 visually disabled viewers. It demonstrated that AD could be transmitted via analogue television being carried over the air along with the conventional television signal. As well as attempting to overcome the various technical difficulties of setting up an AD service, the project looked at the marketing of the service in addition to determining any legislative measures, which could foster and accelerate the dissemination of audio described television. The project was, however, superseded by the introduction of the 1996 Broadcasting Act, which mandated audio description via terrestrial digital transmission.

The 1996 Broadcasting Act legislated that ten per cent of programmes on digital terrestrial television should be broadcast with AD by the tenth year of a digital license being issued. The subsequent 2003 Communications Act extended the 1996 legislative requirements to include digital cable and digital satellite providers. In 2004, the Office of Communications (Ofcom, the independent regulator and competition authority for the UK communications industries) published its Code on Television Access Services, which advised that ten per cent of programmes had to be audio described by the fifth anniversary of a digital license being issued. This was to have a great impact on the further evolution of AD.

In 2000, a digital terrestrial AD trial was launched by the Digital Network, a consortium of the principal broadcasters in the UK (BBC, ITV, Channel 4, ONDigital, etc.) to provide feedback on the quality of AD provided at the time. The trial was conducted in 45 households that included a blind or visually impaired person selected at random from the London and southeast areas. In 2003, the digital terrestrial trial came to an end but the general public were still unable to access AD, as receiving equipment was not yet available. Nebula Electronics, a British multimedia company, marketed the first commercially available equipment able to support the audio description service provided by the major television channel operators. Its DigiTV PC card – a fully featured digital television receiver for use with personal computers – would deliver AD. It also provided the means to record and playback digital TV programmes using the PC's hard disk. The receiver's interface was designed to be both simple to use and comprehensive in function. Following consultation with the RNIB, Netgem, a French company, launched the iPlayer, the first digital terrestrial set-top box with audio description functionality.

2002 saw the launch by British Sky Broadcasting (BskyB) of an audio description service on a very limited number of its own channels, resulting in it being the first platform to deliver AD to the general public. At this stage, BSkyB was under no legal obligation to provide the service as the legislation applied only to the digital terrestrial platform. BSkyB's assumption was that future legislation would include digital satellite, which indeed it did. A year later Channel Five added its AD to the digital satellite provision and in 2004 the BBC, together with Channel 4 and ITV, announced that it would be making AD available via digital satellite television. Finally, in 2005, Ofcom decided that the standard abbreviation for TV audio description should be 'AD' and that this now had to be used in the programme synopsis on digital electronic programme guides, thus providing viewers with information about which programmes carry audio description.

2.2 Receiving AD for television

There are three ways in which audio description can be received on digital television in the UK: via a terrestrial rooftop aerial (Freeview), a satellite dish (BSkyB) or cable (NTL/ Telewest).

In the case of a terrestrial rooftop aerial (Freeview – a non-subscription service), the AD track is sent as a separate low bit rate signal and the set-top box receiver decodes both the programme sound and the audio description. This system, known as 'Receiver Mixed Audio Description', was the only system that fully met the RNIB specifications, having the advantage that the user can adjust the sound levels of each track independently. The Netgem iPlayer Plus [AD] is currently the only type of 'receiver mixed' set-top box on the market in the UK that delivers AD. It offers additional facilities such as a spoken electronic programme guide, which speaks the channel names and provides on-screen scheduling information, which is an advantage as no accessible navigation system exists for remote controls.

For satellite distribution (BSkyB – available as both a subscription and non-subscription service) the AD track and programme sound are pre-mixed and then broadcast as an additional high bit rate 'narrative' bit stream. The set-top box receiver then makes the mix available for use, turning it into a broadcast mixed audio description. Every BSkyB set-top box receiver in the UK has the ability to receive AD, the user simply needs to change the language setting to 'Narrative' but has no control over the relative sound levels of the audio description versus the original soundtrack, which may be a disadvantage.

At the time of writing this article, cable (NTL/Telewest – a subscription service) was about to launch its AD service on BBC1 with the intention of rolling out the service on all other channels during 2006 with total coverage of the UK by 2007. It will initially be a broadcast mixed audio description service. However, should cable providers decide to adopt receiver mixed audio description, cable set-top boxes will also have this capability.

2.3 The current situation of AD in the UK

Currently, around eight per cent of programmes are being broadcast with AD in the UK. Three out of the four major UK broadcasters – the BBC, ITV and Channel 4 – have also been broadcasting on-screen promotion of AD on both analogue and digital television. These promotions demonstrate the service and how to access it. This has generated interest from the general public and has resulted in increased take-up.

The final switchover from analogue to digital is due to start in 2008 and will be completed by 2012. However, 63 per cent of UK households already have digital television today. The RNIB is currently lobbying to have the percentage targets for AD on digital television increased from ten per cent to twenty per cent.

2.4 Challenges and lessons learnt

Good and comprehensive legislation is of great importance. The first major problem occurred in the drafting of the 1996 Broadcasting Act. The Act stated that AD should be broadcast but no mention was made as to how it had to be received. A group of dedicated engineers worked to find a solution, but there was a dispute over who was actually responsible for developing the equipment: the broadcasters or the manufacturers. These issues took so long to resolve that any solutions that were developed became obsolete. For example, it was originally proposed that the common interface slot would be utilized to deliver AD via a plug-in module, but before the technology was finalized, common interface slots had become obsolete. This resulted in AD being broadcast for several years without the equipment being available to receive it.

Technology is a blessing and a curse. Bandwidth is both expensive and at a premium, and with the introduction of high definition broadcasting, bandwidth will become even more of an issue. It is therefore important to opt for audio description delivery methods that correspond to the bandwidth space available. With the receiver mixed option, AD is broadcast as a mono, speech quality audio channel together with the necessary information for the receiver to dip the main stereo soundtrack and mix in AD. The broadcast mixed option re-broadcasts a pre-mix of the original stereo soundtrack together with AD. With this option, the original stereo soundtrack is broadcast twice and consequently the bandwidth required is much greater than with receiver mixed.

Satellite has opted to broadcast AD using the broadcast mixed option. Terrestrial has elected to use the more economical receiver mixed option. The new generation of cable set-top boxes will have the capacity to deliver both options, but currently they are opting for broadcast mixed audio description. As government legislation does not cover the provision of equipment capable of receiving AD, the digital terrestrial audio description service is very dependent on the goodwill of TV receiver manufacturers. However, the competition between set-top box manufacturers is such that every penny counts and the extra cost, no matter how small, of including the AD capability means companies are not willing to invest. Consequently, there is currently only one digital terrestrial set-top box that receives AD.

Promotion among the blind and partially sighted is vital. Audio description is such a new service that many blind and partially sighted people have never heard of it. On-screen TV promotions on analogue and digital television have helped to get the message out to the general public, but there is still a great deal of work to be done to promote the service. Although every digital BSkyB set-top box in the UK has the ability to deliver AD, BSkyB does not actively promote the service. Therefore many blind and partially sighted customers are unaware that their set-top box has access features. Also BSkyB chose to call its audio description service 'narrative' making matters rather confusing for the public.

In addition, there is the issue that some blind and partially sighted people feel they can 'manage' to watch the television without AD. 'Managing' may mean sitting close up to the screen and scanning across it in an attempt to capture the action. It is a case of convincing these people that AD can make watching television a much more rewarding and relaxing experience. However, access to programme listings is almost impossible for most blind and partially sighted people. Finding out which programmes are being broadcast is difficult enough but to then find out which of those programmes are audio described is even more difficult unless access to the internet is available. The best solution would be a web-based audio described programmes listing service that would also be accessible via an automated telephone service. Although this is technically possible, the funding for this initiative still has to be found.

More care should be given to the choice of programmes for AD. Broadcasters have sometimes selected inappropriate programmes to audio describe – a quiz programme where all the questions and answers are read out is perhaps not the best use of AD. The first series of programmes to be audio described has tended to be the soap operas and popular weekly dramas. However, with the recent two per cent increase to eight per cent of programmes being broadcast with AD, the broadcasters are looking at more quality drama/thriller programming.

2.5 Consumer feedback

The following comments have been selected from the many received by the RNIB from television viewers giving spontaneous feedback on the value of AD. Viewers indicate in their comments how they welcome the addition of AD and that AD was noted to enhance the enjoyment of television viewing by blind and visually impaired people:

> I really do have to say what a wonderful advance it is to have audio description on television at home. I started to watch *Bleak House* last week and cried out with delight when it turned out to have audio description. I don't think I would have persevered with it otherwise, as there are a lot of rapid scene changes, and some things communicated only by expression or gesture.

> I cannot describe what it's like to understand fully what is happening. I have never had sight and really didn't realize what a large part of a TV programme I actually missed out on. My husband, who is also blind, and I would like to thank you for making this fantastic service available to many visually impaired people, you have made a real difference.

> For the first time last night, we saw audio description broadcast on *A Touch of Frost*. I have always enjoyed this programme, but found it very difficult to follow because of the visual elements that often give the crucial information. My husband is not usually keen on this programme but last night he was glued to it. Audio description makes such a huge difference to the accessibility of a programme and, hence, our enjoyment of it.

3. Cinema

3.1 Background and some history

Margaret Rockwell and Cody Pfanstiehl pioneered live description in theatres in the USA in the 1980s. The idea was subsequently adopted in the UK and rolled out to include cinemas. A team of trained describers provide the commentary from a soundproof box at the back or side of the stage or screen. It is relayed through a headset or earphones. Before the performance begins, the audio describers provide programme details together with, in the case of theatre productions, descriptions of costumes and scenery. Throughout the show concise descriptions of actions, expressions and gestures are transmitted during gaps between the actors' dialogues.

The service proved to be very expensive and was therefore offered only occasionally. In 2000, Napier University, in collaboration with the RNIB, the International Audio Description Agency and the Glasgow Film Theatre, was given the brief to develop a product that would open the cinema experience for blind people. This led to the development of the Cinetracker, a separate player that delivered the AD track from a CD in the projection box via infrared headphones. However, there were problems of synchronization with the film. As the reels went through the projector the AD started to lose synchronization with the film, resulting in the film sometimes becoming totally incomprehensible.

In September 2001, a system was developed by US based company DTS (Digital Theatre Systems). The AD track was now linked to the DTS time code on each reel of film. Consequently, at the start of each new reel, a new section of audio description was triggered, thus ensuring that the film and AD were always synchronized.

The first film using this system, *Harry Potter and the Philosopher's Stone*, was screened in the UK in January 2002 and since then over 350 films have been audio described in UK cinemas. Dolby subsequently developed the Dolby Screentalk system, which works by tying the AD to the Dolby time code. A major breakthrough was realized in 2003, when the UK Film Council agreed to partially fund equipment in 78 cinemas around England. These installations kick-started the project and there are now over 170 cinemas in the UK with an accessible screen equipped with either a DTS or Dolby delivery unit. Wales and Scotland are in the process of funding more installations.

3.2 The current situation

There is no UK government legislation covering the provision of AD in cinemas. It is the enthusiastic backing of the UK cinema exhibitors, the film distributors and equipment manufacturers that has driven the project and ensured its success. The AD is delivered through an infrared headset with the main film soundtrack coming from the cinema surround-sound. Around eighty per cent of all major films are now released with AD in the UK. Buena Vista International and Warner Brothers describe one hundred per cent of their UK film releases including their foreign language films. Until now most blind and partially sighted people have been unable to access foreign language films, as neither the visuals nor the language are accessible. It is therefore necessary to audio describe the film as well as simultaneously voice the subtitles.

The RNIB is lobbying for the production of an advertisement, which would run in every cinema with AD facilities, advertising the fact that blind and partially sighted people can access films in that particular cinema. The advertisement would be targeted at sighted people who may have friends or family who are visually impaired as, historically, most people with a serious sight problem do not go to the cinema. The concept already has backing from the UK Cinema Advertising Association and the Vue Cinema chain has expressed interest in funding and screening the advertisement.

The UK Film Council has meanwhile agreed to spend £11.5 million on 250 digital projectors (d-cinema) which are to be installed around the UK. The RNIB has been investigating the access capabilities of these new projectors and has been assured that they will be able to deliver AD as part of the server package. However, for this to work, the auditorium will still need to have a dual infrared system installed and infrared headsets will still need to be purchased. The AD will have to be written and recorded earlier in the process than is currently happening for standard film projection.

3.3 Challenges and lessons learnt

Staff knowledge and attitudes need to be improved. There have been tremendous problems with box office and other operational staff in cinemas denying all knowledge of AD. A blind person may have travelled several kilometres to get to the cinema to be told that the film is not available with AD or that the disk has not arrived or the headphones are not working. This, invariably, is not the case. Cinema staff have been known to direct a blind or partially sighted person to a subtitled screening for the deaf. High staff turnover in the cinema industry increases the problems of in-house staff training. Just because AD is available in a particular screen in a cinema does not mean that a specific film with audio description will ever make it onto that screen. This can be very frustrating for the blind or partially sighted person who wants to see a particular film and knows that the AD disk is in the projection box but not being utilized.

Technological needs must be incorporated into the process. AD tracks need to be available prior to the hard-drive film being mastered for d-cinema. Therefore current film industry audio description planning and production practices will have to be changed to meet the new time pressure. The RNIB is encouraging the cinema, DVD and television industries to investigate whether it is possible for AD used for the cinema release at 24 frames per second to be utilized on the DVD at 25 frames per second and then passed through for the TV broadcast. There was recently a rather ridiculous situation where *Lord of the Rings   Fellowship of the Ring*, which was audio described for cinema release, had been re-written by the BBC for broadcast and then re-written again by BSkyB for its satellite film channel.

The BBC, Channel 4 and Five are keen for a solution to be found, as it will, in theory, reduce the costs to broadcasters. ITV has already agreed that if the costs for this process can be kept to a minimum, they will broadcast films in addition to their legal obligation. Buena Vista has agreed to include the AD script and voice as part of their TV contract. This means the film can be broadcast with no audio description copyright issues.

Since blind and partially sighted people are not natural cinemagoers, because of the inaccessibility of the moving image, promotion is of the essence. AD in the cinema is a relatively new service and the challenge is to raise awareness of its availability and to build a new audience. There has been some success in certain cinemas but this seems to be dependent on the enthusiasm of the venue manager.

3.4 Consumer feedback

Cinemagoers have also given spontaneous feedback to the RNIB about how AD is considered essential for a more complete viewing experience. The following recent comments indicate that it is essential to enable them to get the full picture:

> I was absolutely blown away by the whole experience. I got really emotional and actually did burst into tears. The audio description was so good; it was as if I could see again for the duration of the film. Everybody I met who worked at the cinema was lovely and so helpful and my husband, who usually describes things for me, really enjoyed the film, even though he found it a bit strange at first because I wasn't asking him questions!

> The only time I lost concentration was half way through *Spiderman*, when I suddenly realized how great it was to be in a cinema, watching a film without having to rely on someone else describing the visual scenes to me, it gave me a wonderful sense of independence. For

the first time I could talk to sighted friends about the film in its entirety, not just the plot and dialogue but also the visual aspects that I saw through the description.

I went to see the *Matrix Re-loaded* last night and thought the audio description worked brilliantly with it! I thought the detail of the description was really amazing and gave such a graphic sense of the action taking place, of which there was loads!! I wanted to see how it worked with a film like this, as I'd seen the first film in the trilogy and knew it was incredibly visual.

4. Video and DVD

4.1 Background and current situation

The RNIB runs an audio described purchase and rental scheme of over 170 film titles on video including the *Lord of the Rings* trilogy, three *Harry Potter* films, *Casablanca* and some Alfred Hitchcock classics. This is a special product available only from the RNIB. However video is fast being overtaken by DVD and will soon be phased out in the UK. No new titles will be added to the RNIB service from 2006.

A number of the films that have been audio described for the cinema now have AD on the DVD release. There are currently around 100 DVDs available in the UK with an optional AD track in addition to the standard soundtrack. Films include *Spiderman 2*, *Cold Mountain* and *The Aviator*. Companies including Buena Vista Home Entertainment, Pathé, Columbia Tristar and, most recently, Warner Home Entertainment are leading the field. However, there is a great amount of work to be done with the other major DVD distributors.

Broadcasters such as the BBC, ITV and Channel 4 also produce DVDs. Although all three broadcasters audio describe programmes for transmission on digital television, they have not been including the AD tracks on the DVD releases. Following pressure from the RNIB, the BBC has recently agreed that the five-DVD-boxed version of *Dr Who*, will include AD and negotiations are in place for several high profile releases in 2007. Channel 4 is in the process of releasing two of its comedy series with AD, and ITV is looking into releasing some of its classic TV back catalogue on DVD with audio description tracks.

A recent breakthrough has been the commitment from one of the UK's largest online DVD rental companies to host a specific area on their website for audio described DVD titles. The RNIB is in close contact with this company to ensure titles are added as soon as they are released.

Audio navigation (or talking menus) is another hot topic in relation to DVDs in the UK. The RNIB is involved in negotiations with one of the major DVD distributors to look at developing simple and straightforward audio navigation that mirrors the visual menus on all DVD releases. This would make access easier for many people including older people, people with learning disabilities, people with English as a second language as well as people with a serious sight problem. Granada Ventures, a film and television DVD distributor, has already released one DVD with AD, *Shawshank Redemption*, which also has audio navigation.

4.2 Challenges and lessons learnt

The major DVD distributors in the UK are controlled by the Hollywood Studios and it is extremely difficult, if not impossible, to find the person who can authorize the AD track produced for the UK film release to go onto the UK DVD release.

It should be clear by now that promotion to blind and partially sighted is of the utmost importance, but retailers, both high street and on-line, do not include AD in the technical information relating to individual film titles – therefore it is difficult for users to find out which DVDs have audio description tracks.

Navigation of the complex DVD menu structures can also prove difficult for blind and partially sighted people. As video becomes obsolete it will be necessary to persuade DVD distributors to make their products more accessible and to encourage visually impaired people to use DVD.

4.3 Consumer feedback

The following comment, received by the RNIB shows that the addition of audio description on DVDs is warmly welcomed:

> The recent *Hitchhiker's Guide to the Galaxy* film was a must for someone like me who has such fond memories of the original 1978 radio series. But, of course, it's a modern, pacey, noisy science fiction film and if you can't see what's happening on the screen it would be impossible to follow. So it is fantastic that this title has recently been released in the UK on DVD with an audio description track.

5. Conclusion

The RNIB's sole purpose is to benefit blind and partially sighted people in the UK. However, the RNIB is also in the unique position of being able to bring together the key players and competitors in the market to find a solution that can benefit the entire media industry. The RNIB has a long-term strategic commitment to AD and this sends a clear signal to the industry and to decision-makers about the importance of the service. It has a dedicated

Broadcasting and Talking Images Team working on the development and promotion of AD on TV, DVD and in cinema. Having this dedicated team has enabled the development of good working relationships with the broadcasting, film and DVD industries, as well as government departments, regulators and funding bodies. Consequently, if a problem or issue arises, the contacts and relationships are in place to deal with it. In the unlikely event that the necessary connections do not exist, financial and staffing resources are available to spend on building them.

It is clear that ways of promoting AD among the blind and partially sighted could and must be improved, especially as the evidence from consumer feedback indicates a high level of satisfaction when AD is accessed. It would appear therefore that the model taken in raising awareness of audio description is beginning to be effective and should continue to be followed if access to the media by the blind and partially sighted is to be further improved.

---

[1] The Royal National Institute of the Blind (RNIB) is the UK's leading charity offering information, support and advice to an estimated two million people with sight problems. It was founded in 1868 by Dr Thomas Rhodes Armitage. In 1992, the RNIB launched the UK's first audio described video film *Hear My Song*. It currently has over 130 titles, which are produced in-house and available to rent or buy. It is a campaigning voice for the introduction of legislation designed to make AD more widely available.

References

Ofcom. N.d. *Guidance on Standards for Audio Description*. London.
    www.ofcom.org.uk/static/archive/itc/itc_publications/codes_guidance/au dio_description/introduction.asp.html
Ofcom. 2004. *Code on Television Access Services*. London.
    www.ofcom.org.uk/tv/ifi/codes/ctas

Towards a European guideline for audio description

Gert Vercauteren

University College Antwerp, Belgium

Abstract

Although audio description (AD) has been around for almost 25 years now, the number of European countries providing guidelines with regard to this new service is still very limited. Moreover, since the turn of the century, various international organizations have been advocating the creation of an international guideline on audio description. This paper compares some of the existing guidelines with a view to provide a first possible outline of such an international guideline. It solely focuses on the description of recorded audiovisual material, and given the diversity of this type of material, the article suggests a subdivision of the guideline into one general section containing standards that are valid for all categories and various sections dealing with genre-specific issues. The present article deals with only the general section, and in addition to suggesting a possible structure of this section, it also points to a few new avenues for further research.

1. Introduction

In 1989, the EU *Television without Frontiers Guideline* made universal media accessibility – including audio description – an official priority. Since that time, different institutions have pointed out the need for structured, European guidelines on this new technique, making audiovisual products available to blind and visually impaired audiences. In his paper presented at the Open Workshop on Standardization in the Field of Subtitling[1] in Seville, Spain (2002), President of the European Union of the Blind, Sir John Wall, made some recommendations on how to ensure that blind and partially sighted people are not left out of the digital revolution, which is currently taking Europe by storm. In addition to the standardization of various technical issues regarding terminal equipment and the international alignment of user requirements, he considered a united standard in audio description of key importance to guaranteeing accessibility. In a 2003 study on accessibility made by Dr Ruth-Blandina M. Quinn, Research Officer of the Broadcasting Commission of Ireland, we read, with respect to actions taken on a European level the following: "Developments are indeed unfolding and discussions are taking place but decisions made have yet to be formulated into a single set of recommendations". Finally, in September 2005, a communication issued by the European Commission[2] mentions as one of the many practical challenges in the field of accessibility "the lack of European-wide standards".

When we look at the guidelines that are available at present in Europe, we notice that only Spain and the United Kingdom have official guidelines and that in a few other countries, such as Belgium (Flanders) and Germany, guidelines were drawn up by individual professionals.[3] In most countries, however, no guidelines exist whatsoever, so there clearly is a gap that has yet to be filled, that is, the lack of one international set of guidelines on audio description. It seems obvious that such guidelines would provide various advantages and be beneficial to different target groups. First of all, as Ivarsson (1992) put it, "viewers are creatures of habit" and an international guideline would ensure a consistent viewer experience of high quality, regardless of that viewer's location. Furthermore, broadcasters would know what they are purchasing or lending from each other (Wall 2002). The future development of audio description will also rely on the organization of courses – as the ones already organized at different universities in Spain and the United Kingdom – requiring a set of structured, clear guidelines. Finally, as increasingly more countries are passing accessibility laws, an international convention would avoid that the same effort of drawing up national guidelines is repeated in all those countries. This would save countries where no audio description exists valuable time and prevent them from falling even further behind. In addition to all these practical benefits, scholars might benefit from an international standard as well, as it would provide them with a tool on which to base their evaluations or descriptions of described texts.

The main aim of this article is to present a first outline of a slightly adaptable set of guidelines based on a comparison of some of the existing European standards and guidelines. Contradictions in the existing guidelines, vagueness or items obviously relying on personal preference rather than research, automatically point to useful research topics. Drawing up a comparative survey of existing guidelines can therefore also produce a catalogue of items to be researched.

2. The different target groups

Ideally, any set of guidelines should be tailored to the needs of the target group for which it is drawn up. In her article on the future profile of the audio describer in Spain (and by extension dubbing countries in general), Orero (2005) distinguishes no less than ten different types of audio describers. She bases her classification on the different tasks audio describers may have to perform, which can be divided into four categories: (a) creation (of new audio descriptions), (b) translation (of existing audio descriptions and/or film dialogues to be dubbed or subtitled for the deaf and hard-of-hearing), (c) recording (of the audio description) and (d) synchronization.[4]

Based on this classification, a practical guideline should at least comprise three modules: one central module dealing with the creation of audio descriptions, one covering the work of voice talents and a third one describing specific issues to be observed when translating existing audio descriptions.

When we look at the different existing guidelines and, in particular, at the German and the English texts, a possible fourth module could be added, that is, one covering the technical work involved in describing audiovisual programmes. This would include the material needed to carry out the description, possibly some software-related elements (file types, time codes, etc.) and guidelines regarding the studio work (adjustment of sound levels, mixing of the different tracks into one soundtrack, digitalization of the work, etc.). Although part of this work will probably not be carried out by the describers themselves, it might give them a better understanding of the technical possibilities and restrictions when creating the text for the description. A last element that could be added to the guidelines – although this is more of a national matter than an international one – are the legal aspects involving audio description (e.g. requirements regarding the description of credits, guidelines on who can record an audio description[5]).

Consequently, any guideline should therefore, at least, discuss the following elements to cover all the describer's possible tasks:

a) the creation of new audio descriptions;
b) the translation of existing audio descriptions;
c) the recording of audio descriptions by voice talents;
d) the technical aspects related to creating audio descriptions;
e) the (national) legal requirements related to making audio descriptions.

3. The creation of audio descriptions

The remainder of this article will be dedicated to the first element mentioned in the list above, i.e. the creation of new audio descriptions. Existing guidelines regarding the creation of new audio descriptions typically consist of two parts: one section dealing with the different phases involved in making a description (from forming a team and watching the material that has to be described to the revision of the final version and its recording in the studio), and a second section dealing with the practical principles of writing an audio description. It is this second section that I will pursue in greater depth here.

One of the main problems raised in the guidelines is the diversity of the material to be described. The Spanish guideline distinguishes three broad categories: (a) recorded audio description for television, video/DVDs and cinemas, (b) live audio description for plays, operas and other live events and (c) audio guides for visits to buildings, museums, exhibitions, and natural spaces. First of all, it hardly seems feasible to merge these three categories into one single set of guidelines as they are defined by completely different constraints. Furthermore, and regardless of the question whether or not all these types of descriptions can be done by the same describer or not, given their quite different nature, there is the fact that the English guidelines for one, mention no less than twelve different categories of programmes eligible for description within the domain of television or cinema alone (including feature films as one category, with specific guidelines probably applying to different genres within this category). In what follows only recorded AD will be considered.

To counterbalance the wide variety of source material in this category of descriptions, the part of the guideline concerning the practical principles could be further subdivided into two parts, as is also suggested by the English standard: one general section dealing with guidelines that are valid for any kind of programme, and a set of modules dealing with rules and problems related to specific categories of programmes (such as musicals, soap operas, children's programmes). This subdivision will provide an additional benefit, as will be explained later on.

3.1 The structure of the general section

When comparing the different existing guidelines, all their instructions can be reduced to four essential questions: (a) What should be described?, (b) When should it be described?, (c) How should it be described? and (d) How much should be described?

3.1.1 What should be described?

With regard to the first question, most of the current guidelines seem to agree that everything that happens on the screen should be described. However, as is pointed out in the Flemish style sheet, for example, there is much more to be described. Sounds can be important in the description, on-screen text should not be neglected, etc. Summarizing the different elements mentioned in the guidelines, there are three types of information that should be discussed.

(a) images: This comprises describing *where* things are taking place, *when* things are taking place,[6] *what* is happening and *who* is performing the action and *how*.

(b) sounds:[7] This concerns the description of sound effects of the programme (that are difficult to identify), song lyrics and languages used other than the source language of the programme.

(c) on-screen text: This includes logos, opening titles, cast lists, credits and text on signs that might be shown on-screen as subtitles.

One general remark that could already be made here, although it will be repeated later on in the section on how much should be described (3.1.4), is that the information given should be relevant. On the one hand, there is usually not enough time to describe everything. On the other hand, not all the time available between dialogues should be filled with description. This general remark points to two elements that definitely require further study: what is relevant and how much information should be given.

Another issue that was already raised by Orero (2005) is what should be done when various things that have to be described happen simultaneously (e.g. opening titles shown during an important action scene).

3.1.2 When should the description be given?

This section does not address questions such as "when do characters get names", but refers to the moment when the descriptions are heard.

As a general rule, descriptions are inserted in the gaps or silences between dialogues. In theory, the production should be completely silent when descriptions are given, but in practice it has proved impossible to avoid descriptions being inserted over sounds or music. In some instances it might even happen that descriptions replace parts of the dialogue. However, this is a very delicate issue, and when drawing up guidelines, it should be absolutely clear whether describing over dialogues should be allowed or not and if so, when.

In addition to these general guidelines regarding when the description should be inserted, two specific elements should be mentioned in the guidelines. Firstly, can scenes be announced beforehand?[8] One element that is of paramount importance and should be pointed out here is that although scenes or actions can be announced beforehand, the information must never give away the plot and announcing can be done only when synchrony is not an issue. Secondly, can information be given before the programme starts or after it is finished, for example, for reading credits (over a blank screen), as mentioned in the English guidelines?

3.1.3 How should the visual and aural information be described?

The majority of the elements covered in the different guidelines existing at present deal with how the different aspects mentioned under 3.1.1 should be described. They can be classified into two categories: one covering general language and style issues and another covering the use of the different word classes.[9]

Language/style of the description

- The language used in descriptions should be clear and precise, appropriate yet varied.
- A description is made to be read, which means that it must sound natural and that unusual vocabulary or formal phrasing have to be avoided. This does not mean, however, that metaphors or descriptive words enhancing the overall text cannot be used.
- A natural-sounding text also implies that sentences should be kept simple. Complex sentence structures including many subordinate clauses must be avoided and there should not be too much information in one sentence (the current German guidelines even recommend one piece of information per sentence).
- Descriptions should be objective, which means on the one hand that no personal opinions/preferences/preconceptions should be expressed and there should not be any interpretations. On the other hand, objectivity also means that censorship has to be avoided.
- The guideline should discuss the register to be used.[10]
- The wording of the description should match the style of the film or other programme or show that is being described.
- The wording and phrasing should match the audience of the programme.[11]
- Even though the effects used by the director serve a purpose, the use of film terminology should be limited to well-known terms.

Specific word classes

(a) Verbs: The guidelines should specify the tense and voice to be used. With respect to verbs, the current guidelines also seem to agree that hyponyms are preferable to general superordinates combined with adverbs.

(b) Adjectives: As already mentioned under the section dealing with the language and style of the description the adjectives used should be objective, descriptive and specific. Metaphors can also be used. One specific category of adjectives should be addressed separately here: adjectives referring to colours. The German and Spanish guidelines do not specifically mention the use of colours in descriptions, but the Flemish and English guidelines rightly ask why colours should be described to people who cannot see anymore or have never seen at all. They both bring forward different reasons to justify the use of colours in descriptions: (i) people who were not born blind may preserve a visual memory and know perfectly well what colours are, and even people who were born blind understand what colours stand for. Given that only fourteen per cent of the blind population is 100% blind and the rest are partially blind, meaning that they see or have seen colour, colours have to be described whenever they are relevant

(c) Adverbs: When adverbs are used, they should be objective, descriptive and specific, but as stated under (a), the use of adverbs with general verbs should be avoided when a more specific alternative not requiring an adverb can be used.

(d) Personal pronouns: Here, we have to make a distinction between the use of personal pronouns to address the audience, and personal pronouns used to refer to characters in the programme. With regard to the use of personal pronouns to address the audience the following general rule may be formulated: the use of personal pronouns to address the audience (or involving the audience in the description) has to be avoided. There might be some exceptions, however, such as children's programmes. As far as the use of personal pronouns to refer to characters in the description is concerned the following considerations should be taken into account: when using personal pronouns, it has to be absolutely clear to whom the pronoun refers, and personal pronouns should not be overused. It is important to regularly repeat the names of characters to remind the audience of who they are.

(e) Nouns: None of the guidelines enter at length into the use of nouns in descriptions in general, but when looking at the general guidelines on the use of language and style, we could say they have to be objective, descriptive/vivid and precise. A few specific categories of nouns, however, deserve special attention.

- specific terminology

This does not refer to film terminology but to terminology used in films or programmes dealing with a specific subject. The existing guidelines tell us to gather the necessary information (dictionaries, encyclopaedias, reference works...) to be able to describe specific terms adequately. They do not specify, however, how specialized the descriptions can be (e.g. use only terminology that is generally known).

- people[12]

With regard to characters, the guidelines mention different items. There is no agreement on when to provide the characters' names. The German guidelines suggest that, in general, characters should only be given names, after they have been named in the programme. The Flemish guidelines suggest naming people early on in the pro-gramme "unless their identity should remain a secret", and experi-ence from English descriptions shows that characters are often named before their names are given in the dialogues. An interna-tional set of guidelines should try to come to an agreement on this point. There are a few additional elements that could make things easier: (i) when important characters are named only later on in the programme, it can be helpful to give them names earlier on (it avoids confusion among the audience members and it facilitates the describer's work) unless their identities must remain a secret, as mentioned before, (ii) famous people can be named immediately, (iii) when various (new) characters are introduced at the same time, it can be helpful to give them (or the most important ones) names to avoid confusion, and (iv) when several characters are involved in the same dialogue and/or talking at the same time, it is important to name them to make sure the audience knows who is talking.

This section could also be the place to tackle another tricky problem regarding the description of people: how do we describe fa-cial expressions and gestures? A first guideline says that descrip-tions should be objective, but this kind of description will often in-volve a degree of interpretation.

(f) Articles: The guideline should also give information on what articles to use. It would be logical – as is also suggested in the English guidelines – to use an indefinite article the first time something or someone is mentioned, and to use a definite article once it is clear what or who is mentioned.

3.1.4 How much should be described?

When comparing the different guidelines, a few essential lacunas stand out, and one of *the* issues that should be studied in greater detail is how much should be described. The current guidelines mention, for example, that "too much description can be exhausting or irritating" (English guideline), "describing too much just because time allows should be avoided" (Flemish guideline) or that "this is a question that cannot be completely answered" (German guideline). But none of these standards provide any guidance on how much information can be given or how much is too much. Can more information be given at the beginning of the programme to give the audience 'a rest' later on (i.e. if we quantify the 'how much', should it be applied to the movie as a whole, to single scenes, etc.)? Would it be possible to define a maximum amount of description? These and other questions will have to be answered.

4. Modules

The idea of subdividing the guidelines for the creation of audio descriptions into a section dealing with general characteristics and variable ones relating to different genres and categories of programmes will have to be studied as well, but a few advantages of this modular structure seem to be apparent. On the one hand, they improve clarity as no genre-specific problems have to be addressed in the general guidelines. Furthermore, this subdivision could provide a (partial) answer to another problem that is occasionally referred to but not really answered in the existing guidelines, namely the prioritization of information. This matter is certainly too complex to be included in a general guideline. On the other hand, given the unique nature of every programme (and, by extension, probably every scene) even modular guidelines may not be able to cover every specific case. Still, the analysis of screenplays and "insight into genre-related characteristics can be an important guideline for establishing what is significant or not" (Remael 2005).

5. Conclusion

The current guidelines in Flanders, Germany, Spain and the United Kingdom are definitely valuable tools in the promotion of accessibility and the development of (recorded) audio description, but they are little more than a starting point since they remain rather vague on some issues, whereas in other instances they lack structure and even miss some basic information. Indeed,

147

some questions are left unanswered and various issues have to be studied, not only with regard to how to describe (e.g. what to do when opening titles coincide with an action scene, how should facial expressions be described), but also regarding how much should be described or how information can be prioritized.

In order to speed up the accessibility process in countries where audio description is not or hardly existent, it would be useful to draw up one set of international guidelines catering for the needs of all the different types of describers and containing all the information necessary to provide high-quality descriptions. The present survey can be used as a starting point and as a first outline for the delineation of research topics.

---

[1] EBU Newsletter No 37 (www.euroblind.org/fichiersGB/news37TV)

[2] Communication from the Commission to the Council, the European Parliament and the European Economic and Social Committee and the Committee of Regions – eAccessibility [SEC(2005)1095]

[3] The following guidelines served as a basis for the framework of the present article: (i) Spanish Standard UNE 153020:2005, (ii) ITC Guidance on Standards for Audio Description, (iii) Dosch and Benecke (2004) and (iv) Remael (2005).

[4] Although the exact definition of these terms will be different in subtitling countries, where translation will not include dubbing but, in addition to subtitling for the deaf and hard-of-hearing, subtitling for the public in general, the tasks audio describers have to perform there will basically be the same, except for the synchronization, which is an activity inherently linked to the dubbing process.

[5] In Spain, for example, the dubbing union protects the rights and conditions of its voice talents (Orero 2005)

[6] The time factor is seen to be at least part of visual narration.

[7] It should be pointed out that silences can be important as well, or that at least it can be important to describe them in order to add to the drama of a certain scene. In one scene of the Dutch film *Karakter* an angry mob storms the office of one of the main characters, bailiff Dreverhaven, late at night. Just as they are about to batter down the door, he comes out, stark naked. Immediately, the crowd turns quiet. To emphasize this sudden silence, the describers announce it by saying 'A deadly silence falls'.

[8] Although the English guidelines suggest that announcing scenes beforehand might bother some (partially) sighted viewers, there is general agreement that announcing scenes should be allowed. It also depends on the target audience of the description, but as Remael (2005) points out in her stylesheet: "[…]. Since at this stage it is impossible to create AD adapted to this mixed audience's varied needs, a blanket form will be our primary target."

[9] When talking about guidelines referring to language usage, at least some of these (e.g. the use of articles, the type of verb to be used) will of necessity be language-specific. See also Bourne and Jiménez in this volume.

[10] The English guidelines state that "occasionally a slight regional accent may fit the bill, but each programme has to be assessed separately", and in her article Orero (2005) wonders whether or not slang can be used in descriptions.

[11] Like the previous element, this one can be further developed into the modules dealing with the different genres and programme categories.

[12] This part of the guideline deals only with general elements. For soap operas, other guidelines may apply with regard to characters.

References

AEN/CTN 153. Norma Española UNE 153020:2005 (2005). *Audiodescripción para personas con discapacidad visual. Requisitos para la audiodescripción y elaboración de audioguías.* Madrid: AENOR.

Dosch, Elmar and Bernd Benecke. 2004. *Wenn aus Bildern Worte werden – Durch Audio-Description zum Hörfilm.* 3rd ed. Munich: Bayerischer Rundfunk.

ITC Guidance on Standards for Audio Description. 2000.

Ivarsson, Jan. 1992. *Subtitling for the Media.* Stockholm: Ljunglöfs Offset AB.

Orero, Pilar. 2005. "Audio description: professional recognition, practice and standards in Spain". *Translation Watch Quarterly.,* 1(1): 7-18.

Remael, Aline. 2005. *"Audio description for recorded TV, cinema and DVD – Experimental style sheet"*: Flemish guidelines for students of the HIVT.

Wall, John. 2002. TV Broadcasting for All. Audio description and its potential (Part II). *EBU Newsletter.* 37.

A corpus-based analysis of audio description

Andrew Salway

bbrel, Burton Bradstock, UK

Abstract

This paper presents the beginning of a corpus-based investigation into the language used for audio description (AD). The automated analysis of audio description scripts for 91 films was successful in characterizing some idiosyncratic features of what appears to be a special language. Our investigation also began to create an empirically-grounded overview and classification of the main kinds of information provided by audio description. The existence of a special language is explained, in part, by the fact that audio description is produced by trained professionals following established guidelines, and its idiosyncrasies are explained by considering its communicative function – in particular that it is being used to tell a story. Encouraged by the relatively high degree of regularity observed in the corpus, we go on to speculate about the application of language technologies for 'assisted audio description' and for repurposing audio description as a basis for indexing digital video archives.

1. Introduction

The relationships between the visual and the verbal, between vision and language and between image and text have fascinated scholars in many disciplines for many centuries. Audio description (AD) provides a novel, tangible and important scenario for exploring these relationships and it presents immediate and stimulating challenges for research in audiovisual translation (AVT). Audio description is a description of visual information delivered via an audio channel and it is crucial for improving media accessibility for blind and visually impaired people. Recent social, legal and technical developments have led to a steep rise in the global production of AD, and this offers exciting and important challenges for research in audiovisual translation (see Greening and Rolph in this volume) for information about the current state of AD, especially in the UK). The production of audio description fits well within Orero's (2004: viii) definition of audiovisual translation which encompasses "all translations – or multisemiotic transfer – for production or postproduction in any media or format, and also the new areas of media accessibility". It is important to note that source texts such as films combine different kinds of information through audio and visual channels, so that AD, acting as a surrogate for the visual, must interact appropriately with the existing dialogue and sound (Ballester Casado, forthcoming).

In the gaps between existing speech, audio description for films provides enough information about what is depicted on-screen for the audience to follow the story being told in the film. The description is restricted by the amount of time available between the dialogues. Since audio description acts as a surrogate for the visual components used to tell stories in film, we predict that the language of audio description is shaped in part by its narrative function. Narrative is usually defined as involving chains of events in cause-effect relationships, occurring in space and time. Bordwell and Thompson (1997: 90-96), discussing narrative in films, append to this definition a statement about how the agents of cause and effect are characters with goals, beliefs and emotions. Thus, we expect that AD will concentrate on providing sufficient information, complementary to the dialogue so that audiences are able to understand who is doing what, where and why.

Guidelines for audio description, such as those provided by the Office of Communications (Ofcom),[1] give advice about what to describe and how. They recommend the use of the present tense, the avoidance of potentially ambiguous pronouns, the use of adjectives only where they convey essential information and the use of adverbs to enhance the description of an action, for example, 'she stamps her right foot impatiently' – but it is stressed that care must be taken not to use subjective adjectives and adverbs. The guidelines also note that using verbs that refer to specific ways of doing something can be an effective way of enhancing a description. For example, rather than simply saying 'she walks' a describer could say 'she swaggers / lopes / tip-toes / marches'. Three issues that recur whenever audio describers discuss the question of best practice are: (i) how to ensure that description strikes the right balance between frustrating the audience with insufficient information to follow the story and patronizing them by spelling out obvious inferences; (ii) how to maintain objectivity in audio description; and, (iii) how to voice audio description appropriately. Of course, these are problematic questions, the answers to which vary with audiences' needs and cultural experiences, and with the kind of material being described.

This paper is concerned with the language used in the audio description of films. Specifically, it investigates the hypothesis that audio describers use a special language that is shaped by the communicative needs of its users. In so doing, it also overviews the kinds of information that AD provides. So-called functional explanations of language registers, such as special languages, consider the mapping between the communicative needs of language users and the prevalence of idiosyncratic linguistic features in the language (Hoffman 1984). Our approach is to use automated corpus analysis techniques to identify idiosyncratic linguistic features in a collection of AD scripts.

Recently, two papers have analysed samples of AD to investigate what information audio description provides. Working in the context of media accessibility, Piety (2004) adapted spoken discourse analysis techniques in his analysis of the audio description of four films, totalling 23,000 words. He proposed a set of concepts to analyse the structural and functional properties of AD and these concepts included: four structural elements – insertions, utterances, representations and words – and seven types of information – appearance, action, position, reading, indexical, viewpoint and state. Piety went on to discuss how these concepts could be used to compare and evaluate AD practices. Working in a rather different context, Turner (1998) was interested in the potential to reuse audio description scripts as a basis for automatically indexing television programmes and films in digital video collections. His analysis focused on two issues that would determine this potential: (i) how well aligned audio description is with the visual contents; and, (ii) what aspects of visual contents are described. He analysed the AD and accompanying visual contents in 27 minutes of each of a television documentary, a television drama and a feature film. For this analysis, 15 types of information conveyed by AD were defined: physical description of characters, facial and corporal expressions, clothing, occupations and roles of the characters, attitudes of the characters, spatial relationships between characters, movement of the characters, setting, temporal indicators, indicators of proportions, decor, lighting, action, appearance of titles, and text included in image. While the ideas proposed by Piety and by Turner both provide good starting points in elucidating what AD does and how it works, they are limited by the relatively small samples of audio description available.

The research presented in the current paper was carried out as part of the three-year TIWO (Television in Words) research project at the University of Surrey.[2] The overall aim of the project was to develop a computational understanding of storytelling in multimedia contexts, with a focus on the processes of AD. The research team at Surrey worked in conjunction with a project Round Table comprising senior representatives of organizations that produce audio description (ITFC and BBC), a manufacturer of technology for the production and delivery of audio description (Softel) and the Royal National Institute of the Blind (RNIB). There were three main strands to the research: first, a corpus of audio description scripts was gathered and analysed to investigate the language used in AD; second, ideas for increasing the role of information technologies in the production of AD were developed; and third, systems that repurposed AD as a basis for retrieving and browsing video data were prototyped and evaluated.

Section 2 presents and discusses results from the analysis of a corpus of AD scripts for 91 films. The discussion concentrates on relating the observed idiosyncratic linguistic features to the communicative needs of the users of AD, and overviews the kinds of information commonly conveyed by AD. Encouraged by the relatively high degree of regularity observed in the language of AD, Section 3 speculates about the application of language technologies for 'assisted audio description' and for repurposing AD as a basis for indexing digital video archives. Section 4 closes the paper with some conclusions and notes the need and opportunity for diverse research strategies to understand more about the fascinating processes by which the visual is made verbal.

2. Analysing a corpus of audio description scripts

Some factors that may impact on the language used for audio description of films are that

- it refers to a restricted domain of discourse, which is what can be seen on-screen in films;
- it fulfils a communicative function, which is to provide enough information, objectively, for the audience to follow the story told by a film, without patronizing the audience by spelling out obvious information that could be inferred;
- specifically, it should include information about events in cause-effect relationships occurring in space and time, and about the characters involved in the events and their emotional states;
- it must combine with existing dialogue which means, among other things, it must be concise; and,
- these requirements are embodied in the training and guidelines followed by the professionals responsible for producing AD.

The use of language, by trained professionals, to communicate about a restricted field of discourse and for a specific purpose, normally results in a 'special language' characterized by a preponderance of linguistic features that are idiosyncratic in comparison with everyday general language (Hoffman 1984). Here, we investigate the hypothesis that the language used for AD is a special language, in other words, that there exists a 'language of audio description'. Following the kind of corpus linguistics approach described by Biber, Conrad and Reppen (1998), the analysis presented here begins to identify and describe a special language in terms of statistically significant differences between linguistic features in a corpus of AD scripts and a general language sample.

Crucial to such an approach is the compilation of a representative corpus, that is to say, a collection of texts that adequately represents the language in question. The corpus analysed here is limited to British English AD for films, but within this we sought to select audio description scripts that would cover the different ways films are described. In consultation with two senior audio describers, nine film genres were defined, not so much in terms of the properties of the films, but in terms of how the describers thought the language used for AD would vary. The TIWO Audio Description Corpus includes complete AD scripts from all these genres which were acquired from three major producers of AD: RNIB, ITFC and BBC Broadcast. The corpus comprises 91 audio description scripts totalling 618,859 words (Table 1). Our analysis was automated using the text analysis package *System Quirk*.[3]

Table 1. Composition of the TIWO Audio Description Corpus (September 2005); see the TIWO project website for more details.

Genre	Number of films
action	10
children's (animation)	8
children's (live action)	4
comedy	13
dark	8
period drama	9
romantic	11
thriller	7
miscellaneous	21
TOTAL	91

2.1 Unusually frequent words

Let us start by examining the most frequent words in the corpus (Table 2). As in all corpora, both general and special language corpora, the most frequent words are grammatical words like *the, in, and, a,* etc. The first sign of a contrast with general language is the relative preponderance of non-grammatical words within the top 100. In general language corpora such as the British National Corpus there tend to be two or three such words in the top 100. Many of the top 100 words in the TIWO corpus look like concrete nouns and verbs that refer to material processes. This reflects the aim of audio describers to describe only what can be seen on screen. Right away, these words give an impression of what is commonly referred to by audio description (the numbers in brackets are the frequencies of the words in the TIWO corpus):

- Characters and their body parts: *man* (1491), *head* (1268), *face* (1145), *eyes* (1111), *hand* (1089), *hands* (814), *men* (742), *woman* (573) as well as character names.
- Actions: *looks* (2482), *turns* (1400), *takes* (1074), *walks* (986), *goes* (728), *stands* (721), *steps* (711), *smiles* (689), *stares* (659), *puts* (649), *watches* (646), *opens* (623), *looking* (620).
- Objects and scenes: *door* (1913), *room* (1099), *car* (922), *window* (685), *table* (635), *water* (616), *bed* (577), *house* (574).

Of course, when analysing these words out of their contexts, we must not be too hasty to assume anything about their usage. Many of them are, in general language at least, highly polysemous, members of several word classes and often used in phrases. In the next section, we will analyse some of these words in their contexts but for now note that most of the non-grammatical words in positions 101-300 also fit comfortably into the same groupings as above:

- Characters and their body parts: *man, head, face, eyes, hand, hands, men, woman, hair, arms, arm, feet, girl, mouth, boy, crowd, shoulder, officer, people, lady, body, police, soldiers, father.*
- Actions: *looks, turns, takes, walks, goes, stands, steps, smiles, stares, puts, watches, opens, looking, runs, sitting, comes, picks, sees, holds, wearing, smile, nods, standing, leans, glances, gives, holding, watch, beat, grabs, leaves, falls, reaches, watching, drops, closes, lifts, throws, shakes, passes, run, follows, climbs, kiss, pushes, kisses, walk, lies, staring, carrying.*
- Objects and scenes: *door, room, car, window, table, water, bed, house, floor, gun, boat, street, road, ground, horse, phone, desk, hat, office, book, bag, stairs, chair, seat, sky, fire, jacket, bedroom, corridor.*

Table 2. The 300 most frequent words in the TIWO Audio Description Corpus (September 2005)

Position in frequency-ordered word-list	The 300 most frequent words in the Surrey Audio Description Corpus
1-100	the, in, a, and, out, of, to, his, he, her, 's, on, at, she, up, with, as, is, him, it, into, down, back, from, looks, they, over, then, by, door, off, through, are, man, you, them, turns, for, away, an, head, one, i, their, face, eyes, room, now, hand, towards, takes, around, walks, who, two, car, behind, that, sits, across, hands, other, but, look, 't, white, pulls, men, goes, front, stands, side, steps, smiles, onto, tom, window, outside, open, inside, stares, has, puts, another, watches, table, all, round, opens, looking, water, along, again, way, bed, house, woman, black, music, later
101-200	runs, gets, john, under, young, stops, this, sitting, slowly, comes, some, red, david, change, picks, still, moves, floor, light, dark, sees, against, next, go, holds, small, its, which, after, just, no, beside, starts, little, me, long, where, right, hair, past, himself, arms, before, gun, top, wearing, what, not, there, wall, arm, boat, heads, each, street, mike, smile, large, nods, scene, more, feet, be, see, howard, standing, about, jack, can, get, like, above, road, come, have, girl, forward, blue, leans, ground, glances, gives, mouth, holding, watch, beat, grabs, horse, we, night, george, leaves, falls, grace, reaches, here, so, phone, close, boy
201-300	willard, desk, jim, harry, was, when, watching, shot, moment, glass, crowd, gerry, makes, drops, old, do, air, closes, lifts, end, throws, grey, shakes, stand, your, shoulder, green, left, while, danny, hat, lights, passes, run, appears, been, annie, office, book, three, follows, high, bob, between, officer, people, wooden, bag, lady, stairs, chair, suddenly, home, paper, seat, climbs, postman, kiss, something, pushes, others, kisses, body, will, both, don, take, dormer, lying, tries, robin, oh, my, walk, together, sky, fire, police, soldiers, if, guard, tears, move, lies, jacket, staring, michael, cole, leaving, bedroom, ellen, johnny, mr, corridor, carrying, father, stop, frank, almasy

Note: Words that were obviously artefacts of how audio description scripts are written and formatted have been removed, for example, a describer's notes that are not spoken when the audio description is recorded. Other words, such as *in* and *out*, have had their ranking boosted because they are used in formatting, but they are also frequently spoken. Some AD scripts include fragments of film dialogue used by the describers to cue the re-cording of the AD – these are included, but we believe they do not have a significant effect on results.

Frequency alone draws an interesting set of words to our attention and gives us some insight into the vocabulary of AD. However, we are also interested in words that, whilst not highly frequent in the audio description corpus, are used in AD much more than they are in general language. A statistic proposed in Ahmad and Rogers (2001) identifies words that, whilst not necessarily among the most frequent in a corpus, nevertheless appear at much higher rates than they do in general language. The statistic is sometimes referred to as the SL/GL ratio (where SL refers to special language and GL to general language) and it is calculated by dividing the relative frequency of a word in the special language corpus by its relative frequency in a general language corpus. Relative frequency is calculated by dividing the frequency of a word in a corpus by the total number of words (tokens) in the corpus. An SL/GL ratio equal to 1 means that a word is being used 'normally', i.e. as relatively often in the special language corpus as in the general language sample. In contrast, an SL/GL ratio of say 50 means that a word is being used relatively 50 times more often in the special language. If a word has a high SL/GL ratio, it suggests idiosyncratic usage in a special language corpus and there-fore demands closer inspection. Table 3 shows a selection of words with high SL/GL ratios in the TIWO corpus. Here the general language sample is the British National Corpus. To bring to attention words that are used across more than a few AD scripts, only words with a frequency in the corpus of at least 30 are included; some rogue words, for example *llama* and *periscope*, still appear because they are used frequently in the AD of one film.

Table 3. Words with SL/GL ratios greater than 25 and frequencies rates greater than 30 in the Surrey Audio Description Corpus (September 2005).

SL/GL Ratio	
>100	saunters, hurries, stares, shoves, clambers, straightens, gazes, kneels, scrambles, leans, glares, nods, periscope, strolls, crouches, tosses, blinks, trots, frowns, hurls, clunk, grabs, pulls, llama, watches, smashes

50-100	unlocks, hauls, staggers, heaves, minion, stumbles, <u>shakes</u>, wipes, hesitates, pats, <u>haired</u>, <u>lowers</u>, <u>pushes</u>, wanders, crawls, <u>grins</u>, <u>glances</u>, flings, <u>picks</u>, flicks, slaps, hugs, <u>smiles</u>, sniffs, glides, scarecrow, <u>sits</u>, slams, rubs, pours, squeezes, diner, <u>postman</u>, spins, shuts, salutes, drags
25-50	rips, <u>walks</u>, <u>climbs</u>, <u>closes</u>, sips, <u>strides</u>, slumps, gallops, flashback, <u>leaps</u>, <u>knocks</u>, <u>throws</u>, fades, stirs, <u>rushes</u>, <u>kisses</u>, tugs, creeps, <u>jumps</u>, dives, shrugs, crashes, <u>lifts</u>, <u>turns</u>, licks, <u>opens</u>, silhouetted, elevator, <u>pauses</u>, <u>swings</u>, sighs, bounces, <u>stops</u>, dials, swims, bangs, <u>presses</u>, <u>slips</u>, removes

Note: The words are ordered by their SL/GL ratios. Words with frequency rates greater than 100 are underlined. Character names which typically have high SL/GL ratios have been excluded.

Table 3 includes some words that we saw already in Table 2. However, the SL/GL statistic highlights other words, many of which refer to actions. The need for concision in descriptions may account for the high occurrence of troponyms here. Troponyms are verbs that express a particular manner of doing something: *saunters, hurries, shoves, clambers, straightens, gazes, kneels, scrambles, glares, strolls, crouches, tosses, blinks, trots, frowns, hurls, smashes, unlocks, hauls, staggers, heaves, stumbles, wipes, hesitates, pats, lowers, wanders, crawls, grins, flings, flicks, slaps, hugs, sniffs, glides, slams, rubs, pours, squeezes, spins, shuts, salutes, drags, rips, sips, strides, slumps, gallops, leaps, knocks, stirs, rushes, tugs, creeps, jumps, dives, shrugs, crashes, licks, pauses, swings, sighs, bounces, swims, bangs, presses, slips, removes.*

2.2 Concordances of some unusually frequent words

By examining concordances of some of the words identified above, we learn more about how they are being used in AD and we can begin to characterize the kinds of information that audio description commonly provides. It must be emphasized that this is very much a preliminary analysis of what is a vast quantity of concordance data: there are over 27,000 instances of the 29 top 100 non-grammatical words alone. The focus here is on commonly occurring phrases that include the frequent words. These have been grouped, in a preliminary attempt at a classification, according to how they give information about:

- Characters' appearances;
- Characters' focus of attention;
- Characters' interpersonal interactions;
- Changes of location of characters and objects, and
- Characters' emotional states.

Often when characters first come on screen in a film they are introduced in the AD with a relatively simple description of their appearances, e.g. their age, clothing or some distinctive features. Some common phrases are: *woman in* and *man in* followed by an item of clothing, or an age; *woman / man wearing* followed by an item of clothing; and *woman / man with* followed by a distinctive physical feature. In some cases *man* and *woman* are preceded by an adjective relating to the character's appearance, e.g. *young, old, elderly, short, tall, burly, and bearded*:

> A man in a white T-shirt leans towards Jim.
> He sees a man and a woman in a red suit walk by.
> The door of a low-rise brick apartment building opens and a woman in her thirties steps out.
> A dark-haired man with a moustache stands at the door.
> An old woman with a pointed nose and wild, white hair stands in a gloomy room.

The words *looks* and *looking* are often used in phrases like *looking at, looks at, looks up at, looks down at* and *looks around*. These all tend to provide information about a character's current focus of attention. Consider, for example, some concordances of *looks at*, which appears 487 times in the corpus:

> Corelli looks at his men.
> Samuel looks at the blue and black picture.
> Iris looks at John curiously as he puts down his cup.
> Memphis looks at the five young men.
> He looks at Harry thoughtfully.
> Lucy looks at him for a moment, then kisses him.

Other words appear to be used in a similar way but are more specific about the manner in which the character is looking – *stares at, glances at* and *gazes at*. Phrases formed with the words *eyes* and *head* also indicate focus of attention:

Young Parker keeps walking, his eyes fixed on Mary Jane.
Keeping her eyes fixed on Ben, she walks over.
Willard opens his eyes and absently regards the fan.
Slowly she turns her head to face the door.

A preliminary examination of the concordances of *looks at* and the like suggests that they are used when a character's attention is on another character or object. In contrast, *watches (...) as* seems to be used to indicate a character's attention to something happening:

The girl watches closely as he carefully puts the needle on the record.
David watches through his binoculars as Kirgo puts the coin in a flight bag.

Many instances of characters' attention of focus involve them focusing on other characters. There is some overlap then with our proposed category of 'characters' interactions'. However, certain phrases like *turns to, shakes hands, sits next to, their eyes meet, puts hand on, gaze into each others eyes* and *turns away* are perhaps more indicative of key moments in an interaction:

The captain turns to Gatlin.
She turns to Drosoula, who glares at her.
Pelagia moves forward into the room, then turns to look back at him.
They shake hands, Diane nods once quickly, smiling.
Stitch sits next to an elderly lady and takes her hand.
Their eyes meet for a moment, then she turns to close the curtain.
Jules puts her hand on Ellen's shoulder.

Other key information about how an interaction between characters is proceeding is commonly given with phrases like *smiles at, shakes his / her head* and *nods* with an adverb:

Luc smiles at her conspiratorially.
As Ellen smiles at her father, her eyes moisten.
Tess shakes her head and swallows nervously.
Ellen looks steadily at him and shakes her head.
Michael nods, tentatively.
Prince John nods, approvingly.
Annie nods and Tom grins to himself.

For the audience, it is crucial to keep track of the location and presence / absence on-screen of characters and key objects. This broad class of information is expressed with quite a large number of frequently occurring phrases in

AD. Characters' changes of location, typically within a scene, are expressed with phrases including *goes to / into / off / out, walks away / off / out / over to* and *steps towards / into / onto*. These actions may be preceded by a character standing up – *stands up* occurs frequently in the corpus, or completed when a character *sits down*. The opening and closing of doors are frequently described – *opens / closes the door, door opens / closes*, as a characters moving *through the door*, and are often connected with characters entering and leaving scenes; similarly, when a vehicle *pulls up* or *drives off*. Objects change location, and sometimes ownership, when one character *hands* something to another, when a character *picks up / pulls out* an object, and when a character *puts* an object somewhere:

> Quietly she gets out of bed and goes to the window.
> Luca hangs his head solemnly and steps towards a bench with Mary.
> Corelli looks at him coldly, then turns and walks away.
> He stands up and goes back into the main room.
> Gogan steps in through the door.
> The next day, a white car pulls up at the house.
> She picks up a jar from the kitchen table.
> She hands him a rucksack.

As well as keeping track of where characters are, what they look like and who they are interacting with, in order to appreciate a story properly an audience must understand something about the characters' emotional states. Of course, in some instances it will be possible for the audience to infer this either because of what has happened to a character or from the dialogue. However, our corpus analysis reveals some commonly recurring phrases that seem to be used to convey characters' emotional states. The most straightforward way this is described is by saying a character *looks* or *is looking* followed by an adjective such as *confused, shocked, surprised, thoughtful, troubled, uneasy, annoyed, puzzled, concerned* or *dejected*:

> Mrs Mills looks confused, then recovers herself.
> Rebecca looks blissfully happy, Samuel doesn't.
> Noelle's looking faintly embarrassed and puts her hand over her lips.

The verbs *smiles, stares, looks* and *walks* all occur very frequently in the corpus and can be modified with adverbs to indicate an emotional reaction to the events affecting a character – *smiles contentedly / fondly / happily / sadly / shyly / wryly, stares blankly / coldly / curiously / proudly / uncertainly / in confusion / in disbelief, looks anxiously / nervously / desperately, walks briskly / calmly / slowly / stiffly*. Less frequent than *smiles* are *frowns* and *grins*.

Vianne closes the window and turns to Anouk who smiles contentedly.
Her smile fades and she stares blankly upwards.
He stops walking and stares in confusion at the mass of demonstrators.

Actions involving the characters' heads, faces and eyes also give information about their emotional states:

Billy's young face breaks into a wide smile.
She leans back and her face crumples in despair.
Thurman strides across to the dock, his head held high.
Ellen's eyes fill with tears and she smiles sadly at Kate.

There is a great deal of scope for much more detailed investigations in order to describe more precisely the way in which frequent words and phrases are used, and to refine the classification of what kinds of information AD provides. A colleague on the TIWO project at the University of Surrey, Andrew Vassiliou, will shortly complete his doctoral research, which has focused on a more systematic and in-depth analysis of concordances and collocation data from the TIWO corpus. A by-product of analysing the kinds of information commonly provided by AD is that we also learn something about what events commonly happen in films. Consider, for example, phrases that describe characters looking at each other and at key objects, phrases that indicate characters changing location and phrases that describe characters' expressions of emotions. It could be argued that the preponderance of the actions described by these phrases makes them important narrative elements for story-telling in films (Salway, Vassiliou & Ahmad 2005). For this, and other reasons, the analysis of AD could be of interest to narratologists.[4]

2.3 The expression of temporal information in audio description

A key aspect of the definition of narrative is that it involves events organized in a temporal sequence. We found the usage of grammatical features and words that express temporal information to be restricted in AD compared with general language because, for the most part, AD describes something happening in the present time. The written audio description script contains time codes which synchronize the speaking of utterances with the film. In effect, the order of speaking is the major source of temporal information for the audience – if one event is described before another, it is assumed to have happened (in film time) before the other. AD guidelines specify the use of the present tense and this seems to be used in the vast majority of audio description utterances: the simple present tense is used interchangeably with the present continuous. Occasionally, the present perfect is used when only the end-state of an event is depicted on-screen, or to identify unnamed characters:

Pike has killed Grueller, but another vampire is after him, as Buffy stakes her opponent.
The short man who has been pursuing Darby meets with Sneller.

There are, however, other indicators of temporal information that seem to be favoured by audio describers. The verbs *stops, starts, begins* and *finishes* all occur relatively more frequently than in general language as evidenced by their SL/GL ratios (Table 4). They are often used to indicate the end points of events:

Jerry skips for a while, then stops and stares at the rope.
Lynn stops fiddling with the wall temperature gauge.
He walks back to the party and starts dancing.
Slowly she starts to climb the stone staircase.
She discovers it is a letter and begins reading.
The guard moves again, and Griff begins to climb the ladder.
Hester finishes decoding the Kestrel signals with the Enigma machine.

Table 4. Verbs for expressing temporal information that are unusually frequent in the Surrey Audio Description Corpus (September 2005).

Word	*Frequency*	*SL / GL Ratio*
stops	519	28.9
starts	426	9.3
begins	140	3.8
finishes	31	5.0

The use of other words that can indicate when events happen was reported by Salway and Tomadaki (2002), who analysed a corpus of audio description for twelve films comprising 70,852 words. A first analysis of the current TIWO corpus supports the previous findings. Although words to express temporal information did not appear unusually frequently compared with general language, and in fact words like *before* and *after* were relatively infrequent, they did appear to be used in more restricted ways compared with general language. The words *then* (2086) and *now* (1090), when used, were redundant as far as adding information about temporal ordering, because the order of events is implicit in the ordering of the utterances. However, *then* often implies the completion of the first event and *now* suggests a contrast with a previous state or event:

> He watches for a moment then continues walking.
> The major throws the towel to the ground, then dives in after Miss Bentley.
> The businessman is now rather less smug.
> The terrified prisoners are now running as they go about their work.
> Boulton walks into the common room, now wearing a Royal Navy lieutenant commanders uniform.

Both *as* (3651) and *while* (257) were used to express the simultaneity of two events but only *as* implies a causal connection between the two events:

> The gang take aim as the brothers run up a ladder.
> He jumps as the troll gives a snort.
> Lady, Tramp and Jock all giggle, as the puppies play.
> Buddy follows Ray Bob onto the bus while a couple of musicians bid farewell.
> Sully hauls himself back inside, while Boo starts hitting Randall with a baseball bat.

The timing of one event relative to another was also expressed with *when* (290) and *until* (109). The inclusion of one event within another can be expressed by using a non-finite verb with a subordinate clause:

> She walks off then pauses when she realises Jack is lagging behind.
> Ives looks tense, and when they move off, he's holding his arms.
> The others watch until Ned interrupts.
> They attack it with their rifle butts until the door panels smash in and they gain access.
> Coughing, Mary gives the medicine to Tom.

The word *again* (593) was generally used to indicate a second instance of an event within a scene of a film:

> Bending forward, he kisses her again and goes.
> A rhino-like dinosaur knocks Aladar over again as it plods slowly past.

To give information about when events occur in 'story time' rather than in 'film time', times of day, like *morning*, *evening*, *dusk* and *dawn*, are sometimes used in the AD to introduce a new scene, as is *later*. Words referring to specific festival days, months, seasons and years were infrequent. This is perhaps because a lot of information about such things is conveyed in films by costumes, props and lighting and the AD will concentrate on describing these and allow the audience to infer historical periods, times of year, etc.

3. Audio description and information technology

In anticipation of a sharp increase in the demand for AD and the need for organizations to deliver to tight deadlines whilst maintaining, if not improving, the quality of their descriptions, it is important to consider the possibilities for information technology to assist in the production of AD. A backdrop to the discussion here is the limited achievements of automatic translation systems in the past, and the observation that video data are generally considered to be less computationally-tractable than text data. To a computer, moving images consist of pixels of some 32 million different colours, organized into frames of say 800x600 pixels, with typically 24 or 25 frames per second. The mapping from this mass of pixels to the meanings inherent in the moving image for a human viewer has been termed the 'semantic gap' (Smeulders *et al.* 2000). The state-of-the-art in computer vision technology is a long way from successfully bridging this gap and being able to recognize large sets of objects and actions in relatively unconstrained video data such as films.[5] This rules out, for the meantime, the possibility of anything close to fully automating the generation of AD from video data. On a positive note, the relatively systematic nature of the language of AD observed in Section 1 is encouraging for the application of language technologies to assist in the production of audio description. Furthermore, the problem of the semantic gap creates a great potential added-value for AD to be reused as a basis for indexing moving images in digital archives.

3.1 Some possibilities for assisted audio description

This section discusses requirements and desired functionality for software to assist in the production of AD, and the opportunities and feasibility of applying state-of-the-art language and multimedia technologies. These ideas were developed during the TIWO project in consultation with members of the Round Table. Currently available software, such as Softel's *Adept* system, assists in the preparation of audio description scripts, the recording of audio description and its synchronization with programme and film material. It presents the material on-screen alongside a window that marks time-coded speech-free intervals into which describers can type their descriptions. Once the script has been completed and reviewed, it is spoken, recorded and synchronized with the video data by the time codes. In considering further functionality that could be provided by information technology, it is crucial to remember that any gain in efficiency (speed) of producing AD is instantly negated by any lowering of quality, which points to human editors always having the final word. The ideas for further functionality are discussed here in order of how technologically feasible I think they are.

A relatively simple addition to current software would be online access to lexical resources such as specialist terminologies and thesauri to help describers find the best words for their descriptions, and to avoid too much repetition. A system could also be proactive in providing links to relevant information on the web, such as pages related to the subject matter of a documentary being described, or online plot summaries and scripts of a film. Describers could also be provided with access to previous descriptions in order to see how certain things have been described before, either for inspiration for their description or to ensure consistency with previous descriptions within a TV series or film.

A key aspect of guidelines for maintaining the quality of AD is the specification of preferences for certain linguistic features including vocabulary and grammar. This raises the possibility for automatic style-checking whether to give feedback to novice describers, to assist editors or as a tool for organizations, such as the RNIB, that monitor the output of organizations producing AD. For example, it could be feasible for a system to check for vocabulary that is inappropriate to the genre or period of a film, for confusing use of pronouns, for the over-repetition of vocabulary items and for the use of inappropriate tenses and overly complex utterances. For novice describers the feedback could be given as they work, for editors it would be given on a script by script basis, and monitoring organizations may wish to analyse corpora representative of an organization's output to get an impression of how guidelines are being followed.

For some material, such as films, pre-existing descriptions of on-screen scenes, characters and actions are available, e.g. film screenplays. This led us to the idea of creating a first draft AD automatically from such texts. This can be conceived of as a text summarization task, for which there is already an established body of research and technology. On average, screenplays contain about three times as many words as the equivalent AD, but a corpus-based analysis reported by Salway, Vassiliou and Ahmad (2005) suggests that both text types concentrate on providing the same kinds of information – though of course screenplays also contain dialogue. As a follow-up to the TIWO project we are currently working with the audio description team at BBC Broadcast to develop and evaluate technology for creating a first draft AD automatically from a screenplay. Our focus is on algorithms to identify the most important things to describe, and then to edit utterances from the screenplays to fit the time available for description and to ensure an appropriate style of AD. If successful, such algorithms might contribute to technology for near live AD so that describers could speak their description during a first viewing of material, and a system with speech recognition could automatically transcribe and edit what they say. This would also require the application of existing multimedia techniques to detect scene boundaries and dialogue-free intervals in video data.

The final set of opportunities and challenges for information technology to be considered here relate to the adaptation of AD. It is recognized that it is not possible to produce a single AD that would meet all the needs and preferences of all audience members, so perhaps in the future it would be possible to customize descriptions to better suit individuals. Technological developments, such as DVD, and its possible successors like BluRay, offer new ways to deliver AD. For example, users may be able to choose alternative description tracks, or access more detailed descriptions whilst pausing a film. Tracks could be provided with alternative vocabularies for different age groups, or different quantities of descriptive and interpretive information to suit personal preferences. The cost of producing multiple versions manually would be prohibitive, but perhaps language technology can be used to adapt a 'master' description automatically either at the time of production (giving the option for human editing) or at the point of delivery (giving full control to the audience). Any kind of adaptation would benefit from audio description scripts being marked-up, for example using XML, to make explicit to the machine the relative importance of, and interdependencies between, AD utterances and dialogue. Such mark-up may also be a starting point for a kind of template-based translation of AD into different languages, allowing the translator to see quickly what needs to be described. Perhaps the relatively restricted nature of the language of AD makes automatic translation into a first draft feasible. The hardest adaptation-related challenges come from the prospect of programme and film material being edited for reuse after the AD has been produced. Ideally, the original description would be reused but after editing the space available for description may alter, visual content may change, and the original speaker of the description may not be available to record changes.

3.2 Using audio description to increase the understanding of films by machines

Whilst improving media accessibility will always be the primary motivation to produce AD, the coming years may also see interest in it for another reason. As it becomes easier to store and share vast quantities of video data, so the need increases for technologies that can assist in the indexing and retrieval of television programmes and films from digital libraries. In the past, archives such as that of the BBC have been for in-house use only, but the advent of the web creates the demand and opportunity to make them available for public access. A minimal requirement is to store production details such as title, director and genre with every programme and film. More useful though is shot-level or scene-level indexing whereby keywords are associated with shots and scenes, enabling users to retrieve precise intervals of video data that match their queries, for example 'find me all scenes showing a woman on a horse'. Creating such indexes manually is prohibitively expensive in many cases, and the challenge of the semantic gap limits the scope for machines to generate keywords by analysis of the pixels in the video data. An increasingly popular strategy is to automate video indexing by exploiting so-called collateral text associated with video material. For example the research prototype *Informedia*[6] and the commercial *Google Video*[7] use keywords from closed subtitles to index television programmes. Closed subtitles can work well for some kinds of programmes, such as news broadcasts, where there is a reasonably close correspondence between the spoken words of presenters and what is depicted in the moving image. However, that correspondence is often more ad-hoc, especially in other kinds of programmes and films, and so the advent of AD seems especially timely as an alternative source of indexing information.

By definition AD includes a temporally-aligned verbal account of the most important aspects of visual information. Developing an idea first proposed by Turner (1998), in TIWO we demonstrated promising results for keyword-based video indexing using AD. In ongoing work with the BBC Archive we are evaluating the use of AD for indexing television programmes. The TIWO project also explored new ways of accessing films stored in digital libraries, beyond keyword-based retrieval. Imagine in the future asking your computer to find you a film with a similar kind of story to the one you just watched, or asking it to show you a summary of a film containing the key parts of the story. Such functionality would require the machine to understand, in some sense, narrative aspects of the film. In TIWO we found that some narrative-related information could be extracted quite simply from audio description scripts, for example, information about the emotions being experienced by characters at different points in time (Salway & Graham 2003). Figure 1 shows plots for two different films that were generated automatically from their AD. The technique was based on mapping the occurrences of about 600 emotion tokens (keywords in the AD) to one of 22 emotion types. The plot shows each time an emotion token occurs in the AD. This simple technique achieved about 65% accuracy. The extracted patterns of emotion are suggestive of some key aspects of the stories in the films. For example, in the plot for *Captain Corelli's Mandolin* a high density of positive emotion tokens appears 15-20 minutes into the film, e.g. JOY and LIKE, corresponding to Pelagia's betrothal to Madras. The negative emotion tokens which immediately follow are associated with the invasion of their island.

The cluster of positive emotions between 68-74 minutes occurs during scenes depicting the growing relationship between Pelagia and Corelli. The group of FEAR, DISTRESS and SELF-REPROACH tokens between 92-95 minutes maps to a scene in which German soldiers are disarming their former Italian allies, during which a number of Italians are gunned down. Towards the end of the film, the last DISTRESS token appears, followed by a RELIEF token when Pelagia discovers her father has survived an earthquake, and a LIKE token as Pelagia and Corelli are reunited. Our more recent work is extending the range of narrative-related information we can extract from AD in order to generate richer machine-processable representations of stories (Salway, Vassiliou & Ahmad 2005).

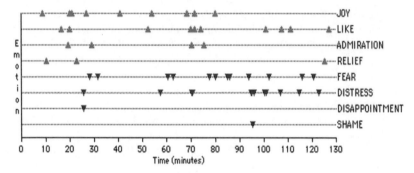

Figure 1a. A plot of emotion tokens found in the AD of Madden's *Captain Corelli's Mandolin,* from Salway and Graham (2003).

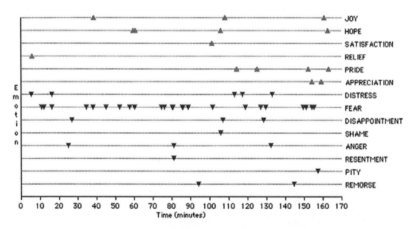

Figure 1b. A plot of emotion tokens found in the AD of Costner's *The Postman,* from Salway and Graham (2003).

4. Conclusions and closing remarks

The automated corpus-based approach reported in this paper was successful in characterising some idiosyncratic features of what appears to be a special language of audio description. These features can be explained by considering the communicative needs of the users of AD. Further analysis, for example of spatial information, and analysis with part-of-speech tagging and lemmatization are required to strengthen the case for a language of audio description. It is also important now to analyse corpora of AD produced in different countries, where different guidelines and practices apply, and in different languages. Our investigation also began to create an empirically-grounded overview and classification of the main kinds of information provided by AD. The degree of systematicity observed in the audio description scripts should be encouraging to those who produce guidelines for AD and those who train audio describers. It is also encouraging for those seeking to develop language technologies for 'assisted audio description' and for repurposing AD to index digital video archives.

There is a trade-off between the wholly automated large-scale analysis of text corpora and in-depth analysis of smaller quantities of data. Corpus-based approaches must be complemented by other ways to understand the processes of AD. Future investigations would do well to follow the advice of Piety (2004) and analyse AD with respect to the visual and audio contents of the films it describes. Also, the argument and suggestions made by Remael (2004) for attending to the narrative functioning of film dialogue in audiovisual translation is highly pertinent to the study of AD. The need for interdisciplinary research into audiovisual, or multimedia, translation was articulated by Gambier and Gottleib (2001:xii). Synergies with four of the subject fields that they mentioned have been hinted at in the current paper, namely film studies, semiotics, information science and computer science. To this list it may be appropriate to add the field of narratology – itself highly interdisciplinary – in order to understand more about how AD works or should work. Of particular relevance are developments concentrating on the cognitive processes by which stories are understood (Herman 2002) and the ways in which stories are told in different media (Ryan 2004).

---

[1] www.ofcom.org.uk/tv/ifi/guidance/tv_access_serv/audio_description_stnds
[2] www.computing.surrey.ac.uk/personal/pg/A.Salway/tiwo/TIWO.htm
[3] www.computing.surrey.ac.uk/SystemQ
[4] Narrative is a multi-faceted phenomenon studied by philosophers, literature and film scholars, linguists, cognitive scientists and computer scientists (Herman 2002). Because AD has to concentrate on the essential information required to tell a story, its analysis could help to answer

questions identified in Ryan (2004) such as how different kinds of media can convey the same stories, and what information is essential to understand a story. It is also interesting to compare the ways in which AD gives information about the characters and events of films with other kinds of text that serve similar functions, for example screenplays and plot summaries, and perhaps even novels where applicable. Vassiliou's work, mentioned previously, includes the analysis of a corpus of film screenplays. Another colleague on the TIWO project at Surrey compared how AD and plot summaries refer to the same events (Tomadaki 2006).
[5] Perhaps the most recent advances in this area have been realized in the Cognitive Vision Systems project (http://cogvisys.iaks.uni-karlsruhe.de).
[6] www.informedia.cs.cmu.edu
[7] http://video.google.com

References

Ahmad, Khurshid and Margaret Rogers. 2001. "The analysis of text corpora for the creation of advanced terminology databases", in Sue Ellen Wright and Gerhard Budin (eds) *The Handbook of Terminology Management*. Amsterdam and Philadelphia: John Benjamins, 725-760.

Ballester Casado, Ana. Forthcoming. "La audiodescripción: apuntes sobre el estado de la cuestión y las perspectivas de investigación". *Cadernos de Tradução*.

Biber, Douglas, Susan Conrad and Randi Reppen. 1998. *Corpus Linguistics: Investigating Language Structure and Use*. Cambridge: Cambridge University Press.

Bordwell, David and Kristin Thompson. 1997. *Film Art: An Introduction*. 5th edition. New York: McGraw-Hill.

Gambier, Yves and Henrik Gottlieb. 2001. "Multimedia, multilingua: Multiple challenges", in Yves Gambier and Henrik Gottlieb (eds) *(Multi)Media Translation: Concepts, Practices, and Research*. Amsterdam and Philadelphia: John Benjamins, viii-xx.

Herman, David. 2002. *Story Logic: Problems and Possibilities of Narrative*. Lincoln, Nebraska: University of Nebraska Press.

Hoffman, Lothar. 1984. "Seven Roads to LSP". *Fachsprache: international journal of LSP* 6(1-2): 28-38.

Orero, Pilar. 2004. "Audiovisual translation: A new dynamic umbrella", in Pilar Orero (ed.) *Topics in Audiovisual Translation*. Amsterdam and Philadelphia: John Benjamins, vii-xiii.

Piety, Philip. 2004. "The language system of audio description: An investigation as a discursive process". *Journal of Visual Impairment and Blindness* 98(8): 453-469.

Remael, Aline. 2004. "A place for film dialogue analysis in subtitling courses", in Pilar Orero (ed.) *Topics in Audiovisual Translation*. Amsterdam and Philadelphia: John Benjamins, 103-126.

Ryan, Marie-Laure. (ed.) 2004. *Narrative Across Media: The Languages of Storytelling*. Lincoln (NE): University of Nebraska Press.

Salway, Andrew and Mike Graham. 2003. "Extracting information about emotions in Films". *Proceedings 11th ACM Conference on Multimedia 2003*, 299-302.
www.computing.surrey.ac.uk/personal/pg/A.Salway/pdfs/Extracting_Info rmation_about_Emotions_in_Films.pdf

Salway, Andrew and Eleftheria Tomadaki. 2002. "Temporal information in collateral texts for indexing moving images", in Andrea Setzer and Robert Gaizauskas (eds) *Proceedings of LREC 2002 Workshop on Annotation Standards for Temporal Information in Natural Language*, 36-43.
www.computing.surrey.ac.uk/personal/pg/A.Salway/pdfs/temporal_infor mation.pdf

Salway, Andrew, Andrew Vassiliou and Khurshid Ahmad. 2005. "What happens in films?". *Proceedings ICME 2005: International Conference on Multimedia and Expo* IEEE. Electronic publication.

Smeulders, Arnold W.M. *et al.* 2000. "Content-based image retrieval: the end of the early years". *IEEE Transactions Pattern Analysis and Machine Intelligence* 22(12): 1349-1380.

Tomadaki, Eleftheria. 2006. *Cross-document Coreference Between Different Types of Collateral Texts for Films*. Guildford: University of Surrey. PhD Thesis.

Turner, James. 1998. "Some characteristics of audio description and the corresponding moving image". *Proceedings of 61st ASIS Annual Meeting*, vol. 35. Medford, New Jersey: Information Today, 108-117.

Acknowledgements

This research was conducted as part of the Television in Words (TIWO) project, funded by the UK's Engineering and Physical Sciences Research Council (EPSRC). I have enjoyed and learnt from discussions about the language of AD with two TIWO colleagues, Andrew Vassiliou and Eleftheria Tomadaki, who also helped to compile the TIWO corpus. Their own analyses, which go much further than the work presented here, are mentioned in Section 1. Early versions of this paper were presented in the form of a seminar at Universidad de Granada, and a talk at the *Media for All* conference in Barcelona. I am grateful to all those present who offered comments, questions and suggestions.

Throughout the project, the TIWO Round Table was an invaluable source of AD expertise and provided texts for the TIWO corpus. I give many thanks to, in alphabetical order, Marie Campbell (BBC Broadcast), Martin Davies (BBC Broadcast), Garry Duguid (ITFC), Denise Evans (RNIB),

Claude Le Guyader (ITFC), James O'Hara (ITFC), Dave Harris (ITFC), Jane Westrop (BBC), Jill Whitehead (RNIB) and Russ Wood (Softel). I have also learnt about AD in conversations with Joan Greening (RNIB), Veronika Hyks (IMS) and Joel Snyder (Audio Description Associates).

From the visual to the verbal in two languages: a contrastive analysis of the audio description of *The Hours* in English and Spanish

Julian Bourne

Universidad de Granada, Spain

Catalina Jiménez Hurtado

Universidad de Granada, Spain

Abstract

This paper offers a contrastive analysis of the audio described scripts of *The Hours* in English and Spanish, with a view to predicting some of the challenges that could arise when translating this type of text from English into Spanish. After arguing that audio description (AD) should be considered as a distinct text type, the paper suggests that different conventions have evolved in English and Spanish regarding both the content and expression of ADs. These differences are illustrated with reference to the English and Spanish ADs for *The Hours*, which are analysed at the level of the word, sentence and larger units of discourse. It is subsequently predicted that the different conventions may create difficulties for the translator both in terms of linguistic transfer and of extra-linguistic considerations such as receiver expectation. Nevertheless, such problems also occur in other translation modes and should not be considered as barriers to translating ADs from English into Spanish, which would undoubtedly bring benefits in terms of time and cost as well as allowing Spanish receivers to experience a different style of AD.

1. Introduction: definition and general considerations

The concept of text is presently undergoing a revolution owing to new electronic and multi-media formats, and to the application of new technologies to many different modes of communication. Both Translation Studies and Linguistics are concerned with the new phenomena resulting from such profound changes, of which one example is audio description (AD). Although AD has been practised for a number of years,[1] it is only recently that such texts have become the object of academic study, and publications on the topic are still scarce.

An audio described text is verbal information inserted between the screenplay dialogues in order to help blind or visually impaired people[2] appreciate what is happening on the screen. Different aspects of AD may be usefully described by different academic approaches, such as semiotics, translation and linguistics. For example, from a semiotic point of view, AD may be viewed as the translation of images to words and is therefore a type of intersemiotic translation, within which two subordinate modalities are possible: on the one hand, intralinguistic (from the images on the screen via a written text to an oral text emitted simultaneously with the image); and, on the other hand, interlinguistic (from the images on the screen to an AD written in one language and later translated into another).

As a text for translation, AD represents a particular case with specific constraints, although similar to those in other types of audiovisual translation, such as dubbing. The translated text is primarily conditioned by the visual information offered on the screen, and by the amount of time/space available in between the dialogues to insert the description.

Finally, from a linguistic point of view, there is some doubt as to whether AD should be considered as an independent text, since it makes sense only in conjunction with the accompanying film and therefore seems to lack certain Hallidayan textual criteria (Halliday & Hasan 1976), such as coherence. Nevertheless, within the field of text linguistics, various authors (Faber Benítez & Jiménez Hurtado 2004; Poethe 2005) have attempted to establish AD as a distinct text type. In this respect, Poethe (2005:40) observes:

> Mit der aus spezifischen kommunikativen Bedürfnissen des Alltags entstandenen Audiodeskription hat sich zugleich eine neue Textsorte etabliert, deren Besonderheiten u.a. in ihrem engen intertextuellen Bezug zum Filmtext besteht, ohne den der Audiodeskriptionstext nicht möglich und nicht sinnvoll wäre.
>
> [With audio description, which arose from specific communicative needs in everyday life, a new type of text was established. One of its characteristics is its close intertextual relationship with the filmic text, without which the audio described text would neither be possible nor make sense. (Our translation)]

In support of the idea of AD as a separate text type, Poethe argues that when formulating a new AD, audio describers resort to a sort of abstract prototype AD manifesting the main features which need to be incorporated (Poethe 2005:40). While this may seem intuitively convincing, certain differences seem to have arisen between countries with regard to the conventions (to be) followed when writing AD scripts, in terms of both content and style, and it is reasonable to predict that such differences may acquire particular relevance when translating AD scripts.

Although not at present a generalized practice, translating ADs would seem to offer considerable advantages in terms of time and therefore cost in comparison with the present practice by which ADs are written from scratch by professional audio describers in different languages.[3] It is therefore worthwhile to explore the possibility of translating ADs and to identify some of the linguistic as well as extra-linguistic challenges that the translation of this new text type might involve. As a preliminary step, the contrastive analysis in the present article is aimed at highlighting differences in the conventions of writing ADs in English and Spanish and at demonstrating how these may affect the translator's task.

While the analysis is restricted to a single film, *The Hours*, our experience of reading ADs in English and Spanish suggests that the two scripts in question reflect the contrasting approach to AD writing in the UK and Spain, at least with regard to literary or historical films.

2. Contrastive analysis of the English and Spanish ADs of *The Hours*[4]

2.1 The film

Based on the novel of the same name by Michael Cunningham (1998), the film portrays the emotional lives of three women separated by time and space but linked through a series of thematic parallels deriving from Virginia Woolf's novel *Mrs Dalloway* (1925). Virginia Woolf herself features as a married woman living in Richmond in the early twenties, struggling with the threat of insanity as she writes her first great novel. Three decades later, Laura Brown, a housewife and mother living in a residential area of Los Angeles, reads *Mrs Dalloway* and is profoundly and irrevocably affected by it. The third woman is Clarissa Vaughan, a modern version of Mrs Dalloway who lives and works in New York, where she looks after her friend Richard, a poet who is suffering from AIDS. As if dictated by the events in *Mrs Dalloway*, the story of each woman interweaves and moves inexorably towards a conclusion of shared revelation.

2.2 Content

According to Snyder (2004:2), the director of described media for the US National Captioning Institute, the audio description of films should strive to include the following: the characters in the scene, the location of the scene, who is speaking, what the characters are doing, what the characters are wearing, facial expressions and body language, text shown on objects in a scene or as subtitles, and colours. Clearly, time constraints force all audio describers to prioritize the information offered at any one moment. However, our experience suggests that while both English and Spanish ADs coincide in describing action and changes of scene, there tends to be comparatively little information in Spanish concerning character and setting. In the present case, this comparative lack of detail with regard to aspects such as clothes, expressions and situational context largely explains the difference in the lengths of the two ADs: approximately 7,800 words in English and 5,000 words in Spanish. As the following extracts illustrate, the English offers quite prolific detail while the Spanish tends towards summarized descriptions:

Outside, a limousine pulls up and Clarissa gets out of the back. Her hair in a neat French plait and wearing an elegant black coat with an orange scarf, she hurries over to the metal door.

Un coche para frente a la casa de Richard. Clarissa sale de él elegantemente vestida.
[A car stops in front of Richard's house. Clarissa gets out, elegantly dressed.]

2.3 Linguistic structures

In the following sections we shall focus on lexical and syntactical elements and on larger units of discourse in which the differences between the two scripts seem particularly relevant to the question of translating ADs from English into Spanish.

2.3.1 Lexicon

In support of the view that ADs in English should be regarded as special language texts, Salway (this volume) and Salway *et al.* (2005) have demonstrated that ADs contain a high proportion of 'weird' words, i.e. words that are infrequent in everyday language as recorded in the British National Corpus. As we aim to show in the following paragraphs, the AD of *The Hours* is no exception. By contrast, the Spanish lexical choices reflect a more restricted vocabulary, with certain exceptions which may be partly attributed to the historical setting of part of the film and to its literary ambience. An example of this is the description, *Virginia vierte agua de un aguamanil en una jofaina y se contempla en el espejo* [Virginia pours water from a jug into a basin and contemplates herself in the mirror]. Here the nouns *aguamanil* and *jofaina* seem markedly old-fashioned against the more familiar *jarro* and *vasija*, while the verb *contemplarse* may be regarded as a somewhat elevated alternative to *mirarse*. As a general rule, however, the lexical resources deployed in the Spanish text suggest a concern to avoid placing excessive cognitive demands on the receiver, whereas the English text seems at times positively challenging in this respect:

The woman's body, face down, is carried by the swift current
through swaying reeds along the murky river bed, her gold wedding
band glinting on her finger, a shoe slipping off her foot.

El cuerpo sumergido de Virginia es arrastrado por la corriente.
[The submerged body of Virginia is swept away by the current.]

2.3.1.1 Verbs

Turning to specific word classes, notable differences may be observed in the
use of verbs in the two ADs. As Snyder (2004:8) has noted with respect to
verbs which express different ways of walking,[5] English is particularly rich
in verbs which simultaneously encode a general action and the manner in
which the action is carried out. In the AD of *The Hours* there is a marked
preference for such semantically complex verbs, which are often monosyllabic (see also Vercauteren in this volume). As ways of taking, for example,
we find 'snatch', 'grab' and 'clasp'; ways of looking are 'gaze'; 'stare' and
'peer', ways of sitting down are 'slump down', 'sink down' and 'flop down'.

By contrast, the Spanish language does not seem to offer such a wide
range of specific verbs and often uses a general verb plus present participle,
adverb or adverbial phrase in order to convey more specific connotations
(Congost Maestre 1994:55). For instance, in the Spanish AD the idea of *to
stare* is rendered as *se queda mirando fijamente* [she stays looking fixedly].
More usually, however, an action described by a specific verb in the English
AD is either not described or rendered by a general verb in the Spanish:

fumbles (with her coat)	not described
slips (into bed)	*se mete (en la cama)*
	[she gets (into bed)]
scampers out	*va (hacia el salón)*
	[he goes (towards the living room)]
scoops (him) up	*saca (a Richie)*
	[she takes (Richie) out]
snatches up (his jacket)	not described

2.3.1.2 Adjectives and adverbs

The fact that the English AD aims to give detailed descriptions of clothes,
setting and facial expressions, necessarily encourages the use of a wide range
of adjectives. Moreover, the AD fully exploits the plasticity of English,

which permits the formulation of highly precise and unusual adjectives simply by compounding two syntactical elements, such as noun or adjective plus past participle. Examples in the AD of *The Hours* are 'gold-edged', 'sun-dappled', 'snub-nosed' and 'mushroom-coloured'. To convey similarly precise ideas in Spanish would necessarily involve the use of longer descriptive phrases. However, it is more characteristic of the Spanish AD to offer less detailed descriptions using fewer adjectives, as illustrated by the following extracts:

> Below, Clarissa takes some keys from her pocket and unlocks a metal graffiti-sprayed door. She takes an unlit lift to a tiny hallway on the top floor and knocks on an internal door.

> *Clarissa abre una puerta pintada con graffitis. Sube en un destartalado ascensor. Saca una llave y llama antes de abrir.*
> [Clarissa opens a door painted with graffiti. She goes up in a ramshackle lift. She takes out a key and knocks before opening.]

Nevertheless, there are cases where the Spanish AD presents adjectives which do not have formal equivalents in the English AD. This occurs when the English AD uses an adverb to describe the manner in which a character carries out an action, particularly when the manner reflects a mood or emotion, as in 'He turns happily to look at her'. In such cases, the Spanish text often uses an adjective qualifying the person rather than an adverb qualifying the verb: *Le mira satisfecho* [He looks at her, satisfied]; cf. 'He stares at her mournfully': *mira pensativo* [He looks, thoughtful]; 'She stares helplessly': *le contempla compungida* [She contemplates him, sorrowful]. More usually, however, the adverbs in the English text, which are again conspicuous for their abundance and concision, have no formal or functional equivalents in the Spanish AD:

> He goes in through the door and closes it carefully behind him.
> *Entra en el chalet.* [He goes into the chalet.]

> She slips carefully into bed.
> *Se mete en la cama.* [She gets into bed.]

> Lottie, the undermaid, forcefully breaks an egg into a bowl.
> *La otra sirvienta casca huevos.* [The other servant breaks eggs.]

> Richie methodically assembles the toy building blocks.
> *Richie construye una casa con las piezas.* [Richard builds a house with the blocks.]

Virginia's head is tilted to one side as she looks wistfully at her sister.
Not described.

2.3.2 Syntax

In a noticeably high proportion of sentences in the English AD, the report of
an action is accompanied by one or more subordinate clauses whose function
is to describe another action taking place at the same time. This way of expressing simultaneity relies heavily on connecting words such as 'as' or
'while': 'As he starts up the car, she bites her lip'. Alternatively, if the two
actions are carried out by the same person, subordination may be achieved
through the use of the present participle: 'Clarissa, putting ice into a glass,
turns away self-consciously'.

The first type of structure is also frequent in the Spanish AD – although
it rarely links the same two actions as is the case in the English AD – and
commonly involves the conjunction *mientras* or *cuando*:

> *Virginia lee mientras fuma un cigarrillo.* [Virginia reads while she
> smokes a cigarette.]
> *Cuando el marido parte, ella ensombrece su rostro.* [When her husband
> leaves, her face saddens.]

It is also possible to find examples of present participles used to link two
simultaneous actions carried out by the same person, although this is less
common: *Laura camina hacia el coche intentando no llorar* [Laura walks
towards the car, trying not to cry.] More usually, the Spanish AD prefers to
use coordinated sentences to convey consecutive or near-simultaneous actions performed by the same person:

> *Cierra los ojos y apoya su espalda en la puerta.* [She closes her eyes
> and leans her back against the door.]
> *Coge un cigarrillo de liar y lo enciende.* [She takes a roll-up cigarette
> and lights it.]

Occasionally, each action is expressed in a separate sentence with no con-
nective:

> *Leonard mira el suelo. A duras penas puede contener el llanto.* [Leo-
> nard looks at the floor. He can scarcely stop himself from crying.]

In a second type of subordination, highly frequent in the English AD, the function of the subordinate clause or clauses is to convey information regarding some aspect of the character or setting. This type of structure often relies on prepositions and past participles with an adjectival function, as in 'In New York, Sally, loaded down with parcels and dry cleaning, comes into the apartment'. Often, one and the same sentence uses several subordinate clauses both to express simultaneity of action and to convey detail, thereby attaining considerable syntactical complexity: 'Virginia, wearing a floppy brown hat and a grey shapeless cardigan over her dress, sits down on a bench, her shoulders hunched as people mill past her'.

Again, although the Spanish AD presents a limited amount of subordination to describe detail, the marked preference is for a more linear style, achieved through coordinated structures and/or the use of independent sentences expressing only one or two ideas each. For instance, the Spanish description corresponding to the extract quoted immediately above is as follows: *Se sienta en un banco. Habla sola mientras la gente pasa a su alrededor.* [She sits on a bench. She talks to herself as the people pass around her.]

2.3.3 Pragmatic coherence

Turning to larger stretches of discourse, it is arguable that the relative abundance of detail offered in the English text enables the receiver to perceive thematic connections which would be lost on the receivers of the Spanish AD. One such example is the food which Clarissa has prepared for the party she intends to give for her friend Richard, a writer who is dying of AIDS. The main course is an elaborate crab dish, which is mentioned in the screenplay as one of Richard's favourite dishes, and it is implied that he and Clarissa used to eat it in their student days. Early in the film we are shown Clarissa's kitchen sink writhing with live crabs (an image which is described in the English AD but omitted in the Spanish) and later, seeing that Richard is highly reluctant to attend the party, Clarissa resignedly tells him: 'Just to let you know that I am making the crab thing. Not that I suppose it makes any difference to you' to which Richard replies: 'Of course it makes a difference. I love the crab thing!'

In the event, Richard kills himself and the party is cancelled. Later that evening, as Clarissa and her daughter are glumly clearing up in the kitchen, the camera lingers on the crab dish before Clarissa picks it up and tips into the rubbish bag. The association between Richard's death and Clarissa's disposal of his favourite dish is suggested to the receiver of the English AD through specific mention of the food: 'Clarissa stares at the crab dish...and pours the contents into a black rubbish bag'. By contrast, the Spanish AD does not specify the food involved, and it seems unlikely that the receiver would perceive any special meaning in the sequence: *Clarissa coge un gran recipiente lleno de comida y tira su contenido a la basura.* [Clarissa takes a large dish full of food and throws its contents into the rubbish.]

On another occasion, the English AD is able to underscore a further parallel through the use of an unusual compound adjective, as described in section 2.3.1.2, specifically the adjective 'mushroom-coloured'. This rather striking description refers to the car in which Laura drives her small boy, Richie, to spend the afternoon with a neighbour, very much against his will. Moreover, the boy seems to sense his mother's turbulent emotional state; at the time of dropping Richie off at the neighbour's her intention is to drive to a hotel and book a room in which to kill herself. Once left at the neighbour's, Richie begins to play with a toy house and car which resembles that of his mother's, and this scene is mixed with images of his mother recklessly driving her real car towards the hotel. By means of the detailed description and particularly the use of the memorable adjective 'mushroom-coloured', the English AD succeeds in conveying this association: 'As she manoeuvres the mushroom-coloured Dodge, Richie pushes a toy, a mushroom-coloured car with white-wall tyres, past the house he has built'. This undoubtedly adds dramatic tension to the sequence, particularly as Richie later crushes the house he has constructed. However, the Spanish AD makes no mention of the toy car at all, and offers only a general description by which it would be difficult to appreciate any intended parallel: *Mientras Laura recorre las calles a gran velocidad, Richie construye una casa con las piezas.* [While Laura drives through the streets at high speed, Richie builds a house with the blocks.]

3. Implications for translation

We hope to have shown that the English and Spanish ADs of *The Hours* differ quite substantially with regard to both content and style. In the following section we shall consider some of the implications of these differences from the point of view of translating ADs from English into Spanish. These may be broadly divided into questions of linguistic transfer and wider considerations concerning convention and receiver expectation surrounding this type of text.

3.1 Linguistic transfer

It has been asserted by authors like Herman (1993:10) that English has more words than any other language. It is also noted for concise expression (Congost Maestre 1994:97), particularly in comparison with Spanish, which is why Spanish translations of English texts are generally longer than the origi-nals. Although these considerations are relevant for all types of Eng-lish/Spanish translation, they are particularly so for this type of text, in which the writer of the English AD has fully exploited both the lexical resources and the concision of the language. Given the constraints of time and space particular to ADs, it is apparent that this would pose difficulties for the trans-lator who would want to offer a comparable amount of information in a Spanish target text.

With respect to the abundant use of semantically complex monosyllabic verbs, for instance, it would not be easy to convey all the connotative infor-mation encoded in verbs such as 'peer', 'snatch' or 'scoop', owing to the relative scarcity of such verbs in Spanish, while the option of using a more general verb with a descriptive phrase may exceed the available amount of space. This consideration also applies to the frequent use of compound ad-jectives such as 'mushroom-coloured' or 'graffiti-sprayed', which would inevitably require longer formulations in Spanish. With regard to the high proportion of adverbs, the difficulty may seem less acute: although there does seem to be a comparative restriction in written Spanish on the use of adverbs (Congost Maestre 1994:55), the preference noted above (1.3.1.2) for using an adjective to describe the character rather than an adverb to describe the action may be exploited by the translator, without affecting the length of the description. However, the same cannot be said for another frequent alter-native to adverbs in Spanish written texts, i.e. the use of a descriptive phrase with an adverbial function, as in *de forma local* for 'locally'.[6] In this case, the longer formulation of the Spanish construction would limit its applicabil-ity when translating ADs.

On the basis of these considerations, it seems likely that a Spanish AD translated from English would present some loss of information with respect to the original text. As noted above, this phenomenon is by no means re-stricted to this type of text: according to Hervey *et al.* (1995), some loss of information is inevitable in *all* types of translation, while marked constraints in time and space are also characteristic of other modalities of translation such as dubbing, subtitling and simultaneous interpreting. However, even if it were possible to offer a similar quantity of detail in the Spanish AD, the question arises of how far this would be desirable, in view of the different conventions with regard to ADs which seem to prevail in the UK and Spain.

3.2 Convention and receiver expectations

Our contrastive analysis of the two ADs has highlighted certain aspects of content and style in the Spanish text, such as its relative scarcity of detail, the use of a comparatively familiar vocabulary and the preference for short coordinated sentences over longer subordinated ones. Insofar as these characteristics are representative of Spanish ADs in general, it may be felt that receivers of ADs in Spain have become accustomed to them and that a translated AD manifesting opposing characteristics, such as abundance of detail, elevated register and complex syntax, would defraud the expectations of target receivers with respect to this type of text.

A further consideration is that ADs in Spain are now subject to specific quality standards established by the *Asociación Española de Normalización y Certificación* (AENOR). These have developed from a tradition of approximately ten years of writing ADs in Spain and reflect a specifically Spanish approach, which could perhaps conflict with the UK tradition. With regard to style, for instance, the first part of the Spanish standard (section E) stipulates that this should be "fluent, simple, with sentences containing no subordinated clauses".[7] The translator undertaking the translation of an English AD into Spanish would thus need to take this legal dimension into account in addition to the question of target receiver preferences.

Again, it is important to stress that the extra-linguistic constraints envisaged here are by no means exclusive to translating ADs. Adapting a translated text to receiver expectations in terms of appropriate vocabulary and sentence structure forms part of the process of translating many types of text from English into Spanish, such as medical leaflets, tourist guides or academic and scientific articles. Similarly, the content and style of several types of translated documents are subject to different legal requirements in the source and target language community, as occurs for example with contracts and patents.

However, it should also be observed that while the AENOR standards are held to reflect user preferences regarding the offer of information and style of ADs, these preferences do not seem to have been demonstrated in any published study. Thus while fully accepting the possibility that the offer of information in the English AD may prove to be excessive to receivers of a translated version in Spanish, it seems equally possible that some receivers would actually welcome the abundance of detail which, as we hope to have shown with regard to certain symbolic elements in *The Hours*, may facilitate a deeper understanding and appreciation of the film. In this sense, it may even be argued that restricting the amount of detail offered to the receiver can have the effect of limiting accessibility to the artistic product.

4. Concluding remarks

It seems fair to conclude that the translation of ADs from English into Spanish is worthy of further exploration, both for the financial advantages it would offer over the present practice of creating ADs from scratch in the two languages, and with a view to enabling Spanish receivers to experience a markedly different type of AD. As with other types of translation, there would undoubtedly be some loss of information with regard to the original, and the translator would need to modify certain aspects of the lexicon and syntax to conform with the conventions of written expression in Spanish in general and with the specific conventions and target receiver expectations regarding this type of text. In this respect, however, there is a clear need for clarification based on empirical research, for in the absence of published studies it is difficult to ascertain the extent to which the conventions of AD in Spain are based on the actual preferences of receivers. An appropriate starting point might be a pilot study in which Spanish receivers were asked to evaluate an AD translated from English and to compare it with the Spanish AD of the same film. Although it is probable that the results of such a study would reflect a variety of opinions and preferences, this in itself might underscore the need for a greater diversity of AD styles, and thus enhance accessibility for different sectors of the blind and partially sighted community in Spain.

---

[1] AD is generally thought to have originated at the Arena Stage Theatre in Washington DC in 1981, as a result of work by Margaret and Cody Pfanstiehl (Independent Television Commission 2000: 4).

[2] AD, however, may also be of interest to sighted people, as demonstrated by McKivragan (1995).

[3] According to the Independent Television Commission (ITC) guidelines (2000: 12) it may take up to 60 hours to prepare the AD script for a two-hour film. The AD script for a film in English may contain around 6,000 words. If we accept that professional translators habitually translate at least 2,000 words in a working day, translating the AD script would take around 24 hours, i.e. one third of the time.

[4] *The Hours* (2003) was presented by Paramount Pictures and Miramax Films. A Scott Rudin/Robin Fox Production, starring Meryl Streep, Julianne Moore and Nicole Kidman, directed by Stephen Daldry. The English AD is credited to IMS, with studio production at Aquarium. The Spanish AD was written by José Luís Chavarría, co-ordinated by Javier Navarrete and produced at Aristia studios.

[5] Snyder remarks: 'Why say "walk" when you can more vividly describe the action with "sashay", "stroll", "skip", "stumble" or "saunter"?

[6] Example taken from Congost Maestre (1994: 56).

[7] *'El estilo de escritura del guión debe ser fluido, sencillo, con frases de construcción directa.'*

References

Asociación Española de Normalización y Certificación (AENOR). 2005. *Audiodescripción para personas con discapacidad visual. Requisitos para la audiodescripción y la elaboración de audioguías.* UNE 153020.

Congost Maestre, Nereida. 1994. *Problemas de la traducción técnica: los
textos médicos en inglés.* Alicante: University of Alicante.

Cunningham, Michael. 1998. *The Hours.* New York: Farra, Strauss and
Giroux.

Faber Benítez, Pamela and Catalina Jiménez Hurtado. 2004. *Traducción,
lenguaje y cognición.* Granada: Comares.

Halliday, M.A.K. and Ruqaiya Hasan. 1976. *Cohesion in English.* London:
Longman.

Herman, Mark. 1993. "Technical translation style", in Sue Ellen Wright and
Leland D. Wright (eds) *American Translators' Association Scholarly
Monograph Series* 6. Amsterdam and Philadelphia: John Benjamins, 11-
20.

Hervey, Sándor, Ian Higgins and Louise M. Haywood. 1995. *Thinking Spanish Translation.* London: Routledge.

Independent Television Commission. 2000. *ITC Guidance on Standards for
Audio Description.* London: ITC Monograph.

McKivragan, Gavin. 1995. *Audetel: Potential among the general population.*
London: BBC Broadcasting Research.

Poethe, Hannelore 2005. "Audiodeskription - Entstehung und Wesen einer
Textsorte", in Ulla Fix (ed.) *Hörfilm. Bildkompensation durch Sprache.
Linguistisch-filmisch-semiotische Untersuchungen zur Leistung der Audiodeskription in Hörfilmen am Beispiel des Films* Laura, mein Engel *aus
der* Tatort-*Reihe.* Berlin: Erich Schmidt Verlag, 33-48.

Salway, Andrew, Andrew Vassilou and Eleftheria Tomadaki. 2005. *Analysing Collateral Text Corpora: Excerpts of Results.* Guildford: University
of Surrey. Manuscript.

Snyder, Joel. 2004. "Audio description: the visual made verbal". Paper presented at the conference *In So Many Words: Language Transfer on the
Screen.* London, 5-7 February.

Woolf, Virginia. 1925. *Mrs. Dalloway.* London: Hogarth Press.

Intersensorial translation: visual art made up by words[1]

Karin De Coster

Vrije Universiteit Brussel, Belgium

Volkmar Mühleis

Institute of Fine Arts Sint-Lucas in Ghent, Belgium

Abstract
With this article we would like to offer a contribution to the development of and reflection on the verbal description of works of art. Verbal description or audio description is a means of translating the visual impression of an object into words. In this paper, we emphasize the complexity of this type of translation. We do this by describing the importance of concepts such as visual intensity and the narrative of the work of art. We also make a distinction between clear signs and ambivalent signs as possible features of a particular work of art. Finally, we concretize these reflections with four practical examples. The first two examples are descriptions of paintings, one by René Magritte and another by Rik Wouters. In the latter, visual intensity is higher than in the painting by Margitte. We conclude with two examples of descriptions of sculptures, one by Auguste Rodin and one by Eugène Dodeigne. It is useful to describe sculptures while exploring the object by touch. The tactile dimension of the experience will have consequences for the practice of describing. A good description will then take these tactile sensations into account and will try to establish an intersensorial translation of the art object.

1. The accessibility of works of art

1.1 Changing attitudes

Accessibility is becoming an important issue in museum policy today. This increased attention to the needs of people with disabilities has been prompted by legislative initiatives. In Belgium, the first legal steps are being taken in the direction of increased accessibility in the arts. Its anti-discrimination law was put on the statute books in 2003. It is a general law that states that every organization or institution should make 'reasonable adjustments' for disabled people. Museums and more specifically art museums are therefore implicitly included in this provision.

However, even if – legally – the situation of people with disabilities is improving relatively slowly in Belgium, in museum practice there is already a long history of services for blind visitors. In Brussels, for example, the Museum for the Blind came into existence in 1975. The museum was – and still is – part of the Royal Museum of Art and History. It organizes temporary exhibitions for visitors who are blind.

From around the same time and on an international level, 'the museum' as a particular institution with a specific discourse, has also been devoting much more attention to the needs of the disabled. Several journals such as *The Museum Journal* and *Museum News* started publishing various articles on the subject (Moore 1968; Rowland 1973; Calhoun 1974; Callo 1974; Watkins 1975; Heath 1976; Molloy 1977). These publications make visually impaired visitors one of the new challenges for the educational role of such institutions.

All the same, and in spite of these legal advances as well as the changing attitudes towards visitors with impairments in museums generally,[2] blind visitors in art museums remain a special case. Art is created in a visual world and always has that link with the visual character of society, whether it functions as a criticism, or symbolically. The paradoxical nature of non-sighted audiences in a highly visual institution is hard to ignore. Sociologist Hetherington stresses this problematic nature of visual impairment and the museum as a visual institution. The museum is a space of seeing. The visually impaired visitor introduces ambivalence into an otherwise ordered and known arrangement such as a museum institution. For him, "the visually impaired are *the not* within the museum [...] The reason I suggest that the visually impaired are such figures within the space of the museum is because the museum has principally been constituted as a space of seeing [...] to be without sight in such a space is to present a problem" (Hetherington 2000:446-447).

Why, indeed, should blind people be confronted with art and visit art museums? In everyday life, visual impairments and visual symbols meet on a daily basis. Blind people are used to visual concepts since their lives are filled with them. Some have seen before, others still see a minimum and even people who have never seen realize that vision is very important in the world they live in. For the same reason they are curious about art, as a visual symbol in society, as an essential aspect of life, as a source of information and as a type of experience. In fact, blind people and people who have a severe visual handicap are already visiting art museums, and have done so for some time. Thus, the question becomes: How can we ensure that their efforts are rewarded?

1.2 Accessibility and the role of language

Increasingly more museums in Belgium organize handling sessions for visitors with visual handicaps during which selections of art collections can be touched. These initiatives are very successful since they provide people without vision with a direct contact with the works of art. However, only a minimal proportion of art is 'touchable'. Conservation rules, size, and art form determine the tactility of works of art. Rendering culture and art accessible to all, therefore means including all works of art, even if they are purely visual. In other words, it is crucial to elaborate these first initiatives, the handling sessions, and find ways to open them up to two-dimensional works of art or objects of art that one is not allowed to touch.

The crucial element in enabling blind people to interact with two-dimensional works of art is language, since it is through verbal description that one can try to translate the visual sensation of works of art that museum visitors cannot touch. However, such an intersensorial translation process is a highly complex matter. A satisfying translation of a visual work of art has to take into account the visual intensity of the work under discussion, as well as the role visually rendered information plays in the narrative the work of art may be telling.

In order to tackle the complexity of this particular branch of verbal description, we will first distinguish 'clear signs' from 'ambivalent signs' in works of art and then discuss the importance of this distinction for an effective description. We will make use of paintings by two Belgian artists, René Magritte (1898-1967) and Rik Wouters (1882-1916), to elaborate these concepts. The paintings that we propose to use are: *The Region of Arnheim* by Magritte and *Lady in Blue in Front of the Mirror* by Wouters (see Illustrations).[3]

Secondly, we would like to share some thoughts on the description of three-dimensional art that actually can be handled by visitors, because a tactile exploration too should be accompanied by visual orientation or translation. This type of verbal translation differs from the translation of a painting, since tactile sensations are equally at play here and need some visual guidance. In short, audio description in this case no longer functions as a translation from a visual image into language, but becomes a form of interplay between the visual image and the tactile sensation that needs to be put into words. An example of a work by Auguste Rodin (*One of the Burghers of Calais – Jean D'Aire*) and one by Eugène Dodeigne (*Hand on the Thigh*) will demonstrate this.[4] The examples used are based on the authors' experiences with groups of blind visitors in the Royal Museums of Fine Arts in Brussels.[5]

It is worth mentioning here that, besides the use of language in audio description, the technique of raised line drawing is another method for rendering two-dimensional art accessible. What this technique amounts to is that a painting is translated tactually into a simplified drawing that can be handled by the visually impaired visitor. The technique is quite well-known, especially in the United Kingdom[6] and the United States[7] (Salzhauer & Levent 2003) but is relatively new in Belgium. There are also specific problems related to this technique. For example, it takes some training on the part of the users to learn to 'read' these type of drawing, and many blind people find them very difficult to use. In other words, even though the technique can be extremely helpful to give visitors an idea of the composition of the work of art or of its general structure, in many cases it is simply easier, cheaper and more effective to describe. The major advantage of description is its interactive nature. Through direct contact with a museum guide there is always the possibility to ask questions and to correct. In this paper, we will therefore limit ourselves to audio description, leaving other, possibly rewarding, techniques to one side.

2. Visual intensity and the work of art

In our contacts with art we take the visual for granted. It is always there. A work of art is created using sight and it is evaluated using visual phenomena. Indeed, it is only in confrontations with blind people that we stop and think about this matter. Practice has taught that verbal descriptions for blind people should always start from questioning the visual intensity of the works of art under discussion, besides their narratives, if these are to be found at all. This visual intensity is defined by the sensual characters of the objects, while the narratives cover all aspects which can possibly be translated into words. It is clear that visual intensity will vary a great deal, depending on the art objects themselves and the contexts in which they were created. Conceptual works of art, like the standardized *Brillo Boxes* created by the pop artist Andy Warhol require an approach which differs from, for example, the sensual paintings created by the impressionist Claude Monet.

The question is: how do we approach this intersensorial translation, given the wide spectrum of visual intensity and narratives. Every work of art deals with signs. Generally speaking, two kinds of signs occur: on the one hand, there are signs that can directly be identified, that give clear pieces of information, and on the other hand, there are signs that are ambivalent, that communicate different levels of meaning. Clear signs are perfectly translatable into words. As for the meanings of ambivalent signs, these can also be put into words, but not always without difficulty, especially if the visual effects cannot be represented through others fields of sensual imagination (such as touch or hearing). A picture puzzle that evokes two different images with one structure, for example, the classic picture of a head that might be that of a duck as well as a rabbit (Gombrich 1959:4) is a purely visual phenomenon with strong intensity. As long as a picture can be translated into another sensual representation (a relief that can be touched, etc.), it is not purely visual. However, a phenomenon like the picture puzzle that misses any analogy with touch or hearing is not translatable sensually (Mühleis 2005:242-244). So this constitutes the limit of intersensorial comparison: when an analogy with other senses proves to be impossible, one can still give an idea of the different meanings of the ambivalent sign (the narrative), but not a representation of how it works sensually (i.e. its intensity). This is because in order to really imagine the sensual effect of ambiguity one cannot just combine the different aspects of the object and achieve a mental representation of the ambivalent impression of the whole. In order to experience this impression, one has to 'begin' with the whole object as the carrier of ambiguity (as is the case with the picture puzzle and the common structure of the duck/rabbit head). This distinction between translatable and untranslatable visual impressions can be found in the following guideline: every sign or meaning of an object of art that can be clearly identified can be translated into words, but one can give an idea of visual ambiguity only if a comparable ambiguity exists in another sensorial field (touch, hearing).

3. Describing paintings

3.1 René Magritte's *The Region of Arnheim* (1962)

In order to establish a mental image of a painting it is helpful to realize that the blind visitor begins with a completely blank working basis. Imagine, for example, that the describer and the blind person are standing in front of *The Region of Arnheim*, a painting by René Magritte. It is a huge picture, 146 cm high and 114 cm wide. First, the describer must give information about these dimensions. He or she offers their hand to the visitor to allow him/her to get a sense of the height of the painting. Then, the describer uses both hands, grasping those of the visitor to signal the painting's width. This tactile introduction gives the visitors their working bases. After this, the description proper follows. We have found that the following two-step approach works well. First, establish a geometrical structure as a frame of reference, and then refer back to this structure later on in the description, i.e. describe the painting in relation to it. Next, proceed to describe the signs that are clear or relatively unambiguous before tackling the ambivalent signs, if this is possible given the picture chosen.

Magritte's painting (see Illustrations) is based on a extremely clear geometrical shape: at the bottom of the picture – not much higher than 20 cm up from the frame – a small and perfectly horizontal wall of stones is shown. On this wall, exactly in the middle of it, there is a nest containing three eggs. If you imagine a vertical line in the middle of the picture and move upwards along it from the nest, then on this very line, in the distance, where mountains are represented, one sees the head of a bird, which actually is part of the mountain chain. Above its head, in the sky, the moon hangs as a half-round form, like a half-round shape one could make with one's right hand.

Starting from there, the spatial impression of the picture can be described: it seems as if we are standing in front of the wall and that behind the wall there is a steep cliff, and that far away there is this mountain ridge, partly covered with snow. In the middle of this ridge – as a part of it – is the aforementioned mysterious head of a bird. The whole atmosphere is cold. The wall and the mountains are of stone. We see snow and the colours are also cold: grey, white and blue. These are all clear signs. The tricky thing now is the head of the bird. From this point on, the whole ambiguity of the picture can be tackled. What kind of bird could it be? Experience has shown that most of the sighted visitors think of an eagle or a falcon, or a comparable bird – they simply combine the information they have been given: mountain and bird, what kind of bird lives in the mountains? Very often they even think, narrowing down the possibilities: okay, it is an eagle... But if they had looked more carefully, they would have recognized that the bird is in fact a pigeon. That shows that the way we see is often simply a combining of cues (mountain plus bird equals...), and then we go on to think that we have seen what we thought should be there. But in so doing, we have not really 'seen' what is there, we have merely followed our 'idea' of it, believing we have actually seen this idea. By creating this illusion Magritte offers us a special reflection about thinking and seeing.

Having pointed this out, the translator can then proceed to the other paradoxical aspects of the picture, the absurd title, the impression of the stone bird in the ridge with its open wings and its relation to the nest on the wall (Is the bird protecting the nest? But it is of stone, so it cannot return to the nest?). The description ends on the whole surrealistic impact of the picture.

3.2 Rik Wouter's *Lady in Blue in Front of the Mirror* (1914)

Much more difficult is the description of a painting that focuses clearly on visual intensity itself, for example, the picture *Lady in Blue in Front of the Mirror* (see Illustrations) by Rik Wouters. The spatial order can be described by the positions of the objects and the lady in the room. The narrative produced by the clear signs is also translatable: the lady, looking into the mirror, the flowers in the vase, the picture on the left-hand side, a sort of a jug below it. The whole scenery is a calm, intimate everyday moment. The problem for the description is the following: these are not the main elements of the picture. The painting is a visual reflection of the 'ambiguous' character of colours and lines. This representation is not about an 'idea' of reality, like Magritte's painting, it is about the reality of the 'visual impression'. So even for sighted viewers a lot of visual information is not clearly interpretable. It seems that in front of the mirror there is a vessel completely made of glass that is reflected in the mirror, but visually this is simply suggested, not confirmed. And like this, most of the objects are only suggestions of themselves: the picture on the left-hand side, the jug below it, the cupboard to the right of the lady, etc. So the translator needs to talk about the ambiguity in the sensual representation of the given scenery. The vivid colours and lines do not serve to convey clear cognitive information, but communicate their own ambiguity, which results in a beautiful impression for the sighted viewers, a joyful game with the viewer's sense of sight. Here, maybe the analogy with instrumental music can be of help: how, much like chords, the strokes establish an intimate, calm atmosphere that remains vague and offers only suggestions of the objects in the room, the person in it, the room itself. The jug, for example, has been drawn with only three, four lines, it seems to be a sketch of a jug, reminiscent of how only one or two cues can remind us of a person, like, "Ah, you mean the one with the big nose!". Seeing and thinking is based on combining aspects, and Wouters plays with this in the field of sight. So visually, the narrative side of the picture (geometrical order, clear signs) is less strong. It is much more based on the feature of visual intensity. This intensity can be rendered verbally by giving comparable examples of ambiguity in touch or hearing, and also by simply explaining the difficulty – and therefore the pleasure – the painting presents even for sighted viewers.

In the end, the mental image blind visitors construct of this painting will be less strong than the one they get from the description of the Magritte painting, but they will have an idea of the spectrum that that painting in general can offer.

4. Three-dimensional art: touch and sight

For describing sculptures or other works or art that visitors are allowed to touch, the approach is somewhat different as a result of this added tactile dimension. Starting with the characteristics of the work of art itself, our first question regards its tactile dimension and the role of this tactility in its narrative. Are tactile sensations of a particular work of art relevant to the narrative of the work of art? Or should they, in some way, be translated into the relevant visual sensations of the same work of art in order to tell the object's story? Before answering these questions we will have a look at some theories about art and touch.

Several philosophers have studied the relationships between the senses and art, and – more specifically – have reflected on the relationship between touch and art. A contemporary author with a great interest in the relationship between art and the senses is Robert Hopkins (2004). For Hopkins, painting is clearly a specifically visual art. The visual status of painting resides in its having to be seen in order to exist. Sculptures, like paintings, exploit vision since they are usually appreciated by looking at them. Unlike paintings, however, they can also exploit touch since they can equally be appreciated through tactile exploration. Hopkins's conclusion (2004:166) is that sculpture is not linked to either vision or touch in the way that painting is linked to vision:

> Sculpture emerges as an art which manages to connect with a super- sensory aspect of experience. In one way this experience is visual; we see the space around the sculpture, and in another way it is kinetic since it is about our possibilities for movement and action. Sculpture is neither visual, nor tactile but a complex mixture of the sensory, as standardly conceived, our awareness of our own bodies, and their possible interactions with the world.

Hopkins's contemporary interest in the relationship between art and the senses should be seen in the light of a very long history of attention devoted to this topic. Johann Gottfried Herder, for example, already discussed the relation of art and touch in the eighteenth century and has been followed by many others in art history, such as Diderot, Alois Riegl, Herbert Read, etc. For this paper it suffices to point out that sculpture has tactile dimensions besides visual ones. Therefore, it is highly recommended that museum guides who are to provide a description have also experienced the tactile sensations of the work to be discussed. This experience will help them find vocabulary related to the tactile to describe the work and will therefore improve the mutual understanding of guides and visitors.

5. Describing sculptures

The description of sculptures has specific requirements that guides must take into account, especially in the case of objects that can be handled. Indeed, the blind visitor receives important tactile information about the object, while the museum guide helps this tactile exploration by providing visual orientation. The aim is again a jointly constructed mental image of the original object. Thus, the audio description becomes an intense interactive experience in which the museum guide's words will be the ultimate link between the tactile sensations and the visual narrative of the work of art.

Since three-dimensional works of art have tactile and visual dimensions, an attempt at describing a three-dimensional object should start with some reflection on these dimensions. What is the nature of this particular object's narrative, for instance? What kind of story does it tell? What is the role of the visual impressions in relation to the tactile dimensions? The comparison between two different sculptures below will help to make this distinction clear. In all cases, as was the case with the description of paintings, it is useful to start with a minimal orientation session, indicating the size and the overall subject of the work.

5.1 Auguste Rodin's *One of The Burghers of Calais – Jean D'Aire* (1886)

This sculpture by Auguste Rodin (see Illustrations) is a taller-than-life portrait of Jean D'Aire, one of the Burghers of Calais. It represents a tall man standing up straight with a huge key in his hands. What makes this bronze sculpture interesting in the light of our endeavours is its tension between the tangible deep lines and its expressive visual appearance.

A tactile exploration of the sculpture soon confirms the crucial elements of its narrative: a tall man, with a thick rope around his neck and a giant key in his hands. A more detailed touch guides the attention towards some deep lines that need further verbal guidance. For example, a tactile sensation of the eyes reveals that the eyes are deeply hidden in the head, the head itself feels like a skull, the lines of the cheeks are so strong that one has the idea of touching a skull. The mouth is one deep horizontal line. All these sensations should be further placed within the visual narrative of the object. Especially characteristic is the determined stressful expression on the man's face, his empty gaze. A visual glance of the man conveys this impression of despair and determination straight away. A tactile exploration is a much slower process, every single tactile element being successively used to build a coherent image. It is the task of the museum guide to follow this slow tactile process and to provide the visual impressions on the basis of which each tactile element that is brought up is given its place in the whole: the lines around the mouth, the cheek, the eyes, etc.

5.2 Eugène Dodeigne's *Hand on the Thigh* (1965)

Next, we would like to offer some thoughts on a meaningful description of a work by the Belgian sculptor Eugène Dodeigne, *Hand on the Thigh* (see Illustrations). It will contribute to further clarifying what we mean by the visual and tactile dimensions of a work of art and how these dimensions influence the description of this particular piece. The main difference with Rodin's work, in as far as description is concerned, is the amount of tactility in Dodeigne's work. *Hand on the Thigh* seems to be almost made for touch. The only thing you see is a kind of ghost-like figure, a little smaller than human size. You can tell it is a figure by the deep holes which one can presume to be the eyes. However, there is little to visually distinguish besides that, whereas a tactile experience will directly move the attention to the stone. The actual figure is inferior to the power of the stone. Consequently, except for the two holes that are presumed to be the eyes, there are no tactile details or elements in the stone that need further verbal guidance. The main story that must be told here is that of the stone itself. The material determines the form, whereas in Rodin's work the material serves the figure of the man. Or, as we would like to put it, the tactile dimension is greater in the narrative of *Hand on the Thigh* than it is in the narrative of *Jean D'Aire*. The stone and its power are the essence of this particular work.

Each work of art that can be touched hides tactile and visual information. It is the museum guide's job to translate 'meaningful' tactile elements into visual information. A thorough reflection on the amount of visual and tactile elements in the narrative of the work of art must precede the actual description. An efficient description then starts with the size of the object and its general subject before the tactile exploration takes place. During the tactile exploration the visitor(s) will have various impressions. It is the guide's task to use these tactile impressions and, if possible, incorporate them into his/her talk about the work. This talk thus becomes an intersensorial reconstruction of the original work of art.

6. Conclusion

When describing a work of art that relies (mainly) on visual perception, it is useful to reflect on the following questions:

1. What can be translated into words? The dimensions, the spatial structure, the narrative of clear signs and the 'meanings' of ambivalent signs.

2. Which visual impression can be compared with an experience of touch or hearing? The intersensorial dimension of the description. In the case of touching a sculpture this also means: what is perfectly perceivable with the hands, the body and what is not?

3. Which of these visual impressions 'cannot' be compared? For instance, the effects of a mirror, the sparkle of light on water, a puzzling picture, etc. In this last case, the guide can talk with the blind visitors about their visual imagination, what is still concrete to them and what is not?

In short, words can give a great deal of information but if visitors are to have a vivid mental image of the work of art, it is necessary for the guide to explore the field of intersensorial possibilities. Besides, in so doing, the sighted guides too will discover qualities in sculptures and paintings that they had never identified before.

¹ This article is the outcome of theoretical reflection in response to several practical initiatives implemented in the Museum of Fine Arts in Brussels.
² In recent years, museums in Belgium have been taking their educational role more seriously. In addition, museums are paying more and more attention to visitors with visual impairments. The *Diamantmuseum* in Antwerp has a new project for visual impaired people, as have the Antwerp Fashion Museum and the Museums of Fine Arts in Brussels and Antwerp. These are just a few examples.
³ Both paintings are part of the collection of the Royal Museums of Fine Arts in Brussels. *The Region of Arnheim* was made in 1962 and it measures 146 x 114 cm. *Lady in Blue in Front of the Mirror* dates from 1914 and measures 123 x 125 cm. In both cases the technique that was used is oil on canvas.
⁴ These two sculptures are also part of the collection of the Royal Museums of Fine Arts in Brussels. The bronze sculpture *Jean D'Aire* dates from the period of 1886-1890. It measures 204.5 x 71.5 x 66.5 cm. *Hand on the Thigh* was made in *soignies* stone in 1965 and it measures 139 x 72 x 72.5 cm.
⁵ The visits are part of a pilot study organized by the *Ligue Braille*, a non-profit organization for the benefit of blind and visually impaired people. The aim of this pilot study is to reflect on the accessibility of visual culture for people who are blind or visually impaired. The group consists of legally blind people. Legally, blind individuals can be defined as best-corrected vision of 20/200 or less in the better eye or a visual field of twenty degrees or less in the widest meridian. A person who is classified as legally blind can therefore still have usable vision.
⁶ For example Tate Modern launched a project in 2002, entitled i-Map. It was an interactive project, using raised line technology to make the work of Picasso accessible for visually impaired people. It was awarded an Interactive BAFTA Award for Accessibility.
⁷ The American organization Art Education for the Blind has an excellent reputation in producing and supporting raised line technology in art (www.artbeyondsight.org).

References

Calhoun, Sallie N. 1974. "On the edge of vision". *Museum News* 52(7): 36-40.

Callow, Kathy B. 1974. "Museums and the disabled". *The Museum Journal* 74(2): 70-72.

Danto, Arthur C. 1986. *The Philosophical Disenfranchisement of Art.* New York: Colombia University Press.

—. 1997. *After the End of Art: Contemporary Art and the Pale of History.* New Jersey: Princeton.

Gombrich, Ernst H. 1959. *Art & Illusion. A Study in the Psychology of Pictorial Representation.* London: Phaidon.

Heath, Alison. 1976. "The same only more so: museums and the handicapped visitor". *The Museum Journal* 76(2): 56-58.

Hetherington, Kevin. 2000. "Museums and the visually impaired: the spatial politics of access". *The Sociological Review* 48(3): 444-463.

Hopkins, Robert. 2004. "Painting, sculpture, sight and touch". *British Journal of Aesthetics* 44(2): 149-166.

Molloy, Larry. 1977. "The case for accessibility". *Museum News* 55(3): 15-17.

Moore, George. 1968. "Displays for the sightless". *The Museum Journal* 68(4): 154-155.

Mühleis, Volker. 2005. *Kunst im Sehverlust*. Munich: Fink.

Norton, Robert E. 1991. *Herder's Aesthetics and the European Enlightenment*. London: Cornell University Press.

Rowland, William. 1973. "Museums and the blind. It feels like a flower. Some examples of existing facilities for the blind". *ICOM News* 26(3): 117-121.

Salzhauer, Elisabeth and Nina Levent. 2003. *Art beyond Sight: A Resource Guide to Art, Creativity and Visual Impairment*. New York: AFB Press.

Watkins, Malcolm J. 1975. "A small handling table for blind visitors." *The Museum Journal* 75(1): 29-30.

René Margritte

© René Magritte
Le Domaine d'Arnheim/The Region of Arnheim, 1962
c/o Beeldrecht Amsterdam;
foto: Koninklijke Musea voor Schone Kunsten van België, Brussel;
fotografie: Ro Scan, J. Geleyns.

Rik Wouters

© Rik Wouters
Dame en bleu devant une glace/Lady in Blue in Front of the Mirror, 1914
foto: Koninklijke Musea voor Schone Kunsten van België, Brussel;
fotografie: Ro Scan, J. Geleyns.

Auguste Rodin

© Auguste Rodin
Un des bourgeois de Calais : Jean d'Aire/Jean D'Aire, 1886-1890
foto: Koninklijke Musea voor Schone Kunsten van België, Brussel;
fotografie: Speltdoorn.

Eugène Dodeigne

© Eugène Dodeigne
Main sur la cuisse/Hand on the Thigh, 1965
c/o Beeldrecht Amsterdam;
foto: Koninklijke Musea voor Schone Kunsten van België, Brussel;
fotografie: Ludion.

Accessible opera in Catalan: opera for all

Anna Matamala

Universitat Autònoma de Barcelona, Spain

Pilar Orero

Universitat Autònoma de Barcelona, Spain

Abstract
Media accessibility is beginning to have some presence in the world of leisure. Through legislation some countries such as the UK and the USA have made accessibility compulsory on TV and in cultural and artistic life. Other countries are following suit with the slow implementation of accessibility which has an eclectic presence. This is the case of one of the supposedly least popular music performances: opera. This article looks at the different schemes and tests which have taken place at the Catalan Opera House, the *Gran Teatre del Liceu*, to make opera accessible for all.

1. Introduction

In 1994, a large fire destroyed the *Gran Teatre del Liceu* in Barcelona. The subsequent reconstruction work and design of the new building focused mainly on technology. Five years later, in 1999, it opened showcasing some state-of-the-art developments such as the engineering program *Katia* and the subtitling system *Figaro*, which allows every seat in the theatre to follow the libretto in Catalan, English or Spanish.

However, the *Liceu* was rebuilt following the old seating arrangement and thus, as was the case in the original *Liceu*, there are some seats with little or no stage visibility. To compensate for the lack of vision, these seats were fitted with Thin Film Transistor (TFT) screens in order to provide a full view of the stage plus the subtitles.

The new hi-tech *Liceu*, plus the determined attitude of the *Liceu* management to make opera accessible to a wider audience, has placed Catalan Opera at the forefront of a new approach to opera and its reception. This article looks at the different schemes adopted by the *Liceu* to make the Catalan Opera House an accessible theatre for children, students, those on a tight budget, and the physically and sensorially handicapped. Special emphasis will be placed on audio description (AD), since different alternatives are proposed taking into account audience feedback.

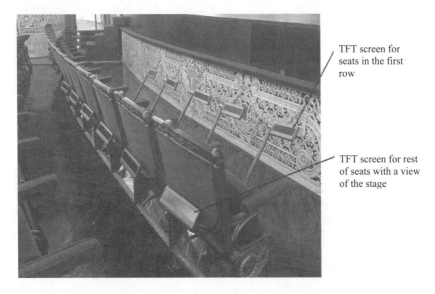

TFT screen for
seats in the first
row

TFT screen for rest
of seats with a view
of the stage

Figure 1. Screens in seats with vision of the stage.
Photo by Bofill, courtesy of the *Gran Teatre del Liceu*.

Figure 2. Screen for seats with no vision of the stage.
Photo by Bofill, courtesy of the *Gran Teatre del Liceu*.

2. Enjoying opera from an early age to over 65

Stimulating children from a young age to enjoy opera and music is the aim of the Education Department within the *Liceu*'s organization. Its many and varied activities are targeted at two different groups: families and schools. Performances, films and concerts are offered at affordable prices for families out at the weekend and on school holidays. Besides, school activities are organized by age. Some simple activities such as tours and dress rehearsals are provided for the younger children, whilst secondary school children can enjoy many different organized activities such as the possibility of climbing onto the stage and singing choral passages from the performances they are attending. There is also a yearly prize for the best opera composed for a young audience.[1]

At a university level the *Liceu* embarked on the project Open Opera,[2] which allows students from 27 Spanish universities to follow an opera with subtitles live via videoconferencing – in 2003 operas at the *Liceu* were subtitled in Galician, Catalan and Spanish for the first time. The *Xarxa Telemàtica Educativa de Catalunya* (www.xtec.es) also offers 25 scenes online, subtitled in Catalan and Spanish.[3]

And finally, for those under the age of 26 and over 65 the *Liceu* offers special tickets with discounts.

3. Opera in Catalan for the physically and sensorially impaired

For those with physical disabilities the building was originally rebuilt with accessibility in mind and it provides access to wheelchairs, prams and pushchairs. For every performance there are seats available for wheelchairs.

For the deaf and hard-of-hearing the *Liceu* projects surtitles in Catalan on a screen over the proscenium.[4] They also offer subtitles in Catalan, Spanish and English, and those can be followed at the back of every seat on a TFT screen.

The translator creates surtitles either from the original opera libretto by editing the Catalan version of the libretto or by creating new surtitles following the stage interpretation. It is also the translator who decides, during the performance, the moment at which a surtitle appears on the screen and at which a new surtitle is projected, following the music score and the stage action.

Since opera is a live performance (although everything is prepared in advance with librettos and music scores) changes may occur at any time. This is why the presence of a person who times and projects the surtitles in real time is so crucial. Surtitles at the *Liceu* can be up to three lines long, and the people who work in the surtitling department believe, based on their experience, the reading of three short lines to be faster and more comfortable than that of two long ones. The number of characters per line is 38-39.[5]

4. Opera in Catalan for the blind and the visually impaired

In October 2004, the *Liceu* signed an agreement with the *Associació Catalana de Cecs i Disminuïts Visuals* (ACCDV) to incorporate AD for the first time in five operas for the 2004-5 opera season (*Boris Godunov, Rigoletto, Parsifal, Roberto Devereux* and *L'elisir d'amore*). This opera AD agreement was a pioneering project in Spain and audience reaction was enthusiastic, as described in Matamala (2005). In other European countries AD is already being offered, but in the UK for example the policy is not to overlap the music.[6] Therefore, opera AD in the UK means patrons can request a cassette tape, which can be obtained from the ticket office and which includes a comprehensive description of the representation. In other words, the AD can be listened to at home before the performance.[7]

This brings us to the next issue, one that mirrors previous dilemmas in opera performances. The issue we would like to discuss is whether an opera should be sung in the source language or in translation. If sung in the source language, should the opera be surtitled in the target language? Or even more interestingly: if sung in the target language, should it be surtitled? Mateo (1998) has given a comprehensive overview of the first question, reaching the conclusion that opera translation is a matter of fashion and socio-cultural issues. She quotes examples such as the different approaches taken in the UK today, where the English National Opera (ENO) and Opera North always stage operas in English translation while the Royal Opera House has a policy of source language performances. Interestingly enough, the much debated issue of surtitling (Dewolf 2001; Mateo 2001) is now much forgotten, since it has been proven that surtitling increases the number of people attending performances, makes opera accessible to those with hearing disabilities and allows the public in general to enjoy opera more.

A similar dilemma as that presented for surtitling has now arisen for audio description, albeit with some different styles or approaches.

5. The two existing approaches to opera AD

As an art form, opera is multisemiotic and multimodal by nature: verbal, non-verbal, visual and auditive. According to Buyssens (1943:56):

> The richest collection of semical facts seems indeed to be that produced by the performance of an opera. The artists communicate with the audience in a variety of ways: through words, music, mime, dance, the costumes of the actors; through the orchestra, the

setting and the lighting on-stage and in the auditorium; through the architecture of the theatre. [...] In short, a whole world here gathers and communicates for the length of several hours (translated by Marvin Carlson).

As Bassnett (2000:96) writes: "The case of opera introduces other issues to the question of the relationship between text, performance, and translation. The libretto can serve both as a text to be sung and as a guide to the audience, to enable them to follow the performance". There is no general agreement as to which of these many features is the most important. While popularly it is thought that music is the crucial element in opera, academics and composers have questioned this, establishing the importance of the text to which composers set their music, and of words as "an intrinsic element not only in the expression of the meaning of what is sung, but of the dramatic action" (Dewolf 2001:182). This satisfyingly expresses the mechanics of the interacting features of an opera, as Dewolf (2001) showed in her study of Wagner's *Parsifal*, and as described by Gorlée (1997:248–249):

> a *Gesamtkunstwerk*, i.e. as, above all, dramatic action, and his [Wagner's]idea that the specific goal of music and words together is "the artistic synthesis in which the music, with its special ability to express what [...] 'we cannot talk about', is called upon to develop the poetic intent of the words into melody and harmony, in interaction with text, gesture and stage action" (quoted in Mateo 2001:32).

Mateo (2001:32) also quotes comments from the Catalan contemporary composer Xavier Montsalvatge:

> In opera, the plot development, the dramatic component, is of utmost importance, I daresay even superior to the music... Neither the score of *Otello* nor that of *Falstaff* or of *Gianni Schicchi* would pass, without difficulty, the test of a concert session dissociated from its dramatic support" (Mateo's translation) (Montsalvatge in MEC 1976:165; 169).

Dewolf (2001:180) defends a comprehensive approach to opera where "words and music interact to create a theatrical effect. Without reasonably full comprehension of the words on the part of the audience, opera inevitably becomes pantomime accompanied by music, not integrated musical drama". With this integral approach in mind we can look at two opposing approaches to opera AD, bearing in mind that audio description is of epigonic nature, and this is due to the fact that audio description is a postproduction activity: it will intrinsically be linked to the language used in the representation, whether it is sung in the source language or target language.

5.1. The Anglo-Saxon opera tradition in AD

As we have already seen, and as York (this volume) confirms, opera in the Anglo-Saxon world is performed in both English and/or the opera's source language, whereas Dewolf (2001) and Mateo (2001) mention that much debate and opposition were created when opera houses decided to offer surtitling. When it comes to audio description, similarly, some feel that music should not be troubled by description, and that the text should be subservient to the music, which has led to AD in the UK meaning the production and recording of a cassette which is sent – by request – and can be listened to before the actual performance. A partially sighted person who attends an opera representation, having heard this type of description, listens to the performance and is able to follow the plot, but misses the meaning of the words as they are being sung. At the other end of the spectrum, in the USA, some opera houses – as is the case with the Virginia Opera – have up to three people describing independently: the plot, the costumes, and the stage production, while the performance is taking place. This is a service offered by the organization Arts Access,[8] whose fundamental goal is to encourage and enable people with disabilities to have full access to arts programmes.

5.2. The Catalan approach

It is a fact that when opera is sung, it is not easy to understand the words, even when they are sung in the audience's language. When high notes are sung, the lack of understanding is more acute. This is also the case for a chorus or a duet, or when several characters are singing at the same time (Desblache forthcoming). If the words are not understood, as Dewolf (2001:281) points out, "music and dramaturgy are 75 to 80 per cent of the opera experience and the lines account for some 20 per cent. Titles reverse the ratio, the 20 per cent experience becomes the 80 per cent experience, with music receding to the background". The same can be applied to a person with sight problems. They are able to enjoy 100 per cent of the music but they miss out on the dramatic representation, the meaning of the words being sung, and the development of the action. In some cases, such as the December 2004 production of *Boris Godunov* at the *Liceu*, frightening noises were heard from the stage. In the second act, Boris is surrounded by model-size replicas of Russia's emblematic civil and religious buildings so as to represent the map of the land under his control.

Figure 3. Stage production of the model size replicas of Russia's emblematic
civil and religious buildings.
Photo courtesy of the *Gran Teatre del Liceu.*

At one point Boris picks up the buildings and hurls them across the stage
creating a tremendous noise which is part of neither the libretto, nor the
music score. This is only particular to the staging of this performance. Should
what is taking place on-stage not be explained to the person in need of audio
description? Audio describer York (this volume) certainly appears to think
so.

In Catalonia, opera is performed in the source language, which means
that the general public cannot follow the text. As already mentioned, both
surtitles and subtitles are available for every seat in three languages, but for
the blind AD is needed.

The Catalan AD approach is inclined to be a comprehensive description.
Throughout the whole performance the describer – always male – speaks
over the music and on some occasions over songs. He provides information
about what is taking place on stage and also the plot. It could also be said that
opera AD in Catalonia is biased to offer descriptions of the plot and the
thoughts and feeling of the characters that would be banned in the Anglo-
Saxon tradition. Whilst traditionally the Anglo-Saxon listener of the AD will
arrive at the conclusion that Gilda, Rigoletto's daughter, is feeling sad or
desperate because of the facial expressions or the body language, a Catalan

AD will spell out 'Gilda is sad' or 'Gilda is desperate'. Whereas in some cases there is only one possible interpretation of the dramatic actions, in other cases it is up to the spectator to interpret. Nevertheless, in Catalonia AD is filtered through the describer, who interprets the action and tells the result in his locution.[9] In some cases AD at the *Liceu* focuses on describing only the generic plot in the libretto and not the particularities of each production. On some occasions there is a detailed AD as in *Rigoletto*, and even different descriptions can be found, as can be seen in the following ADs by two different blind associations on the same opera production.

ONCE:
L'escenografia ha girat enduent-se'n Gilda, que novament s'havia enfilat a l'arbre per recollir-ne alguns fruits. Mentre, ha entrat Marullo, Ceprano, Borsa i altres cortesans emmascarats. Són davant la tàpia de la casa. Per l'altra banda, entra Rigoletto.

[The stage, where Gilda is on top of a tree collecting some fruit, turns. Meanwhile Marullo, Ceprano, Borsa and some other courtiers with masked faces enter. They are standing in front of the wall of the house. From the opposite side Rigoletto enters.]

ACC
L'escenari evoluciona com un carrusel i es transforma en els afores de la casa on hi ha cortensans partidaris del Compte Ceprano.
Gilda a interior resta confiada.
Una escala està disposada perquè algú salti el pati a raptar la que creuen ser l'amant de Rigoletto.
[The stage changes like a carrousel and it is transformed into the outside of a house where there are some courtiers from Compte Ceprano's party.
Gilda is inside and feels confident.
There is a ladder ready for someone to climb up and jump into the patio to hijack the person they believe is Rigoletto's lover.]

As pointed out in Matamala (2005), the key issue when audio describing opera is the coexistence of different visual elements available to sighted people which have to be brought together in a synthetic narration.

- *Staging*: what is seen on stage, such as movements, set design, costumes, props, facial expressions.
- *Surtitling or subtitling*: operas are performed in the original language with Catalan surtitles.
- *Libretto and leaflet*: sighted people can consult the libretto, which is available on the *Liceu* website, and can also read a leaflet with a

summary of the plot.

Due to the limited gaps available in which opera is not sung, the describer has to choose the most relevant elements and create a vivid description, which will be delivered live and will have to slightly change according to improvisations.

The whole process of audio describing starts at the dress rehearsal, where the audio describer takes notes. Then, making the most of the libretto and the website information, the narrator watches a videotaped copy of the opera four or five times in order to write the description and to decide on when to say it. Since it is a live performance the descriptions are cued in the libretto. Then the describer also prepares the final credits and an introduction. Final adjustments are made during a live performance a few days before the opening night, in which the narrator works from a separate room with two screens offering him a wide view of both the stage and the subtitles. The final stage is audience feedback, collected through different questionnaires in which the blind and the visually impaired have expressed enthusiastic opinions (Matamala 2005).

6. A comprehensive AD: two new possible approaches

Taking into consideration the benefits of the two previous approaches – a description recorded on a cassette which is listened to before the actual performance and a live comprehensive AD which includes a personal interpretation – and source text opera performance as a point of departure, one possible comprehensive AD would entail a combination of elements, as follows.

A visit to the stage, with *in situ* description of the set production: props and wardrobe. Some opera houses offer, previous to some representations, an introduction to the performance in the foyer. Attending this short introduction could also help and enhance the AD. Some minutes before the opening, a short introduction with the first act synopsis, names of singers according to the order of singing and stage production could be audio described. During the performance a balanced AD of the dramatic action and the plot could be given when needed. A short introduction similar to the one preceding the first act could be provided for each act.

A different approach would include the same features as mentioned above, but rather than providing a live comprehensive AD, a recorded audio surtitling or subtitling could be listened to (Orero forthcoming). Though this suggestion will raise many eyebrows, audio subtitling (Theunisz 2002) has been researched in the Netherlands by the Federation of Organizations for Visually Impaired People (FSB) together with the public broadcasting company NOS and the Federation of Dutch Libraries for the Blind (FNB) with such positive results that the service has been implemented on a permanent basis. Portlock, Petré and Pescod (2006:6) describe how other European countries also offer spoken subtitles or audio subtitling nowadays: "The Netherlands provides spoken subtitling on ninety per cent of broadcasts, but only on the public channels. Finland has forty hours of audio subtitled television per week and Sweden has audio subtitling on foreign films on a daily basis."

The Dutch 'Spoken Subtitles' experience for television led us to think of a possible trial and use of audio subtitling for opera. Given the fact that the person who attends an opera performance in Barcelona is in a similar linguistic situation to the person in the Netherlands who is sitting in front of a TV set broadcasting a foreign film in a foreign language, audio surtitling was an avenue to be researched. We asked the *Associació Catalana de Cecs* whether it was prepared to try this possible accessible service. The describer was informed of the system and delivery used in the Dutch 'Spoken Subtitles' and it was agreed that the concert version of Donizetti's opera *Roberto Devereux* would be used as a trial. This opera was chosen because it was a concert version with little stage action, and it was thought to offer all the ingredients to become the perfect case study.

The set-up was an opera being sung, with no dramatic action taking place on stage. Leading singers and choir were in a still position throughout the performance. Sporadically, a character/singer moved, entered or left the stage, sat down or stood up in front of a rostrum with the music score singing. Little else took place on the stage, which had no props, and a backdrop colour was the only change for each act: black and blue, black and orange, and black and fuchsia were the three combinations – hence little AD was needed compared to what might have been the case in a fully interpreted opera.

As can be seen in the three photographs on the following page, singers and choir, dressed in black, stand and, occasionally, a singer may sit down. Stage production and sets are reduced to a change of backdrop colour.

Since surtitles and subtitles are also offered in concert operas we thought of testing the reception by the blind community when the describer reads the subtitles. The describer suggested adding some extra information about the minimal stage change, the situation of characters on the stage, and a brief introduction to the plot at the beginning of each act. This experience would offer the visually impaired the same information as the sighted audience: they would have the comments read on top of the music and singing, whereas the sighted can read them without any sound interference. A similar introduction to that read in opera ADs was prepared and read, and some AD of the stage was also added, along with a straight reading of the surtitles.

Figure 4. Donizetti's opera *Roberto Devereux*
Photo courtesy of the *Gran Teatre del Liceu.*

Figure 5. Donizetti's opera *Roberto Devereux*
Photo courtesy of the *Gran Teatre del Liceu.*

Figure 6. Donizetti's opera *Roberto Devereux*
Photo courtesy of the *Gran Teatre del Liceu.*

The voice reading the surtitles was the same describer, or voice-talent, who had previously prepared and read the three AD operas blind people had experienced, hence the many voice problems encountered by the Dutch research 'Spoken Subtitles' team, who used a mechanical decoder voice in their experience, would not exist. Technically there were no problems, since the voice-talent could broadcast from a separate room where a screen was set up showing the singing taking place on stage plus the Catalan surtitles.

A questionnaire was prepared in advance and was read to the blind by the helpers after the performance. Though, at first, the experiment was greeted with much reticence and scepticism by those who knew about it, the reception by the blind community was welcomed (Orero forthcoming). This has opened, on the one hand, a new accessibility avenue of university research, and, on the other hand, a possible accessibility mode which could be implemented in Catalonia, and a much cheaper and time effective alternative to live opera performance: though audio subtitling will be adequate for concert opera versions further research will have to take place for representations with dramatic action.[10]

As Verboom et al. (2002:297) point out, AD "is a very expensive approach [...] and it is not financially feasible for most broadcasting companies to make a significant portion of their programmes accessible". The new approach to opera accessibility will combine the live description of set, props, wardrobe, synopses, cast, plus the audio subtitling, and at some polyglot places such as Barcelona, the *Liceu* could offer the beauty of a choice of three languages.

7. Conclusion

Media accessibility is a human right that is becoming increasingly important as the information society develops quickly into a multimedia format society. Access to TV and, more importantly, to DTV with all its services will soon be an unavoidable reality. For those with sensorial disabilities, or simply, for people over 60 who also suffer from cognitive impairments, audio description and audio subtitling will be a crucial tool (Moreno 2004; Orero 2005). This article dealt with opera accessibility, but it is only one of the many investigations we are pursuing at the university to make media accessible, and this as soon as possible.

---

[1] For more details about the prize: www.Liceubarcelona.com/infantil/escolars.asp

[2] For the description of the whole project:
www.uib.es/servei/comunicacio/sc/actualitat/arxiu/2003/gener/09/link1.htm

[3] www.xtec.es/cgi/mediateca_crp?NU=MP012393. Operas represented in 1999-2000: *Turandot* ('Gravi, enormi ed impotenti'); *Lucia de Lammermoor* ('Ardon gl'incensi'); *Le nozze de Figaro*

('Cazonetta sull'aria'); *El cas Makropoulos* ('Però en mi la vida s'ha aturat'); *Lohengrin* ('O fänd' ich Jubelweisen'); *Sly* ('Tu! Tu mi salvi! Si...'). Season 2000-2001: *D. Q. Don Quijote en Barcelona* ('Es un héroe, mis queridos invitados...'); *Samson et Dalila* ('C'est toi que sa bouche invective'); *Billy Budd* ('Blow her away'); *Aida* ('Gloria al Egitto'); *Giulio Cesare* ('Cessa omai di sospirare!'). Season 2001-2002: *La Traviata* ('Morró!... La mia memoria'); *Kàtia Kabànova* ('Tant de bo m'agafessin'); *Henry VIII* ('Et vous messieurs, que le roi fit mes juges'); *Lady Macbeth de Msensk* ('Però què és això? Massa tard!'); *Die Zauberflöte* ('Der Hölle Rache'); *Tristan und Isolde* ('Hern Tristan bringe'); *La Favorite* ('Mon châtiment descend du ciel'); *Gloriana* ('England and England's Queen entrust their hopes to you!'). Season 2002-2003: *Ariadne auf Naxos* ('Grössmächtige Prinzessin'); *Don Giovanni* ('Ja la mensa é preparata'); *Norma* ('Casta diva'); *Pikovaia Dama* ('Si les gentils damisel·les poguessin volar com els ocells'); *Orfeo ed Eurídice* ('Che farò senza Eurídice!'); *Il viaggio a Reims* ('Nel suo divin sembiante').

[4] Both Dewolf (2001) and Mateo (2001) have written extensively on opera surtitles and subtitles.

[5] We would like to thank subtitlers at the *Liceu* for the information they provided. Unluckily, we were not able to enter the booth where they work as a result of security measures.

[6] The USA too has a well developed AD policy, and theatre and opera have been audio described there for many years now.

[7] For a discussion of introductory "Talking Notes" see York in this volume.

[8] For more information see www.artsaccessinc.org/index.html

[9] There are some extreme cases when the AD has gone beyond what was taken place, interpreting and spelling out, for example, the contents of the letter a character is reading, when neither the public, nor the describer has access to the contents of the written text, and in fact it is only by the character's expression that it can be assumed that the letter means bad news, but no more than that.

[10] Perhaps an introduction, such as the one prepared by Greg York for "Talking Notes" in the UK, along with an audio subtitling could be a possible solution for live opera AD.

References

Bassnett, Susan. 2000. "Theatre and opera", in Peter France (ed.) *The Oxford Guide to Literature in English Translation*. Oxford: Oxford University Press, 96-103.

Buyssens, Eric. 1943. *Les langages et le discours. Essai de linguistique fonctionnelle, dans le cadre de la sémiologie*. Brussels: Office de Publicité.

Desblache, Lucile. 2004. "Low fidelity: opera in translation". *Translating Today* 1: 28-30.

—. Forthcoming. "Challenges and rewards of libretto adaptation", in Jorge Díaz Cintas and Gunilla Anderman (eds) *Audiovisual Translation: Language Transfer on the Screen*. Basingstoke: Palgrave Macmillan.

Dewolf, Linda. 2001. "Surtitling operas, with examples of translations from German into French and Dutch", in Yves Gambier and Henrik Gottlieb (eds.) *(Multi)Media Translation. Concepts, Practices, and Research*. Amsterdam and Philadelphia: John Benjamins, 179-188.

Gorlée, Dinda L. 1997. "Intercode translation: words and music in opera". *Target* 9 (2): 235-270.

Matamala, Ana. 2005. "Live audio description in Catalonia". *Translation Today* 4: 9-11.

Mateo, Marta. 1998. "El debate en torno a la traducción de la ópera", in Pilar Orero (ed.) *Tercer Congrés Internacional sobre Traducció*. Bellaterra: Universidad Autónoma de Barcelona, 209-221.

—. 2001. "Performing musical texts in a target language: the case of Spain". *Across Languages and Cultures* 2(1): 31-50.

—. 2002. "Los sobretítulos de ópera: dimensión técnica, textual, social e ideológica", in John Sanderson (ed.) *Traductores para todo. Actas de las III Jornadas de doblaje y subtitulación*. Alicante: Universidad de Alicante, 51-73.

MEC (ed.) 1976. *La ópera en España: su problemática. VII Decena de música en Toledo. 1975*. Cuadernos de actualidad artística., 13. Servicio de Publicaciones del Ministerio de Educación y Ciencia.

Moreno, Trinidad. 2004. "Televisión accesible: ¿mito o realidad?". *Faro del Silencio. La revista de las personas sordas* 200: 42-47.

Orero, Pilar. 2005. "La inclusión de la accesibilidad en comunicación audiovisual dentro de los estudios de traducción audiovisual". *Quaderns de Traducció* 12: 173-185.

—. Forthcoming. "Audio subtitling: A possible solution for opera accessibility in Catalonia". *Cadernos de Tradução*.

Portlock, Steven, Leen Petré and Dan Pescod. 2006. "The future of access to television for blind and partially sighted people in Europe". Report of the RNIB to the European Blind Union, May 2006. Manuscript.

Theunisz, Mildred. 2002. "Audio subtitling: A new service in the Netherlands making subtitling programmes accessible". www.sb-belang.nl

Veerboom, Maarten, David Crombie, Evelien Dijk and Mildred Theunisz. 2002. "Spoken subtitles: making subtitled TV programmes accessible", in Klaus Miesenberger, Joachim Klaus & Wolfgang L. Zagler (eds) *Computers Helping People with Special Needs*. Berlin-Heidelberg: Springer-Verlag, 289-303.

Virkkunen, Riitta. 2004. "The source text of opera surtitles". *Meta* 49(1): 89-97.

Acknowledgements

We must thank Greg York – from Talking Notes – for his generosity, openness and willingness to collaborate and help out at all moments. He also sent us his guidelines for the production of Talking Notes, as well as several samples for us to listen to.

Verdi made visible: audio introduction for opera and ballet

Greg York

Talking Notes, UK

Abstract

Talking Notes audio introductions address the needs of vision-impaired patrons at the opera and ballet. They give a coherent account of the plot, and illustrate it with vivid descriptions of sets, costumes, characterization and stage business. The production technique includes research, essential elements of scripting, the use of appropriate presenters, the relevance of musical examples, and methods of reproduction. A comprehensive audio introduction gives enough colourful detail for the vision-impaired patron to visualize the production before curtain up and allows for uninterrupted enjoyment of the performance. In London, for the last thirteen years Talking Notes audio introductions have been a vital ingredient of the access policies at the English National Opera and the Royal Opera House, where they are available at all performances.

1. Talking Notes – Genesis

My route into audio introduction seems, in retrospect, to have had some inevitability about it. After working for six years in orchestral management, I joined the BBC as an announcer on the music and arts network, Radio 3, and spent much of the next twenty years describing operas and concerts for a listening public who, naturally, could not see them. Those radio introductions concentrated on narrating the plot, and there was little time to help listeners to imagine the visual element. Outside the BBC I recorded scores of books for the Royal National Institute of the Blind (RNIB), and began to appreciate the needs of vision-impaired people (generally referred to as VIPs).

By a happy coincidence, when I left the BBC in 1993, the Royal National Theatre was just setting up its first professional audio description (AD) team and invited me to join it. The team was trained by Diana Hull, a charismatic American actress, who had developed her own methodology for audio description in the theatre. Her energy, boundless enthusiasm and sound principles were inspiring. I worked on several productions, including JB Priestley's *An Inspector Calls*, Harold Pinter's *The Birthday Party,* Alan Bennett's delightful realization of *The Wind in the Willows*, and Eduardo de Filippo's *La Grande Magia.* After every audio described performance the National Theatre held a feedback session in which VIPS could pass on their reactions to the describing team. These were extremely valuable and allowed us, the describers, to hone our skills according to the needs of the listeners.

In informal conversation at those meetings several vision-impaired patrons mentioned how much they appreciated the growing trend for audio description (AD) in the theatre. But they all felt that such provision did not go far enough. They expressed a need for AD in the lyric theatre and for some way of making the printed programmes in the concert hall available to people who could not read them. I felt that, given my previous Radio 3 experience, I was being presented with an unmissable opportunity.

After much consideration and discussion with interested parties, not least potential writer-presenters, I decided to offer 'audio introductions' – narration and description provided before the performance begins – rather than simultaneous description. I chose the title Talking Notes because of its play on the word 'notes' and also because the adjective 'talking' has useful connotations for VIPs – Talking Books is a long-established recorded library, part of the RNIB, and there is a network of Talking Newspapers across the country.

As it happened, the English National Opera (ENO) had already been considering audio provision, but did not know where to begin or whom to consult. So when I turned up, they accepted my suggestions straight away over a cup of coffee. The Royal Opera House (ROH) was rather more cautious, and it took a year or so of protracted negotiations before an occasional service began there. From the outset, the ENO insisted that every production have at least one live audio-introduced performance. They were more sporadic at the ROH, but after a couple of seasons they realized that it was discriminatory to be selective.

In the first years, the audio introduction was relayed live in the auditorium. At the ENO the presenter sat in the sound box at the rear of the stalls, had an excellent view of the stage and was in close contact with the technicians, in case there were any problems. Things were less comfortable in the ROH before its restoration. The Talking Notes presenter had to work from an ancient unused BBC studio – all 1940s veneer, massive coat racks and brass waste-paper buckets, and decades of corporate dust. It was set high up behind the amphitheatre, just about as far away from the stage as you could possibly get. The only view was through a dusty double-glazed window, and the only way of hearing the performance was on a crackling show-relay speaker. The quality of the picture on the television monitor also left much to be desired. In both houses the presenter worked with a commentary lip-mike, and his prepared script was relayed via the house's internal transmission system to VIPs listening on headsets in their seats in the house.

With the redevelopment of the ROH and with technological progress, things improved dramatically. For a long time I had felt that the provision of just one or two introduced performances of any one production severely restricted the vision-impaired patrons' choice, but I was well aware of the economic impracticality of engaging a presenter every night. The solution was obviously to record the presentation, in as compact and flexible a form as possible. I suggested that the Talking Notes audio introduction be recorded on minidisc, so that it could be relayed at every performance at minimal additional cost.

Now, thirteen years later, it is a source of some pride that all ENO performances at the Coliseum and all Royal Opera and Royal Ballet performances at the ROH are introduced by Talking Notes – which means that VIPs can go whenever they choose and can rely on being provided for.

2. The advantages and disadvantages of audio introduction

What are perceived as the advantages or disadvantages of audio introduction as against audio description is largely dependent on the listener's needs and preferences. With audio introduction the advantages are that

- You do not need to wear a headset throughout the performance, so you can hear it in natural acoustic stereo;
- You can listen to every note of the music without interruption;
- Your neighbours are not subjected to the squeaks leaking from your headset during the music;
- Perhaps most significantly, the presentation does not have to be delivered live: it can be pre-recorded and made available at every performance (unlike simultaneous AD, which has to be live as it depends on the timing of the dialogue on-stage).

The disadvantages of audio introduction are that

- Everything has to be pre-described, which puts a strain on memory;
- Pre-description also removes any element intended to surprise;
- There is no possibility of reflecting any change on-stage as it happens – simply keeping company with the listener in the event of a delayed curtain, for example, or explaining an unexpected hiccup. There was the occasion (during a performance of Bedrich Smetana's *The Two Widows* with a live audio introduction, as it happened) when the gamekeeper Mumlal fired his gun and his dog took fright and bolted, dragging the chair to which he was tied. He was not the 'principal' dog, as it were, only a late replacement, and the production team had omitted to engage a gundog, which was used to sudden bangs;
- With pre-recorded presentation it is not possible to describe curtain calls as they happen, to enable listeners to express their reactions appropriately.

So a pre-recorded audio introduction has to be considered in the same way as the printed programme: it is complete, finished and published before the run of performances begins.

On balance, I have found that visually-impaired opera-lovers and concert-goers prefer to listen to music without intrusion from the describer – and certainly my experience in the last thirteen years has indicated that, with just a few exceptions, vision-impaired patrons at musical events accept the limitations of the audio introduction.

3. Formula

The formula that we adopt for operas and ballets has remained unchanged since the inception of Talking Notes. We produce a fifteen-minute introduction before Act One (or the first part of the programme), and five minutes before every subsequent act – though this often is not really enough time. Fifteen minutes must be the limit at the top of a show, not least because it might not be possible to open the auditorium earlier, but (more) especially because the listeners have to absorb a lot of information and sit for a considerably longer period than their sighted companions.

Concert presentation is different. In the first place, it is never pre-recorded. Most orchestral concerts are a one-off, as far as Talking Notes are concerned, and there would be no advantage in pre-recording all the introductory notes. Because the presenter keeps the concert-goer company throughout the performance, each work can be introduced before it is played, and platform layouts and alterations can be described. So we generally allow(ed) just ten minutes for the introduction at the top of a concert.

4. Production method

For operas and ballet, the Talking Notes production method is quite simple, and we try to keep our schedule as tight as possible – and not to embark on a new production too early, to allow for inevitable changes when the work reaches the stage. At the ROH I employ a researcher, who attends model shows, makes detailed notes of set layouts, and visits wardrobe, wigs and shoes to compile a thorough impression of every costume. The researcher and I attend stage rehearsals to confirm visual details and to note characterizations and stage business. The ROH publications department provides an authenticated version of the synopsis (which may, of course, differ from the original librettist's), and then I collate all the research, write a script and record it (using minidisc as the preferred medium).

5. Presenters

People generally assume that my presenters and myself must be opera and ballet specialists, hugely knowledgeable about the art forms. Over the years it is true that we have learnt a great deal about the operas and ballets on which we have worked. But any modest scholarship we have acquired is much less important than our ability to tell the story and describe the visual elements vividly.

6. Script

The following aspects will be discussed with reference to the script:

- Compression
- Information overload and how to avoid it
- Main/essential credits
- Nutshell synopsis
- Production concept – sets and costumes
- Making it real
- Identifying with the listener
- Telling it as it is
- Ballet – interviews and musical examples
- Narration
- Scene sympathy
- Literary style
- Vocabulary
- Shapes and textures
- Colours – evocative – resonant adjectives – associations with other senses

Compression

The greatest challenge with audio introduction, of course, is that, because everything has to be said before the music begins, you not only have to pack as much visual information as possible into a fifteen-minute introduction, you also have to sustain interest by varying the density and the tempo of the material and by taking care not to repeat yourself: not to overuse telling words or phrases.

First consideration: avoid information overload – vary density with tangential illustrative material from programme

People often ask how you avoid what they call 'information overload'. It is generally sighted people who make the assumption that this is what VIPs will have to endure. I think that in this context the concept is simply wrong. It is possible (and desirable) to vary the density by tangential reference to the printed programme, quoting salient passages from articles, or alluding perhaps to a significant musical moment, and generally giving your listeners a perspective which they do not need to remember during the performance. I believe that if the plot is coherent, with all its complexities teased out and clarified, and, provided the descriptions are pertinent and lucid, the listeners will absorb them. With luck, they will hang on your every word, just as they would with any other audio work to which they are listening for pleasure.

All basic production information: cast list, production team, music team, sponsors, translators, etc.

At the beginning of a presentation, it can take a few moments for listeners to become accustomed to the reception on their headsets. At the very least, they need time to adjust the volume. In the theatre and opera house, the needs of the stage staff frequently dictate how soon the house can be opened to the public; and it is not unusual for Talking Notes listeners still to be taking their seats when the introduction begins. So I always make sure that the first minute or so is devoted to the main (or essential) credits – comparable to the front page of the programme book – composer, librettist, date of composition, date and place of first performance, sponsors of the current production, translator, director, designers, choreographer, fight director, and so on. I generally leave the conductor until last, since I feel he is the most influential member of the production team. By the time I have gone through all the credits, I hope that the listeners have adjusted their headsets to their own satisfaction and are aurally 'tuned in', as it were.

Nutshell synopsis

Next, if there is time within the opening introduction, it is helpful to include a nutshell synopsis: the plot summed up as concisely as possible and the main characters identified. For example, if I wanted to summarize Gioacchino Antonio Rossini's *The Barber of Seville* I might say:

> It's the story of young Count Almaviva, who's fallen in love with the beautiful Rosina. She's the ward of the crusty old Doctor Bartolo, who keeps her securely locked up indoors. With the help of the crafty barber,

Figaro, Almaviva gains admittance to the house in a variety of disguises, manages to tell Rosina he loves her and persuades her to elope with him. The elopement plan is foiled by Bartolo's crony Don Basilio, arriving with a lawyer to marry Rosina to Bartolo. But Almaviva convinces Basilio that a bribe is a better option than the business end of a pistol. Basilio agrees to be a witness, and Almaviva is married to Rosina.

Production concept

Before I begin to describe the set and costumes in detail, I like to give an overview of the general production concept, sometimes using a recorded interview with the designer. It can be absolutely essential to the appreciation of a production, because there is no use in telling listeners that this is an 18th century piece concerning counts, cloistered maidens and barbers if the production team have chosen to set the opera in the 1970s and everyone is dressed like punks.

It is also useful to map the geography of the stage – the number of levels, perhaps, and the general shapes of performing areas – and to give a general view of the costumes – for example, that because we are in the 1870s all the men are bewhiskered and dressed in frock coats or cutaway tail coats, and all the ladies are in elegant gowns with bustles and short trains. That sets up a general framework for the descriptions of individual costumes, which come later when the characters make their first appearances. At this point, before the narrative begins, I think it is perfectly reasonable to talk in theatrical terms: to refer to 'the stage, the wings and the flies' and to the mechanics of the staging.

This was how we sketched the general concept for the sets of *Figaro's Wedding* (as ENO titled Graham Vick's 1993 production of Mozart's *The Marriage of Figaro*):

After the overture the curtain goes up on Richard Hudson's design for Figaro's quarters in the palace. It gives a glimpse of other rooms, rather like an architect's sectional drawing; it also suggests the layers of palace society. The whole of the visible floor area is covered in a shiny indigo marble with a regular scattering of gold stars; it protrudes out towards the orchestra pit in a right angle just right of centre. The ceiling above is the dark blue of the midnight sky. On the left, running almost diagonally upstage, is a high wall of deep stippled green – as an interior surface you could think of it as marble. The rear wall of Figaro's room runs out at right angles to it and extends some way across the stage to the right. Behind it, and parallel to it are the walls of two other rooms. Each wall is higher than the one in front of it and ends with a pair of double doors, whose architraves are progressively more elaborate – from the simple lines of the doorway in Figaro's room to the rococo excesses of the state apartments. And each wall is in a different and vivid colour: the first one a brilliant ochre yellow, the next room off-white or the palest of greys, and the room beyond – rich crimson.

Similarly, this is how we introduced the designs for Verdi's *Falstaff*, directed by Matthew Warchus at ENO in 1997:

Laura Hopkins was influenced by the little perspective peep-shows of Dutch interiors in the National Gallery: each one a box whose inside is ingeniously painted, so that when you look through a peep hole you get the impression of depth and receding space – as if you were looking into a real life-size room. In her sets, Laura Hopkins has faithfully reproduced several elements of those peep-show paintings – for example, some red leather-backed chairs have found their way from a peep-show by Samuel van Hoogstraten straight into Ford's house in Windsor. And perspective plays a more significant part than usual. It's been suggested that, when he wrote the opera, Verdi was viewing Shakespeare from the distant perspective of his old age.

A similar overview of the costumes is useful as a short-cut at the beginning to avoid the need to describe basically the same dress or suit over and over again. All that is necessary later is to highlight a particular detail, especially if it helps to illuminate the nature of the character – for example, an ostentatiously-trimmed hat might say much about the vanity of its wearer.

This was the brief outline for Andrea Schmidt-Futterer's costumes in Strauss's *Arabella* at the Royal Opera in 2004:

Though the libretto sets the story in the mid-19th century, the production team have chosen to update it to an indeterminate period probably as recent as the 1990s – the eclectic mixture of costume styles ranges from Edwardian to hip hop. Most of the principal men, apart from Mandryka, wear stiffened jackets, giving them a rather two-dimensional appearance. The bell-boys and waiters are in violet livery trimmed with gold braid, and pill-box hats. They wear round red-tinted glasses and black gloves with gold lurex spots. From time to time they pass through the lobby or across the landing. One of them always slides in with smooth robotic movements, his feet never leaving the floor.

Later one can include much more specific descriptions. These were Christine Haworth's costumes, which the ugly sisters (danced by men) wore to the ball in the 2004 Royal Ballet production of *Cinderella*:

The sisters have surpassed themselves. Big-and-Bossy wears an elaborate black wig, shaped like a pagoda, from which starfish are suspended. A large fish is speared across the front of her head. Her cape is a golden net, on which more starfish are mounted round her head and shoulders. Shells threaded on a black ribbon form her necklace. The bodice of her gown is of gold lamé, liberally studded with shells, and the panniered skirt is draped in sea green and coral moiré, with highly-coloured fish appliquéed all over it. To round off the piscene impression she wears black fishnet gloves and stockings, sprinkled with sequins, with lace-up ankle boots.

Tiny-and-Timid favours birds. Her head-dress consists of two stuffed lovebirds on the side of her tall, red coiffure, and lots of ostrich feathers. Her cape is of light blue feathers, over a gown of canary yellow silk, embroidered with pearls and sequins. More lovebirds appear on a front panel of the bodice. She wears long satin gloves, and wires decorated with feathers stand up from the toes of her orange high-heeled shoes.

Making it real

Once I have embarked on the story, I like to treat all aspects of the set as if they are real; so there are no further references to 'backdrops' or to 'props' which only *look as if* they are real. For the rest of the presentation, what looks real is taken to *be* real. I believe this helps to keep the listener focused on the story and the descriptions, and to disregard the theatrical artifice. It assists the suspension of disbelief and makes for a richer experience.

Identifying with the listener

I prefer to address the listener as 'you' in the singular, and to describe things as if we were seeing them together. So, a character does not come 'downstage', but moves 'closer to us'. This is also part of maintaining the illusion of realism and avoiding the sense of theatricality.

Telling it as it is

There are times when one is obliged to describe something accurately, however inappropriate it might seem – a condition which has become known in Talking Notes as 'the bucket syndrome'. Our very first production was an expressionist staging of Verdi's *Simon Boccanegra* at ENO, quite untraditional, heavy with symbolism, and designed with great dramatic blocks of colour, notably scarlet, and black and white. At the very opening,

Paolo sets fire to a document and drops it into a conveniently-placed bucket. An ordinary galvanized garden bucket with a handle. That, we thought, reasonably enough, was the best way to describe it. The dramaturge was alarmed – felt it was rather an undignified expression – suggested we refer to it as a 'metal receptacle'. We represented to him that his description was too vague. It was a bucket, so why not call it a bucket? And that is what we did.

Ballet – interviews and musical examples

With a ballet, pre-describing the set and costumes and stitching them into the storyline is the easy part; what is much harder, yet crucial, is to convey at least a flavour of the choreography *before* the ballet is performed. So how do you manage that in just a few minutes? Unless you can speak perceptively about the dance – and perhaps you need to have been a dancer to do so – the presenter's best option is to go to the horse's mouth and interview the choreographer, or ballet master or mistress. Their unique insights into the overall character of the dance and descriptions of the most demanding moments in the piece can really bring the introduction alive. And of course the personal voice of an authority lends as much colour to the presentation as an illustration in a page of print.

Interviews can be recorded well in advance and tidied up in the studio to eliminate hesitations and repetitions, and then be built into the final presentation. This was part of our *modus operandi* when Talking Notes was running at the Royal Festival Hall, and it brought terrific immediacy to the listener's experience. It made for a very busy, somewhat stressful experience for the presenter, who had to prepare a script as well as record and edit an interview in just a few hours before the performance. But it was worth the effort to be able, for example, to reproduce for our listener an interview with the pianist Mitsuko Uchida about the intricacies of a Mozart piano concerto moments before she stepped onto the platform to play. The sighted concert-goers without headsets did not realize how much they were missing.

Narration

Once the production concept is established, I embark on a detailed narration of the plot, illustrating it as vividly as possible with descriptions of all the visual details – props as they occur, and individuals' costumes and characterizations. These descriptions have to be lucid enough to sustain the listener throughout at least the first act – if not the whole opera. It is also important to describe any business which is likely to get an audience reaction – any extra-musical noise (the jangling of keys, for instance) – as well as noting the musical cue to a salient moment (such as the sombre horn at the end of *La bohème* when we learn that Mimì has died).

Scene sympathy

It is a precept of audio description in the theatre that the language and vocabulary be in keeping with the character of the scene. This is just as important in an operatic audio introduction, especially if the production is set in the period when the piece was written. My feeling is that the spoken description should try to reflect the period setting and the quality of life depicted, even to the extent of using archaic language or slang if it seems appropriate.

The tone of the presentation from moment to moment is critical: it is obvious that the style of description of a tragic death should be grave and formal, rather than casual and light-hearted. Similarly, it would sound idiotic for a comic scene to be described in funereal tones. I also like to name objects accurately. In the second act of the Royal Opera's 2003 production of Mozart's *Die Zauberflöte* the props included a beautiful brass clockwork model of the solar system, and, though I suspected it might be unfamiliar to most listeners, I explained what it was and named it accurately as an orrery. Even recondite words have their own special resonance and add colour to the presentation.

Literary style

A word of caution, though. It is very important that the prose style be as lucid as possible. Since the listener will hear the script read aloud and will not have the opportunity (at least in the opera house) of returning to a passage, it must be straightforward and uncluttered. Any convoluted, over-literary construction will be harder for the listener to disentangle. Even the devices beloved of broadcasting newswriters – such as hanging participles, misplaced adverbs, too many subordinate clauses – should be strenuously avoided. Many people are maddened by them, and they get in the way of good, clear, direct communication. On the whole, I would advise that sentences be as simple as possible, with perhaps only one correctly-placed adjectival or adverbial clause. There is nothing wrong with conjunctions, especially if they clarify the sequence of events.

Scripts are always written in the present tense, for the simple reason that the opera-goer, sitting listening in the auditorium, has to absorb the story prospectively. Clearly, the perfect tense, which is customary for most narratives, would be inappropriate. Similarly, it would be clumsy in the extreme to relate the plot and describe the visual elements in the future tense. Just imagine: "Angelotti will stumble out of the Attavanti chapel and unexpectedly encounter Cavaradossi. Angellotti will be filthy, his hair will be matted, and there will be a bloody bandage around his right forearm.

Luckily, Cavaradossi will recognize him, and, having been a republican sympathizer for the previous twelve years, will agree to help him to hide after nightfall". If you work entirely in the future tense, you make it hard for yourself and for your listener to place other events in time. However, if you stick to the present, you can refer to past and future events from the standpoint of a continually evolving moment.

Vocabulary

I mentioned earlier the risk of repeating yourself, and that risk seems to be at its highest in the use of verbs of motion: when you are describing comings and goings. Since you are trying to create a real event for the listener, it simply is not good enough to say that a character 'enters', and even worse that he 'exits'. Those terms are too 'stagy' and draw attention to the unreality of the situation. You have to characterize the manner in which the character appears, and try not to use the verb again. For example, a strong person might well 'stride determinedly' into the room; but if he 'strides' about every time he moves, the repetition tends to dilute the impact of the description. But it is often hard to find the right verb without resorting to bland terms such as 'comes in' and 'appears'. Words such as 'materialize' should be used only when the character really does appear suddenly out of nowhere. I keep a long list of words to describe a person's gait – and I seem to add to it almost daily.

Your listeners might not notice it, but even the use of the harmless prepositions 'in' and 'out', 'on' and 'off' can suggest theatricality. We use them habitually for entrances and exits on stage, even when the scene is set outdoors. But in everyday speech, you would not describe someone coming 'in' to the middle of a huge open-air space such as Hampstead Heath.

Shapes and textures

The concerns of an audio introduction are really no different from those for an audio description, save, perhaps, that they ought to be more vivid and therefore more memorable. It is useful to draw on allusions which have reference to the senses other than sight, especially touch and smell.

The shape of things can pose problems. The geometry of acting areas, particularly, can be very confusing for anyone who has never been able to see anything in three dimensions. You might try to find a relationship with a familiar object: "it's like a hugely-enlarged flattened spoon with a long narrow walkway opening onto an oval area". Or you could describe a funnel-shaped space in terms of moving through it: "if you walked into it, you would find the walls getting closer to you". The illusion of perspective is often critical to the design of a scene, and, again, it is necessary to explain that "the vista appears to recede away from us, with each successive building smaller than the one before it".

In describing costume, texture is an essential ingredient: your listener will instantly recognize the different qualities of velvet, fur or coarse hair.

Colours – evocative – resonant adjectives – associations with other senses

I have always been given to understand that VIPs – even those who have never had any sight – prefer colours to be given an identity, a character, in addition to their general label on the spectrum. After all, every adjective has its own resonance. 'Moss green' is so much more evocative than simply 'green'; 'magenta' more telling that 'deep pink'. To this end, it helps to decide on a particular discipline or field from which the allusions can be drawn. In this respect the ENO production of Britten's *A Midsummer Night's Dream*, with its wonderful evocation of a sultry Mediterranean summer night, was a gift: we were able to draw on a glorious variety of aromatic herbs to describe the rich blues and greens which formed the production's colour palette. Alternatively, a production of *Lady Macbeth of Mtsensk* at the ROH was dark and largely monochrome, and our colour references were based on metals and stone.

It is sensible to avoid allusions which could sound anachronistic in context. For example, you cannot have 'pillar-box red' either in the 18th century (before pillar boxes were invented), or in France, where mail boxes are yellow now, I believe, though they used to be blue, which is even more confusing.

7. Revivals

Productions which have already been staged and introduced by Talking Notes require less script preparation – because that was done on a previous occasion. It is necessary, though, to compare the existing script with the revival on stage, to make sure that any changes to characterization, business, costumes and props are noted. Most likely, there will be at least some cast changes too. The script will be carefully amended before recording and mastering for reproduction at performances.

8. Pros and cons for use of musical examples

From time to time it has been suggested that the inclusion of short musical examples would make for useful reference points for the listener. We have tried it for a few Royal Ballet introductions (including *Giselle* and *La fille mal gardée*), but would not consider doing it regularly, for several reasons.

Firstly, and most importantly: music clips take up valuable time which could be used for description; secondly, it is necessary to record musical extracts in piano performances (since to record the Royal Opera House Orchestra would be prohibitively expensive); then, there is the matter of audibility in an auditorium where the orchestra is already tuning up; and, not least, there might be problems of performing rights in the use of commercially-recorded material, and, in some cases, of copyright in making our own recordings. So musical examples are very much the exception, and none of our regular listeners have expressed a need for them.

9. Reproduction

Once the script is complete, and other essential details have been checked – such as the number and duration of intervals, which have a bearing on how much material has to be provided – the script is recorded onto minidiscs, and reproduced in the opera house at every performance.

We also produce a parallel recording, including dates and times of performances, details of associated events, and duplicate it onto cassettes for advance circulation to VIPs, so that they can familiarize themselves with it before they come to a performance. They can request a tape from the Access Officer at the respective house and it is mailed to them free of charge.

The London Coliseum has a radio system for broadcasting the audio introduction, which can be heard anywhere in the theatre, including the bar and the cloakroom, so listeners do not need to take their seats in the auditorium in order to hear Talking Notes; the Royal Opera House is still using a very high quality infra-red transmission system – its limitation, of course, being that it can be heard only in sight of its radiators, which are in the auditorium only.

10. Conclusion

It is a source of great pride to us who work in Talking Notes that, in the last thirteen seasons, we will have produced no fewer than 400 opera productions and 175 ballet productions. Almost every opera and ballet has had a number of performances, which means that the Talking Notes introductions have been relayed several thousand times. Quite a lot of the productions were revivals, so we did not have to devise scripts from scratch, but each required careful revision and an up-to-date recording for the performances. They have ranged from Adams to Zimmermann, and included works as diverse in scope and style as Wagner's *Ring* cycle and Bernstein's *On the town*.

Talking Notes has introduced performances by the Karas dance company, the Norwegian National Ballet and Opera North at Sadler's Wells Theatre in London, performances by Glyndebourne Touring Opera and the Northern Ballet Theatre in a number of British cities, productions by the Scottish Opera at the Edinburgh Festival over several years, and two operas mounted by Opera Northern Ireland in Belfast. We also presented 204 orchestral concerts at the Royal Festival Hall during our residency there in 1995 and 1996, and over 150 concerts at The Anvil in Basingstoke between 1994 and 2002.

As far as it has been possible to ascertain, Talking Notes is the only full-time professional audio introduction service working in the lyric theatre anywhere in the world. That makes us unique, of course, but it also imposes a responsibility. Since there is no direct competition, it would be all too easy to become sloppy. It is important that high standards be set and maintained to ensure that vision-impaired patrons are provided with introductions which are vivid, colourful, memorable and, above all, entertaining. We hope that, when the curtain goes up, our VIPs will have a good idea of what the show is about and what it looks like. Verdi made visible.

Audio description in the Chinese world

Jessica Yeung

Hong Kong Baptist University, China

Abstract
There is no provision of audio description (AD) at the institutional level on the Chinese mainland. This is to be expected since most resources in this sector are used on medicines to eliminate curable blindness. By contrast, the lack of provision in the wealthy city of Hong Kong can be attributed only to a lack of awareness of the right to media access for all. There is an attempt to provide training in audio description for university interpreting students, and this has proved to be educationally beneficial. In Taiwan, much advocacy and research have been done and provision is improving dramatically.

1. Visual impairment in the Chinese world

The attempt to present an overall picture of anything at all about China often provokes trepidation before any other intellectual responses. This is due not to China's vast geographical expanse, nor to its flattering long history and intricate cultural system, but rather to the widely diverse ways of life which result from uneven economic development across the country. According to official figures,[1] among the 1.3 billion total population of the country, 42.99% (approx. 561,570,000 people) reside in urban areas while the poor rural areas accommodate 57.01% (approx. 744,471,000 people) of the total population. In the Shanghai region, GDP per capita is RMB18,645 (approx. EUR1,818) in urban areas and RMB8,342 (approx. EUR813) in rural areas. In the southernmost province of Guangdong on the other side of the border from Hong Kong, GDP per capita is RMB14,770 (approx. EUR1,440) in urban areas and 4,691 (approx. EUR458) in rural areas. But the relatively high GDP in urban areas does not reflect an average living standard in China. In the first place, the gap between the rich and the poor in cities is large. The relatively high GDP does not reflect the living standards of everyone in these cities. To further complicate the picture, there is a large number of 'urban dwellers' who are not actually 'urban dwellers' in the normal sense of the word, for these are people without dwellings. They are people who have moved from villages to cities in hopes of finding jobs in factories and mines, in some known cases enduring exploitation and sometimes finding themselves in working environments without proper safety facilities, simply to earn a living. It is estimated by some organizations that, in Guangdong Province alone, this group of mobile workers amounts to 1,500,000 against the total settled population of 91,940,000 of the Province. A most striking picture is revealed if we make a comparison between the far ends of the economic spectrum: the official figure of GDP per capita in Beijing is RMB44,969 (approx. EUR4,386); whereas according to a World Vision survey, about 30 million people in China are living on RMB1.7 (approx. EUR0.17) a day. 6.9% of China's total population is living below the poverty line.

Against this economic background, it is almost predicted that one finds an overwhelming concentration of the visually impaired in the rural areas. According to Orbis statistics, out of the 1.3 billion total population in China, it is estimated that 9 million people are blind or suffer other kinds of visual impairment, including 50,000 children. 80% of these 9 million people are recorded in rural areas. According to Orbis figures, 50% of blind and visually impaired people are curable, given proper medical care. In 2005, Orbis could afford to provide for surgery to only 1,940 people and medical care to only 38,990 people. Unfortunately, the need for audio description for those people whose sight cannot be recovered does not occupy a high priority, given the present lack of resources. Having said that, there is clearly an aspiration at the upper level of state administration to improve provisions for people with special needs. The Law of the People's Republic of China on the Protection of Disabled Persons was adopted on 28 December 1990 and implemented on 15 May 1991. It gives legal protection to the rights enjoyed by people with disabilities to "equal and full participation in social life and their share of the material and cultural wealth of society".[2] It stipulates assistance be given to them to participate in various forms of cultural, sporting and recreational activities, including to "offer TV programmes in sign language and put in subtitles or narrations in some movies and TV programmes".[3] In fact, the diverse dialectal environment across the country has already prompted national and regional television channels to provide full subtitles in order to maximize numbers of viewers. The state-owned national channel CTV also provides sign language interpreting for some news programmes. There are also audio tapes of description of some films for general listeners who have no access to these films, but they do not exclusively target listeners with visual impairments. So far, there is no information indicating any provision of audio description on television or in cinemas on the Chinese mainland.

The correlation between a country's wealth and the level of care and provision received by minority groups is easy to understand. Except in extreme cases of developing countries where the accessibility of medicines and opportunity for surgery are highly restricted, visual impairment is not class-constituted, nor do people with visual impairments always form a consistent class. The visually impaired expect, as the sighted do, a higher standard of life in wealthy societies. China's neighbour Japan offers a good comparison. It provided the first regular service of audio description on television broadcast on NTV for a two-hour drama programme in the entire world in 1983, a period when Japan's economy was doing well. The description was not an optional extra to the television audience. It was simply broadcast with the soundtrack of the programme. There was no means to turn it off and view the programme without the description. Although the technology was not excellent, the fact that AD was provided on an institutional level in Japan showed a high expectation of life style for all. It would take a further study with sufficient data to establish a correlation between a society's wealth and its provision of audio description, but the cases of Japan and China may serve as indications.

2. Audio description in Hong Kong

However, Hong Kong, China's wealthiest city and a special administrative region enjoying a high level of autonomy after being returned to China after 156 years of British colonization, does not have a successful track record in the provision of audio description. The Disability Discrimination Ordinance was implemented in 1996 to protect people with disabilities from any form of discrimination in all aspects of social life. There is, however, no stipulation to ensure provision of services catering for their special needs by venues and organizations. There are NGOs, working alongside the Hospital Authority and the Social Welfare Department, with subsidies from the government and charity foundations, to share rehabilitation work and offer relevant services. But audio description hardly features prominently as a high priority.

Without the support of legislation and institutions, the campaign to promote audio description can only be sporadic and analogous to guerrilla warfare. For a number of years in the 1990s and the early 2000s, Augustine Chiu-yu Mok, then General Secretary of Arts with the Disabled Association (ADA), had attempted more vigorous efforts with audio description. Mok is himself a political activist promoting People's Theatre of the Boal tradition in Hong Kong. His approach to the theatre is one that aims at empowerment of minorities. He has successfully promoted Theatre of the Silence, Hong Kong's deaf people's theatre, and a number of drama productions by people with visual impairments in the international theatre arena. His efforts to promote audio description with the ADA represented a natural development of the project of empowerment for people with visual impairments through theatre. Working alongside Mok was his colleague Janet Mei-hing Tam, who was trained in linguistics and has some experience in interpreting. Her input has been most significant since ADA's plan to bring audio description trainers to Hong Kong to train describers in the early 2000s was hampered because of a lack of funding. But thanks to her background in interpreting, and equipped with training material she found sources abroad and Tam was able to organize self-help training for volunteers. It was also Tam who first advocated audio description to be associated with interpreter training in Hong Kong and who sought to bridge the two areas.

It was under Tam's persuasion that I experimented in teaching audio description to translation and interpreting students at the Hong Kong Baptist University. In 2005, I was able to secure a teaching development grant from the university to develop teaching material for a 30-hour course as part of translation and interpreting training. It was designed in such a way that every three-hour unit of the course can be independent, so that instructors can teach the whole or parts of the course as appropriate for their subjects and also for the time they have. The course makes reference to the training material from a number of sources. Students are familiarized with the general principles of audio description. A substantial part of the course aims at introducing students to different art forms and preparing them for describing a variety of performances and works. Exercises are set to describe two drama productions, two dances, two *xiqu* (Chinese opera), two films, two paintings, two museum tours and two public events. All performances and works are local productions. The structure of the course is similar to the training of audio description in other regions, except that the bilingual situation of Hong Kong and the nature of bilingual training for interpreters are taken into account. Of the two exercises on each art form, one is done in English and the other in Cantonese. The course was first conducted in 2006 for the subject "Translating across Media". The subject as a whole aims at drawing students' attention to the process involved in intersemiotic translation. Nine hours of the 30 hours of material was used. At the end of the course, a focus group discussion was held for student feedback. The students generally enjoyed the training and found it useful as it helps them acquire a number of transferable skills, some of which are similar to those acquired in interpreting training:

A. Skills similar to those acquired in interpreting training:

1. Vocal skills: Almost all students in the discussion were made very much aware of the use of their voice as a communicative tool. They have become less shy about hearing their own voices coming through recording and broadcasting machines, and more comfortable with their sense of presence through the use of their voice. They also found the training helpful in their speech articulation.

2. Command of the languages: The majority of students found the exercises particularly challenging in relation to their command of vocabulary for the material world, since the accuracy of vocabulary in this domain is essential in keeping their description lively and brief. In preparing their scripts, most of them made extensive use of the thesaurus and built up a good vocabulary for certain items that they came across in the exercises.

3. Grasping an overall picture and finding focus in description: One of the major problems students encountered is the selection of material to describe. Some of them found it very frustrating at first when they tried to work on too many details. Then, they gradually got used to the idea of prioritizing and managed to focus on the general picture to maintain the flow of their narrative.

B. Skills not related to interpreting

1. Empathy: Most students reported that the experience of audio description training was the first time they had tried to imagine the experience of other people's bodies. They were encouraged to step into the shoes of people with visual impairments, and to imagine how these people experienced the world through sensations other than visual ones.

2. Awareness of their own bodies: Some students reported that imagining others' bodily sensations has inspired them to be more aware of their own bodily experiences and their own cognitive processes through the different sensations.

3. Awareness of the differences in the operation of semiotic systems: One student remarked that the consistency between visual images and verbal narration is different, i.e. sometimes visual images she saw were consistent, but when she described them in words, she found the connection between information units missing. Another student found visual images more accommodating to ambiguities than verbal language. At one point in our focus group discussion, students digressed to share what they each thought to be the distinctive features of different semiotic systems.

4. Awareness of the interplay between different information sources: All students in the first exercise of describing a drama production talked over the characters' dialogues and other sound effects. They found it difficult to hold back and let the other audio sources occupy the foreground. It showed a lack of knowledge and trust in audio communication except through verbal means. Much time in the sessions was spent on impressing upon the students the importance of listening to other sounds and sound effects and working with them. One student

remarked that this had made her become aware of her own role in a complex communication network, and of the need to work well with other elements in such a network.

5. Knowledge of the arts: One student remarked that one of the most valuable things about the course for her was the opportunity to learn about the various art forms. Others agreed that having to prepare the scripts meant that they had to carry out research into the works and the forms, and that had promoted their knowledge of the arts considerably.

Training for this first batch of students is still ongoing. Some of them are expected to perform audio description for the Arts Festival for the Disabled at the end of 2006. This will be the first time audio description is performed in the theatre in Hong Kong. Until now there has been no audio description provided on television or in cinemas. Neither do DVDs of Hong Kong films provide it. Unlike the situation on the mainland, the failure to provide audio description at an institutional level cannot simply be attributed to a lack of resources.

3. Audio description in Taiwan

In comparison, Taiwan, with a slightly less prosperous economy than Hong Kong, has had more success in developing audio description. My theory is that the different political structures of the two societies have played a part in this. Hong Kong's colonial rule needed to take shelter from the economic success of a radical market economy. Art and culture were deemed inimical to such a setup as its innate critical edge could naturally have led to inquiry into the colonial situation (Ma 2006:79-102). Therefore, art and culture hardly featured as a priority in the colonial government's agenda. 'Post-colonial' Hong Kong[4] simply inherited the prevailing ultra-capitalist ideology. It is not surprising that the provision of audio description, which is associated with facilitating reception of cultural products, has not featured in the government agenda in either the colonial or the 'post-colonial' period. By contrast, culture fulfils a completely different function for the Taiwanese Government. The KMT Party's[5] departure from the mainland in 1949 to settle in Taiwan meant a discontinuity of the history of the KMT's Republic of China. Until the possibility of relinquishing the claims for the mainland in favour of establishing a separate nation state of Taiwan emerged as a popular aspiration in the 1990s, it was important for the KMT to find some ways to legitimize Taiwan as the 'real' China. One possible way was to displace the concept of 'China' from a geographical reality to a cultural reality. There were periods when Communist China renounced traditional Chinese culture as feudal and undesirable, Taiwan, on the contrary, prided itself on being the legitimate heir of the China of *Ru* (Confucian) culture. Culture has therefore been foregrounded in Taiwan's public policy.

In Taiwan, the Council for Cultural Affairs (CCA) under the Executive Yuan [Ministry] is responsible for cultural affairs. In a speech delivered by Chen Yu-chiou, then President of the CCA, in December 2003, the pledge was made that facilitating participation of the minorities in art and culture was a part of the grand vision of a 'cultural Taiwan'. In the same speech, audio description was cited as one of the services the Council pledged to provide. At the time the Council had been supporting the work of the local Audio Description Association, an organization devoted to the sole mission of promoting audio description. The Association started in the 1990s to devise its own training material for audio description and run training workshops for volunteers. It started to provide audio description in the theatre in 2000 and on television in a drama series broadcast in 2001. In 2002, it embarked on the provision of description for museums. The first exhibition with description was the Henri Matisse exhibition at the National Museum of History. Up to 2003, with the collaboration of the National Film Archive and various theatre companies, it produced description for more than 20 films, drama and dance on video and DVD, including for the film *Crouching Tiger, Hidden Dragon*. The most significant achievement of the Association is the development of a 'viewing' system to cater for the special needs of people with visual impairments. It is an apparatus to combine audio description and braille, both designed to synchronize with recorded theatre productions. When there is no dialogue, viewers will hear narration by the describer; when there are dialogues or special sound effects, they will be given braille scripts that describe the mis-en-scene. The system claims to be the first of its kind in the world.

Although the extent of success with audio description in Hong Kong and Taiwan is poles apart, there is one basic similarity in the two places. In both places, introduction and advocacy are down to individual efforts. In Hong Kong, it is individual staff members of Arts with the Disabled Association who have been seeking institutional recognition of the necessity of and support for audio description, although without much success as their work is seriously restricted by external conditions. In Taiwan, it was the American-trained Chao Ya-li, the founder and General Director of the Audio Description Association in Taiwan and present Dean of Communication in Tamkang University, who started the advocacy for, research on and practice of audio description in Taiwan.

4. Towards an ontology of audio description

Compared with her advocacy and practice, Chao's research on audio description is equally successful. Her most important publications in audio description are in Chinese, yet not only do they show a good awareness of other work on the same topic published in the international arena, but it is clear that her studies are at the cutting edge of international research on audio description at present. The record of the surveys and experiments she has conducted and the subsequent theoretical inquiry on the communicative nature of audio description are compiled in a thick Chinese volume. It is the first book-length study exclusively devoted to audio description by a single author that I have come across so far. In order to show how her work is well articulated with the development of audio description internationally, I will take a short detour and map out the directions audio description research has taken so far.

The first academic study on audio description is generally accepted to be the late Gregory Frazier's MA thesis dating back to 1975 and written at the San Francisco State University entitled *The Autobiography of Miss Jane Pitman: An All-audio Adaptation of the Teleplay for the Blind and Visually Handicapped* (Piety 2004:453; Snyder 2005:936). In recent years there has been a plethora of material posted on different websites. Until the mid-1990s the majority of the material available on the internet was about audio description providers and advocates, and training agencies such as the Audetel website and the website of the Royal National Institute of the Blind. These websites are all of an introductory nature. They often contain an introductory section to audio description, including its definition, availability, basic techniques of description and links to other websites about audio description. From the mid-1990s onwards there have been more varied kinds of information available. There are reports and studies on the reception side of audio description. Some map out a profile of audio description audiences (Packer & Kirchner 1997); some evaluate the benefits of the services (Peli, Fine and Labianca 1997; Schmeidler and Kirchner 2001; Petré 2005). The conclusions of these studies are overwhelmingly positive, arguing for audio description's efficacy in facilitating social integration of and education for the visually impaired. There are also studies on audio description from linguistic perspectives. There is a study subjecting audio description scripts to discourse analysis and looking at the language system of audio description and audio description narration as a discursive process (Piety 2004). It is believed that this particular work is the first investigation of audio description as a language system. A recent trend towards a generic approach is observed in the 2005 International Conference on Audiovisual Translation in Barcelona, Spain. A number of studies look at the different requirements and modes of reception of audio description for different forms of experience including the theatre, the opera, the ballet and museum exhibitions (Ania 2005; Matamala & Orero 2005; York 2005). There is also a case study of the audio description script for Almodóvar's film *Todo sobre mi madre*. It offers a look in detail into the techniques of and language used in audio description narration (Ballester 2005). Another paper predicts a future need for the interlingual translation of audio description scripts as the circulation of films and DVDs with audio description is expected to expand (Jiménez 2005). In terms of a large-scale research project, Salway's TIWO – Television in Words at the University of Surrey, has received much attention. It was conducted between 2002 and 2005. Salway and his team approach audio description from the perspective of computational semiotics and multi-modal communication. Making use of a corpus of audio description texts of 500,000 words for 60 feature films and a selection of television programmes, their research looks at the cognition process involved in the reception of films and television programmes with audio description, and the linguistic features of audio description narrations (see Salway in this volume). It is against this background that Chao Ya-li's research in Taiwan should be assessed.

Coming from the perspective of Communication Studies, she sees communication as the foundation of any community. The philosophy underlying her work in audio description is media access for all. One important task she accomplished in her studies was to map out the state of interpersonal communication of the visually impaired in Taiwan. A series of surveys were conducted to provide statistics on the communication habits of the visually impaired in Taiwan. Information gathered indicates their accessibility to the mass media including television and DVDs, their purpose for 'viewing' television programmes, the frequency and modes of communication with family and friends. Her survey shows that over 98% of people with visual impairments in Taiwan have access to radio, over 95% to television, around 70% to video and over 48% to personal computers (Chao 2002:46-47). These figures led her to conclude that the provision of audio description on the institutional level is necessary in order to ensure effective communication and social integration for the visually impaired in a world they cohabit with a majority of sighted people. This series of quantitative data gatherings represents the first stage of Chao's work. They are almost identical to some surveys done in the US and the UK in the 1990s, in the advocacy stage of audio description. The second stage of Chao's research is qualitative. In December 1988 and January 1989, a film clip of about 25 minutes was shown to different groups of people under different viewing circumstances:

1. 'viewing' by audience with visual impairments without audio description;
2. 'viewing' by audience with visual impairments with audio description;

3. 'viewing' by sighted audience blindfolded without audio description;
4. 'viewing' by sighted audience blindfolded with audio description;
5. viewing by sighted audience without audio description.

27 people with visual impairments and 25 sighted people participated in the experiment. Their responses during the viewing were collected with mechanisms of think-aloud-protocols. After the viewing, they told researchers what information, including the general narrative, details of the plot and aesthetic effects they had got from the viewing experience in in-depth interviews conducted with them on an individual basis. The aim of this exercise was to compare the cognitive processes in visual experience and audio description experience. All the 52 audience members were then asked to listen to four different versions of audio description for the same film clip scripted by different people and to give feedback on them. The data collected in this experiment was further analysed for better understanding of the cognitive processes through AD, for both theoretical and practical purposes.

This is where Chao's work departs from mainstream audio description research, which mainly adopts linguistic approaches. According to the bibliography at the end of Chao's book her study has drawn on Gratifications Theory in Communication Studies, Media and Film Studies, Phenomenology of the Merleau-Ponty school and Translation Studies, but it is semiotics that has set the dominant note throughout her inquiry. Her basic assumption is that every medium of communication appeals to a certain human sensation with which the medium was associated at its invention. The formation and operation of the sign systems of every medium is different. The structure of a work made in a particular medium and the meaning created in it naturally tend to conform to the particular sensation with which the medium was associated at its invention. As a result, there will necessarily be an experiential gap when meaning constructed in one medium is translated to be conveyed in a different medium. This assumption prompts her to ask a number of important questions including the following:

1. How do people with visual impairments experience the world with four senses rather than five?
2. What kind of experience is audio description providing for people with visual impairments?
3. What is the best selection of visual elements to be described?
4. How can one convey such information in ways that the special features and needs of the sensations of people with visual impairments can be gratified?
5. What is the role of the describer?

The following are some of the observations made:

1. There is a drastic epistemological difference in the reception of a film by the sighted in 'ordinary' viewing and the unsighted with audio description. The sighted view a film and witness a virtual reality constructed on-screen; whilst the unsighted experience a palpably 'real' reality as they listen to the dialogues and sound effects of the film, which approximate closely to the everyday sounds that they hear.
2. The reception of a film with audio description is different from the reception of a radio play. The audience of the former is aware of "a visual image in the process of unfolding" (Chao 2002:109, my translation).
3. Different features of the visual and verbal sign systems cause major problems in audio description. For example, the more flexible and free syntax of the visual image is difficult to represent through verbal construction.
4. There are two layers on which signs work: the narrative and the aesthetics. The aesthetics of a film are as important as the narrative of the film. The aesthetic elements often generate synaesthetic experiences. Therefore, describers should pay more attention to moods and feelings of the film if they aim at creating comparable experiences for the unsighted as that experienced by the sighted.
5. The reception of a film with audio description by the unsighted requires two semiotic processes to work side by side: the dialogues and the sound effects are deictic whilst the verbal narration of the audio description is symbolic.
6. Describers are the architects who construct a virtual world for people with visual impairments to exercise their imagination in this world.
7. Describers achieve much more than conveying information pieces that stand alone. They facilitate communication between the structure of the world of the sighted and that of the unsighted.
8. There are two possible positions describers can take. They can take the subsidiary role of co-narrators translating certain signs for the unsighted audience. Co-narrators perform a task similar to 'filling blanks'. But describers can also take the pro-active role of independent narrators, taking control of the overall product by making their own narration, the dialogues and soundtrack work together. They might even incorporate an introduction to cinema or the film before the film starts and create a unique experience for the audience.

Much has been done in Chao's study to establish an ontology of audio description. There is no account of how exactly these observations have changed the practice by the Audio Description Association. One expects huge impact to have been exerted and one looks forward to further publications on how such impact is transformed into progress.

5. The future

Although the differences in dialects and cultures among the Chinese communities are enormous, there is much among the Chinese audio description practitioners to share. For one thing, linguistic studies on Chinese audio description scripts would show radically different features from English scripts, since the syntactic structure of the Chinese dialects is different from that of English, and the symbolic mechanisms of the Chinese language systems are also different from those of the Indo-European languages.

While research is being done to improve the practice, much is still needed in advocacy. In Taiwan, where culture is esteemed more highly in its own right than it is in many other Chinese communities, the rights to access culture of people with visual impairments are better represented in government policies. In many other places where governments pay minimum lip service to such rights, when they bother to do even that, advocates resort to other avenues for legitimacy. In Hong Kong, where many are obsessed with the idea of the city's role as the 'window of China' and 'Asia's world city', the language-related transferable skills inherent in audio description training might serve as a first attraction to the practice.

In the summer of 2006 when the World Cup was sweeping the Chinese mainland, an article was posted and circulated on the internet criticizing the lack of provision for people with visual impairments to enjoy the games. A heated discussion was provoked and most discussants agreed that radio broadcast did not target people with visual impairments and that such broadcasts could not serve their special needs. The 2008 Olympics in Beijing could be an excellent opportunity for audio description advocates. Perhaps the Chinese government would like to show the world that they are keen to ensure everybody's rights to access cultural experience.

---

[1] All figures on population distribution and GDP, unless otherwise stated, are quoted from the National Bureau of Statistics of China.
[2] Cited on the website of Chinese Disabled Person's Federation (www.cdpf.org.cn).
[3] Chapter 5, Law of the People's Republic of China on the Protection of Disabled Person
[4] There are critics who purport that Hong Kong's 'return' to China is merely a second colonization by China (Chow 1998:151).

[5] Kuomintang, or the National Party, was the ruling party of the Chinese mainland before the Communist takeover in 1949. Sun Yat-sen, the founding Party Chairman of the KMT, led the 1911 Revolution in which the Manchurian Qing Dynasty was overthrown.

References

Ania, María Josep. 2005. "Museums, galleries and historical sites: Accessibility for the blind and visually impaired visitors". Paper delivered at International Conference *Media for All*. Barcelona, 6-8 June.

Ballester, Ana. 2005. "Almodóvar just in words: audio description strategies in *Todo sobre mi madre* (1999)". Paper delivered at International Conference *Media for All*. Barcelona, 6-8 June.

Chao, Ya-li. 2002. *Yuyan Shijie zhong di Liudong Guangying: Koushu Yingxiang di Lilun Jiangou* [Images Flowing in the World of Language: To Construct a Theoretical Framework for Audio Description]. Taipe: Wunan Publishing Co.

Chow, Rey. 1998. *Ethics After Idealism: Theory, Culture, Ethnicity, Reading*. Bloomington and Indiapolis: Indiana University Press.

Frazier, Gregory. 1975. *The Autobiography of Miss Jane Pitman: An All Audio Adaptation of the Teleplay for the Blind and Visually Handicapped*. San Francisco: San Francisco State University. MA Thesis.

Jiménez, Catalina. 2005. "Audio description: A new form of knowledge representation". Paper delivered at International Conference *Media for All*. Barcelona, 6-8 June.

Ma, Kafai. 2006. *Cong Feixu Li Kanjian Luoma* [Seeing in Ruins a Vision of Rome]. Hong Kong: Cosmos Books.

Matamala, Ana and Pilar Orero. 2005. "Accessible opera in Catalan". Paper delivered at International Conference *Media for All*. Barcelona, 6-8 June.

Packer, Jaclyn and Corinne Kirchner. 1997. "Who's watching? A profile of the blind and visually impaired audience for television and video". American Foundation for the Blind. www.afb.org/section.asp?SectionID=3&TopicID=140&DocumentID=12 32#impaired

Peli, Eli, Elisabeth M. Fine and Angela T. Labianca. 1996. "Evaluating visual information provided by audio description". *Journal of Visual Impairment & Blindness* 90(5): 378-385.

Petré, Leen. 2005. "User feedback on audio description and the case for increasing audio description targets". www.rnib.org.uk/xpedio/groups/public/documents/publicwebsite/public_ userfeedback.doc

Piety. Philip J. 2004. "The language system of audio description: An investigation as a discursive system". *Journal of Visual Impairment & Blindness* 98(8): 453-469.

Salway, Andrew. 2005. "TIWO – Television in Words: Final Report". www.computing.surrey.ac.uk/personal/pg/A.Salway/tiwo/TIWO.htm

Schmeidler, Emilie and Corinne Kirchner. 2001. "Adding audio description: Does it make a difference?" *Journal of Visual Impairment & Blindness* 95(4): 197-203.

Snyder, Joel. 2005. "Audio description: The visual made verbal". *International Congress Series* 1282: 935-939.

York, Greg. 2005. "Audio-introduction for opera and ballet". Paper delivered at International Conference *Media for All*. Barcelona, 6-8 June.

Notes on contributors

Vera Lúcia Santiago Araújo has a PhD from the University of São Paulo, Brazil, with a dissertation on the translation of clichés in dubbing and subtitling (*Meta*, 49/1, 2004). She teaches English as a foreign language and translation at the State University of Ceará. Together with Eliana Franco she carried out research on subtitling for the deaf and hard-of-hearing in Fortaleza in 2002. The results were published in *The Translator* (9/2, 2003), *Topics in Audiovisual Translation* (2004) and *Questões de Lingüística Aplicada* (2005).

Julian Bourne is an associate lecturer in scientific and technical translation at the department of translation and interpreting at the *Universidad de Granada*, Spain. His doctoral thesis (2003) analysed the translation into Spanish of politeness features in the dialogue exchanges of contemporary English novels. He is a member of the research and development team *Tracce*, which aims to promote accessibility in the media for the blind, the deaf and the hard-of-hearing.

Karin De Coster has an MA in adult education and has recently (2007) obtained a PhD in adult education, entitled *Zonder beeld, met titel. Over taal en ervaring van blinde bezoekers in kunstmusea* [Without image, with title. About language and the experience of blind visitors of fine arts museums] at the department of adult educational sciences at the *Vrije Universiteit Brussel*, Belgium. In addition to her scientific work, she is also actively involved in some projects concerning accessibility and audio description in museums.

Jorge Díaz Cintas is programme convener of the MA in Translation at Roehampton University, London. He is the author of several books and articles on subtitling and has recently published *Audiovisual Translation: Subtitling* (2007), co-written with Aline Remael. He has been the president of the European Association for Studies in Screen Translation since 2002.

Joan Greening joined the RNIB's media and culture team in April 2000, having previously worked in the field of disability as a theatre director and a television and film producer. Since joining the RNIB she has been instrumental in the development of audio description on digital television, DVD and in cinemas across the UK, working with the industry to ensure the services are accessible to blind and partially sighted customers.

Catalina Jiménez Hurtado is a lecturer in linguistics and translation at the department of translation and interpreting at the *Universidad de Granada*, Spain. She is interested in the relation between lexical semantics and translation, and in the modulation of both fields in the development of different types of meaning representation and controlled languages. She directs a research and development team called *Tracce*, which aims to promote accessibility in the media for the blind, the deaf and the hard-of-hearing.

Anna Matamala holds a degree in translation from the *Universitat Autònoma de Barcelona*, Spain, and a PhD in applied linguistics from the *Universitat Pompeu Fabra*, Spain. She is presently an associate lecturer at the *Universitat Autònoma de Barcelona*, where she coordinates the MA in Audiovisual Translation. She has been working for more than ten years as an audiovisual translator for Catalan television. Her main research interests are audiovisual translation, media accessibility and applied linguistics.

Clive Miller started his career as an operational engineer in television before doing further study in computer science and accessibility. He then joined the Royal National Institute of the Blind, the leading UK charity for visually impaired people, as a technical consultant with regard to digital broadcasting. He now works as a consultant in a number of fields including accessibility and broadcasting.

Volkmar Mühleis has a PhD in art history and is a lecturer of philosophy at the Institute of Fine Arts Sint-Lucas in Ghent, Belgium. He has published a study about the implications of blindness for the perception of art (*Kunst im Sehverlust*, 2005). From 2004 to 2006, he guided blind visitors around in the Museums of Fine Arts in Brussels.

Josélia Neves holds a degree in languages and literatures and an MA in English Studies. She has a PhD in subtitling for the deaf and hard-of-hearing from the University of Surrey Roehampton, London. She teaches audiovisual translation at the *Instituto Politécnico de Leiria* and the *Universidade de Coimbra*, Portugal. Her main interests lie in teaching audiovisual translation and in developing action research projects in the field of accessibility to the media.

Pilar Orero holds an MA in Translation from the *Universitat Autònoma de Barcelona*, Spain, and a PhD in translation from the former University of Manchester Institute of Science and Technology (UMIST), UK. She lectures at the *Universitat Autònoma de Barcelona*, where she also coordinates the online MA in Audiovisual Translation. She is the co-editor of *The Translator's Dialogue* (1997) and the editor of *Topics in Audiovisual Translation* (2004). She is the leader of two university networks (CEPACC and RIID-LLSS), which group 18 Spanish universities devoted to media accessibility research and quality training.

Aline Remael teaches translation theory and audiovisual translation at University College Antwerp, Belgium. Her main research interests are subtitling, subtitling for the deaf and hard-of-hearing, live subtitling and audio description. She is currently co-supervising a project on live subtitling with speech recognition technology in collaboration with the Flemish public television channel and the University of Antwerp. She is the chief editor of the translation studies journal *Linguistica Antverpiensia New Series*, and a member of the TransMedia research group.

Deborah Rolph obtained a psychology degree and worked in the USA in a project aimed at reintegrating psychiatric patients into the community. Upon returning to Europe she attended the University of London to do an MA in Social Work. After working for several years in the field of mental health, she managed a pioneering scheme of home treatment for people in psychiatric crises. Personal engagements took her to Spain, where she currently works as an English teacher at the *Universitat Autònoma de Barcelona*.

Andrew Salway has recently started Burton Bradstock Research Labs (BBREL) to further his research and development activities in corpus-based multimedia content analysis and new media, with a focus on the themes of multimodality and narrative. Previously, he spent twelve years at the University of Surrey, where he pioneered the computer-based analysis of audio description. He has published 20 papers and has given international keynote lectures, given talks and seminars to audiences in multimedia computing, new media, semiotics, narratology, information studies, corpus linguistics and audiovisual translation.

Christopher Stone is a post-doctoral researcher at the ESRC funded Deafness Cognition and Language (DCAL) research centre at University College London. Trained at the Centre for Deaf Studies at the University of Bristol, he then worked as an interpreter and trainer based in Bristol undertaking work in Uganda and Finland. His PhD at the University of Bristol examined Deaf translators in television news. His research interests include prosody in translation, bilingualism and intensive interpreter training. He still works part-time as an interpreter.

Gert Vercauteren works as a research assistant at University College Antwerp, where he teaches computer-assisted translation, as well as literary and multimedia translation in the Portuguese department. His field of research is audiovisual translation in general and audio description in particular. He is currently working on a PhD about the role of relevance in audio description.

Jessica Yeung is an assistant professor of the translation programme and associate director of the Centre for Translation, Hong Kong Baptist University, China. Her main research interests are literary translation and drama translation, intercultural and interlingual communication in the theatre. She translates both play scripts and texts of *xiqu* (traditional Chinese theatre). She is also a stage actress and theatre critic. In addition to translation and interpreting, she also teaches audio description.

Greg York worked at the BBC for 21 years presenting operas and concerts and then became one of the first professional audio describers at the Royal National Theatre in London. In 1993, he set up his own audio introduction company to serve visually impaired patrons at the opera and ballet, and he now works full time for the English National Opera and the Royal Opera House.

Index

A Ferreirinha, 113
A Midsummer Night's Dream, 227
Accessibility, 13, 14, 15, 16, 17, 18, 19,
    20, 26, 27, 28, 36, 42, 44, 45, 46, 47,
    55, 89, 92, 93, 97, 111, 119, 120, 121,
    122, 123, 127, 132, 139, 140, 147, 148,
    151, 152, 168, 185, 186, 189, 190, 199,
    201, 203, 212, 232, 239, 245, 246, 247
ADA, 117, 118, 233
Ahmad, Khurshid, 158, 163, 167, 170
Akmajian, Adrian, 81
Allen, Woody, 117
Allsop, Lorna, 71
Almodóvar, Pedro, 239
Amerikaans Theater, 114
An Inspector Calls, 215
Analogue, 12, 91, 115, 123, 128, 130, 131
Ania, Maria Josep, 239
Arabella, 222
Arandes, Jorge, 112
Araújo, Vera, 17, 48, 49, 93, 99, 103, 104,
    105, 106, 245
Aristia, 119, 186
Armitage, Thomas Rhodes, 138
Associaçao Portuguesa de Surdos, 25
Associació Catalana de Cecs i Disminuits
    Visuals, 204, 210
Audesc, 112
Audest, 117
Audetel, 112, 113, 128, 238
Audio description
    Art, 189, 190, 191, 192, 193, 194, 195,
        196, 197, 198, 199, 200
    Assisted, 18, 151, 154, 166, 171
    Broadcasting, 112, 114, 115, 116, 123,
        127, 128, 131, 138, 139, 140, 210,
        212, 228
    Characters, 177, 206, 207, 210, 220,
        221
    Corpus, 171, 172, 173, 178, 239, 247,
        249, 250
    Guidelines, 151, 152, 154, 163, 167,
        171, 186, 214
    History, 128, 133, 189
    Introduction, 227, 228, 229, 241
    Language, 242, 243, 244, 245, 246,
        248, 249
    Lexicon, 178, 185
    Live, 113, 115, 116, 131, 141, 168, 203,
        209, 212, 213, 214, 216, 217
    Narrative, 18, 44, 53, 73, 127, 130, 131,
        152, 163, 169, 170, 171, 172, 173,

        189, 191, 192, 193, 194, 195, 196,
        197, 198, 221, 225, 235, 240, 241,
        247
    Opera, 8, 11, 18, 19, 46, 97, 112, 114,
        115, 132, 141, 201, 202, 203, 204,
        205, 206, 207, 208, 209, 210, 211,
        212, 213, 214, 215, 216, 217, 218,
        219, 220, 221, 222, 223, 224, 225,
        226, 227, 228 , 229, 234, 239
    Standard, 120, 121, 124, 138n 139, 140,
        142, 147, 148, 149, 185, 187
    Syntax, 181, 184, 185
    "Talking Notes", 19, 138, 213, 214,
        215, 216, 217, 218, 220, 223, 224,
        227, 228, 229
    Temporal information, 163, 164, 173
    Terminology, 146
    Text type, 167, 175, 176
    Theatre, 11, 112, 113, 114, 115, 117,
        118, 127, 133, 186, 201, 205, 213,
        215, 216, 220, 225, 228, 229, 233,
        236, 237, 239
    Training, 117, 118, 119, 123, 134, 154,
        191, 231, 232, 233, 234, 235, 236, 237,
        238, 242
Baker, Charlotte, 71
Ballester Casado, Ana, 151
Ballet, 19
Basque, 123
Bassnett, Susan, 205
Belgium, 18, 24, 30
Benecke, Bernd, 113, 115, 116, 117, 119
Bennett, Alan, 215
Bernstein, Leonard, 228
Biber, Douglas, 154
Bilingual, 16
Blindenzorg Licht en Liefde, 113
Bobeldijk, Marcel, 28
Bordieu, Pierre, 12
Bordwell, David, 152
Boris Godunov, 204, 206
Bourne, Julian, 18, 115
Brazil, 17, 99, 100, 103, 105, 106
Brillo Boxes, 192
British, 16, 18, 19, 31, 71, 72, 91, 112,
    113, 122, 129, 155, 158, 178, 229, 233
Britten, Benjamín, 227
Broadcaster
    ABC, 93
    ARD, 24, 27
    ARTE, 115, 119
    ATM, 48

BBC, 24, 26
BR, 113, 116, 118, 119, 120
BskyB, 129, 130, 131, 135
Canal Sur, 112, 114
Canale 5, 34
CBS, 91
CTV, 232
Channel 4, 128, 129, 130, 135, 136
Channel Five, 129
Italia 1, 35
ITV, 128, 129, 130, 135, 136
Lusomundo Gallery, 113, 114, 123
Mediaset, 34
MDR, 119
NBC, 93
NDR, 119
Nederlandse Openbare Omroep, 33
NOS, 36
NTV, 232
ONDigital, 128
PBS, 91
Publieke Omroep, 36
Radio Barcelona, 112
RAI, 24, 25, 27
Rede Globo, 99
RTBF, 40
RTP, 25, 28, 30, 31
RTV, 34
SIC, 28, 31
SWR, 116, 119
TV Cabo, 113, 114, 125
TVE, 25
TVI, 28, 31
TV3, 25
VRT, 24, 26, 30
WDR, 119
ZDF, 24, 27, 28, 32
Buyssens, Eric, 204
Calhoun, Sallie, 190
Campbell, Marie, 173
Cantonese, 234
Captain Corelli's Mandolin, 169
Carroll, Mary, 25, 27
Carmel, Simon, 72
Cartoons, 13
Casablanca, 136
Castilian, 123
Catalan, 19, 25, 48, 49, 112, 114, 123, 201,
    203, 204, 205, 206, 207, 208, 210, 212,
    246
Catalonia, 19
CEN, 13
CENELEC, 13

Centro Communicare è Vivere (CECOEV),
    37
Chao, Ya-li, 237, 239, 241
Chekov, Andrei, 115
China, 19
Chow, Rey, 242
Cinema, 45
Cinderella,103, 222
Colby, 37
Cold Mountain, 136
Congost Maestre, Nereida, 179, 183, 184
Conrad, Susan, 154
Cook, Ian, 72
Corbin, Juliet, 72
Corpus-based analysis, 18, 151, 171
Couté Rodriguez, Isabelle, 9, 41
Crang, Mike, 72
Crouching Tiger, Hidden Dragon, 237
Cunningham, Michael, 177
Das Kätchen von Heilbronn, 115
Davies, Martin, 173
De Coster, Karin, 189
De Craene, Guido, 123
De Groot, Vanjia, 36
De Filippo, 215
De Linde, Zoé, 49
De Zaak Alzheimer, 114
Desblache, Lucile, 206
Deutsche Hörfilm GmbH, 116, 119
Dewolf, Linda, 204, 205, 206
Dewulf, Bernard, 24, 26, 30, 40, 45
Díaz Cintas, Jorge, 11, 49, 106
Die Zauberflöte, 213, 225
Diderot, Denis, 196
Digital, 12, 15, 17, 26, 45, 47, 48, 54, 89, 91,
    92, 93, 96, 97, 113, 114, 115, 123, 127,
    128, 129, 130, 131, 134, 136, 139, 141,
    151, 153, 154, 166, 168, 169, 171
Distributors
    Buena Vista Home Entertainement, 134, 135,
        136
    Columbia Tristar, 136
    Granada Ventures, 137
    Pathé, 136
    Warner Bros., 47, 134
    Warner Home Entertainement, 136
Documentaries, 13, 27, 120
Doens, Edwin, 36
Dodeigne, Eugène, 18, 189, 191, 197
Donaldson, Chas, 24, 26, 31, 35, 37, 39,
    42, 43, 45, 46, 52
Donizetti, 210, 211
Dosch, Elmar, 113, 116, 119
Dr Who, 136

Duguid, Garry, 173
DVD 15, 17, 30, 31, 36, 44, 45, 46, 47, 48,
    49, 50, 56, 91, 106, 112, 114, 115, 116,
    119, 127, 135, 136, 137, 138, 149, 168,
    237, 245, 250,
EBU, 148
Eine unheilige Liebe, 113
Ente Nacional de Sordomudos ENS, 37
ETSI, 39, 53, 55, 56
Eugeni, Carlo, 24, 26, 27, 35, 37, 38, 41,
    45
Europe, 13, 14, 15, 16, 19, 23, 24, 25, 40,
    43, 55, 91, 111, 112, 122, 139
European Federation of Hard of Hearing
    People, 48
European Union, 12, 39, 97, 139
Evans, Denise, 173
F.C. De Kampioenen, 114
Falstaff, 205, 222
Faber Benítez, Pamela, 176
Federation of Dutch Libraries for the
    Blind, 210
Federation of Organisations for Visually
    Impaired People FSB, 210
Fine, E.M., 238
Flanders, 26, 31, 32, 33, 36, 40, 42, 43, 45,
    46, 48, 111, 113, 147
Flemish, 24, 26, 40, 41, 48, 52, 113, 114,
    122, 142, 145, 146, 147, 149, 247
France, 24, 41, 46, 49, 52, 53, 213, 227
Frazier, Gregory, 238
French, 24, 46, 59, 91, 118, 129, 178, 213
French Chef, 91
Franco, Eliana, 93, 103, 104, 105, 245
Galician, 123, 203,
Gambier, Yves, 89, 171
Geyskens, Harry, 123, 125,
Germany, 24, 25, 26, 27, 31, 32, 36, 41,
    45, 47, 52, 111, 113, 115, 116, 117,
    118, 119, 120, 121, 123, 125, 139, 147
Giselle, 251
Gombrich, Ernst H., 192
Gorlée, Dinda L., 205
Globalization, 12
Gran Teatre del Liceu, 19, 112, 201, 202,
    204, 206, 207, 208, 209, 211, 212
Graham, Mike, 169, 170
Greening, Joan, 17, 112, 114, 122, 127
Gregory, Susan, 93
Guidelines (see also Standard), 25, 32
    European, 38
    Wenn aus Bildern Worte werden, 119
Gutt, Ernst-August, 76, 77
Halliday, M.A.K, 176

Hand on the Thigh, 191, 197, 198
Harmonisation, 39, 40, 48
Harris, Dave, 174
Harry Potter and the Philosopher's Stone,
    133, 136
Hasan, Ruqaiya, 176
Hatim, Basil, 76
Haworth, Christine, 222
Hear my Song, 138
Heath, Alison, 190
Herder, Johan Gottfried, 196
Herman, David, 171
Herman, Mark, 183
Hernández Bartolomé, Ana I., 112
Hervey, Sándor, 184
Hetherington, Kevin, 190
Hinnenkamp, Volker, 75
Hitchcock, Alfred, 24, 136
Hitchhiker's Guide to the Galaxy, 137
Hoffman, Lotear, 152, 154
Hong Kong, 19
Hopkins, Robert, 196
Hull, Diana, 215
Human rights, 12, 14
Humphries, Tom, 72
Hyks, Veronika, 112, 116, 117, 118, 119
Identity, 87
Imhauser, Corinne, 38, 46, 47, 52
IMS, 118, 125, 174
Inghilleri, Moira, 73, 78
Instituto da Comunicaçao Social (ICS), 37
Interpreting, 16, 79, 80, 81, 82, 83, 84,
    115, 184, 231, 232, 233, 234, 235, 245,
    246, 248
Isham, William. P., 76
Italian, 24
Italy, 24, 26, 34, 35, 37, 38, 41, 45, 46, 49,
    52
ITFC , 153, 155, 173, 174
Ivarsson, Jan, 140
Jiménez, Catalina, 175, 176
Karakter, 114
Kay, Neil, 93
Kirchner, Corinne, 238
Kotelman, Joachim, 27
Kyle, Jim, 71
La bohème, 224
La fille mal-gardée, 227
La Grande Magia, 215
Labianca, A.T., 238
Ladd, Paddy, 71, 72, 75
Lady in Blue in Front of the Mirror, 191,
    194
Lady Macbeth of Mtsenk, 227

Langs de kade, 113
Le Guyader, Claude, 174
Leijten, Marielle, 50
Lentz, Jurgen, 9, 26, 33, 36, 45
Lessing, Gotthold Ephraim, 115
Levent, Nina, 191
Ligue Braille, 18
Lorenzo García, Lourdes, 38
Lord of the Rings, 135, 136
L'elisir d'amore, 204
L'un per l'altre, 112
Ma, Kafai, 236
Magritte, René, 18
McKivragan, Gavin, 186
Majoria absoluta, 112
Marsh, Alison, 33, 44
Matamala, Anna, 19, 112, 115
Mateo, Marta, 204, 205, 206
Match Point, 117
Matisse, Henri, 237
Matrix Re-loaded, 136
Méndez Braga, Belén, 48
Mendiluce-Cabrera, Gustavo, 112
Menina da Rádio, 113
Miller, Clive, 16
Miss Sara Sampson, 115
Mod Squad, 91
Molloy, Larry, 190
Monaghan, Leila, 71, 72
Monet, Claude, 192
Montsalvatge, Xavier, 205
Moore, George, 190
Moreno, Trinidad, 212
Mozart, Wolfgang Amadeus, 224
Mrs Dalloway, 177
Mundovisión, 119
Mühleis, Volkmar, 18, 189, 192, 246
Museum
  Antwerp Fashion Museum, 199
  Diamantmuseum, 199
  For the Blind, 189
  Royal Museum of Art and History, Brussels, 189
  Royal Museums of Fine Arts, Brussels, 191, 246
  Tate Modern, 199
Music, 30, 31
Narrative, 127, 130, 131, 152, 163, 169, 170, 171, 189, 191, 193, 194, 195, 196, 197, 198, 221, 235, 240, 241, 247
National Captioning Institute, 119, 177
Netherlands, 24, 26, 30, 31
Neves, Josélia, 17, 23, 25, 28, 30, 31
Norm

Deaf translation, 16
O'Hara, James, 174
Ofcom, 26, 37, 112, 128, 129, 138, 152
ONCE, 112, 208
On the town, 228
One of the Burghers of Calais-Jean D'Aire, 197
Ong, Walter, J., 82
Opera, 19, 24
  Chinese, 234
Opera companies
  English National Opera (ENO), 204, 216, 217, 221, 222, 223, 227
  Glyndebourne Touring Opera, 229
  Monnaie, 46
  Opera North, 229
  Opera Northern Ireland, 229
  Royal Opera House (ROH), 216, 217, 218, 227
  Scottish Opera, 229
  Virginia Opera, 206
Orero, Pilar, 15, 17, 19, 25, 28
Packer, Jaclyn, 238
Padden, Carol, 71, 72
Pardina i Mundó, Joaquim, 48
Parsifal, 204, 205
Peli, Eli, 238
Pereira, Ana, 25, 28, 38
Pescod, Dan, 210
Petré, Leen, 210, 238
Pfanstiehl, 133
Picasso, Pablo, 199
Piety, Philip J., 238
Pinter, Harold, 215
Plats bruts, 112
Plot, 19
Poethe, Hannelore, 176
Portlock, Steven, 210
Portugal, 14, 24, 25, 28, 30, 31, 35, 36, 37, 42, 44, 45, 46, 52, 90, 96, 111, 113, 114, 119, 120, 123, 125, 246
Prendergast, Roy, M., 96
Priestley, JB, 215
Quality, 26, 34
Quico, Celia, 120, 125
Quinn, Ruth-Blandina M., 139
Quinto-Pozos, David, 82
Rank, Arthur, 90
Read, Herbert, 196
Reading speed, 29, 30, 36, 38, 39, 47, 105
Red Bee, 44
Redig, Joris, 118
Remael, Aline, 11, 15, 16, 23, 171, 245, 247

Reppen, Randi, 154
Rico, Albert, 49
Riegl, Alois, 196
Rigoletto, 204, 208
RNIB, 17
RNID, 55
Roberto Devereux, 204, 210, 211
Robson, Gary, 24, 101, 103
Rockwell, Margaret, 133
Rodin, Auguste, 18, 191, 197
Rogers, Margaret, 158
Rolph, Deborah, 17, 69, 112, 114, 122, 127, 151
Romero, Emerson, 90
Rossini, Gioacchino Antonio, 220
Rowland, William, 190
Royal Festival Hall, 224, 229
Rudvin, Mette, 78
Ruuskanen, Deborah D. K., 76, 77
Ryan, Marie-Laure, 171
Sadler's Wells Theatre, 229
Saerens, Gunter, 30
Salway, Andrew, 18, 151, 163, 164, 167, 169, 170, 171, 178, 239, 247
Salzhauer, Elisabeth, 191
Sánchez, Diana, 117
Sancho Aldridge, Jane, 93
Santamaría, Laura, 49
Schmeidler, Emilie, 238
Schmidt-Futtener, Andrea, 222
Sculpture, 196, 197, 198, 199
See no evil, hear no evil, 113
Senghas, Richard, 71
Shawshank Redemption, 137
Smetana, Bedrich, 217
Snyder, Joel, 119, 174, 177, 179, 238
Sequeiros, Xosé R., 77
Setton, Robin, 76
Sign Language, 1
    Ambivalent, 18
    Bilingualism, 73
    BSL, 73
    Clear, 18
    Interpretation, 16, 35
    Translation, 73
Simon Boccanegra, 223
Skelton, Tracey, 72
Skutnabb-Kangas, T., 75
Slembrouck, Stef, 49
Smeulders, Arnold, W. M., 166
Smith, Theresa, 72, 75
SOAP, 49
Software
    Dragon Naturally Speaking, 33
    Imputlog, 50
    K-live, 33
    Speech recognition, 33
    SWIFT, 33
    ViaVoice, 33
    WinCAPS, 33
Sound effect, 31
Sound system
    Dolby, 133
    DTS, 115, 133
Spain, 15, 18, 24, 25, 28, 31, 37, 38, 39, 42, 46, 49, 96, 111, 112, 114, 117, 119, 120, 121, 123, 139, 140, 147, 148, 177, 184, 185, 186, 204, 238, 245, 246, 247
Speech
    Input, 32
    Recognition, 25
Sperber, Daniel, 76
Spiderman, 135
Spiderman 2, 136
Spindler, George, 72
Spindler, Louise, 72
Spradley, James, P., 72
Squires, Judith, 73
Stallard, Gerry, 93
Standard (see also guideline),
    ES 202, 432
    European Telecommunication Standard Institute (ETSI), 39
    ETSI STF286, 53
    Minimum, 38
    Spanish UNE, 37, 38
Standarization, 53
Stenocaptioning, 101, 106
Steno do Brasil, 100
Stenotype, 100, 101, 102, 103, 106
Stolze, Radegundis, 79
Stone, Christopher, 16
Strauss, Anselm, 72
Style-book, 36
Subtitle
    Assisted, 34
    Audio, 122, 209, 210, 212, 213, 214
    Bitmap, 47
    Block, 29, 30, 48
    Ceefax, 24
    Closed, 31, 32, 47, 51, 89, 90, 91, 99, 100, 102, 107
    Colour, 31, 34, 36, 37, 38, 44, 47, 49, 92, 95, 96
    Edited, 30, 31, 33, 34, 40, 48, 50, 77, 80, 92, 100, 105
    Equipment, 24
    Font, 47, 49, 95, 96

Interlingual, 13, 36, 37, 42, 45, 46, 49,
  87, 94, 100, 106
Intralingual, 25, 32, 37, 42, 44, 49, 50,
  94, 100
Layout, 36, 218
Legibility, 39, 47
Lines, 36, 204, 206
Literal, 30
Live 13, 25, 28, 29, 30, 32, 33, 34, 35,
  36, 40, 44, 45, 49, 50, 203
Open, 24, 30, 31, 32, 46, 49, 76, 91, 99,
  100, 103, 104, 105
Page 888, 26, 98
Paralinguistic information, 30, 31, 36
Pop-on, 30, 31, 34, 48, 50, 102, 103,
  104, 105
Position, 30, 31, 34, 48, 50, 102, 103,
  104, 105
Pre-recorded, 36, 41, 42, 44, 49, 74, 80,
  81
Punctuation, 34, 36, 45, 96
Readability, 39, 47, 104
Real-time, 25, 27, 32, 35, 101
Rear-window, 24
Scroll, 30, 31, 34, 48, 50, 80, 100, 102
Semi-live, 32, 35, 49
Smiley, 31, 96
Snake, 48
"Spoken Subtitle", 210, 212, 214
Stenography, 34
Teletext, 13, 23, 24, 25, 26, 27, 28, 29,
  35, 37, 40, 44, 49, 51, 89, 90, 91
Televideo, 25
Velotype, 33
Verbatim, 30, 31, 34, 46, 47, 48, 50, 92,
  100, 106
Videotext, 24, 32, 36
Supalla, Ted, 76
Symbols
  Accessibility, 7, 16, 39, 53, 54, 55, 56,
    57, 58, 59, 60, 61, 62, 63, 64, 65, 66,
    67, 68, 69, 190
  Audio description, 53, 55, 56, 60, 61,
    64, 68
  Pictogram, 53, 54, 57
  Signing, 53, 55, 56, 61, 65, 68, 81, 86
  Speech output, 16, 53, 54, 55, 56, 60,
    61, 66, 69
  Spoken command, 16, 53, 54, 55, 56,
    61, 69
  Subtitling, 53, 55, 56, 61, 63, 68
Tactile, 53, 55, 97, 191, 193, 195, 196,
  197, 198
Taiwan, 19, 231, 236, 237, 239, 242

Talking Notes, 19, 215, 216, 217, 218,
  220, 223, 224, 227, 228, 229
Tam, Janet Mei-hing 233, 234
Taylor, Philip, 72
Theatre
  Cinema Subtitling System (CSS), 115
Theatre Royal Windsor, 112
The Aviator, 136
The Barber of Seville, 220
The Birthday Party, 215
The Fellowship of the Ring, 135
The Hours, 18, 175, 177, 178, 179, 183,
  185
The Marriage of Figaro, 221
The Region of Arnheim, 191, 193
The Two Widows, 217
The Wind in the Willows, 215
The Subtitling Company, 26
Theunisz, Mildred, 209
Thompson, Kristin, 152
Titelbild, 36, 41,
TIWO, 153, 155, 157, 158, 163, 164, 166,
  167, 169,
Todo sobre mi madre, 239,
Tomadaki, Eleftheria, 164,
Toury, Gideon, 78,
Training, 15, 19, 20, 23, 26, 40, 41, 42, 43,
  44, 45, 72, 77, 94, 97, 106, 117, 118,
  119, 123, 134, 154, 191, 231, 232, 233,
  234, 235, 236, 237, 238, 242
  Hands-on, 40, 43
  In house, 40, 41, 117, 119, 134
  Skills, 15, 30, 34, 41, 44, 45, 49, 75, 82,
    84, 94, 111, 120, 215, 234, 235, 242
  University, 40
Turner, James, 153, 169,
TV, 13, 15, 16, 17, 18, 24, 25,
  Current affairs, 27, 28, 32
  Digital 12, 26
  Fiction, 36
  General interest programmes, 25
  News, 25, 27, 28, 32
  Non-fiction, 36
  Political, pre-election debates, 32
  Series, 25
  Sports, 33
Twelfth Night, 113
UK, 16, 17, 24, 25, 26, 31
Uncle Vanja, 115
USA, 47, 48, 90, 91, 93, 133, 201, 206,
  213, 247
Utray, Francisco, 25, 28, 48, 112, 121,
Valentine, Gill, 72
Van Balkom, Hans, 52

Van Diem, Mike, 114
Van Herreweghe, Mieke, 49
Van Looy, Erik, 114
Van Son, Nic, 36
Van Waes, Luuk, 50
Vassiliou, Andrew, 163, 167, 170
Venuti, Lawrence, 88
Verberk, Susanne, 26, 36, 41, 52
Verboom, Maarten, 52, 212
Vercauteren, Gert, 17, 111, 120, 139, 179, 248
Verdi, Giuseppe, 19, 215, 222, 229
Vermeer, Hans, J., 76
Videogames, 13
Vila, Pere, 112,
Visual intensity, 18, 189, 191, 192, 194, 195
Von Kleist, Heinrich, 115
Vuorinen, Erkka, 75
Wales, 43, 133

Wall, John, 139, 140
Warhol, Andy, 192
Warchus, Matthew, 222
Watkins, Malcolm, J., 190
Websites 13, 16, 56, 238
Weiss, Markus, 113
Westrop, Jane, 174
Wetten dass, 28
Whitehead, Jill, 174
Wilson, Deirdre, 76
Windkracht 10, 114
Woll, Bencie, 71, 73
Woolf, Virginia, 177
Word, Russ, 173
Wouters, Rik, 18
Yeung, Jessica, 19, 231, 248
York, Greg, 19, 205, 207, 213, 214, 215, 239, 248
Yu-chiou, Chen, 237